GOD AND THE REACH OF REASON

C. S. Lewis is one of the most beloved Christian apologists of the twentieth century; David Hume and Bertrand Russell are among Christianity's most important critics. This book puts these three intellectual giants in conversation with one another to shed light on some of life's most difficult yet important questions. It examines their views on a variety of topics, including the existence of God, suffering, morality, reason, joy, miracles, and faith. Along with irreconcilable differences and points of tension, some surprising areas of agreement emerge. Today, amid the often shrill and vapid exchanges between "new atheists" and twenty-first-century believers, curious readers will find penetrating insights in the reasoned dialogue of these three great thinkers.

Erik J. Wielenberg teaches in the Philosophy Department at DePauw University. He is the author of *Value and Virtue in a Godless Universe* (2005) published by Cambridge University Press.

D1225495

GOD AND THE REACH OF REASON

C. S. Lewis, David Hume, and Bertrand Russell

ERIK J. WIELENBERG

DePauw University

CAMBRIDGE
UNIVERSITY PRESS

CAMBRIDGE UNIVERSITY PRESS
Cambridge, New York, Melbourne, Madrid, Cape Town, Singapore, São Paulo, Delhi

Cambridge University Press
32 Avenue of the Americas, New York, NY 10013-2473, USA

www.cambridge.org
Information on this title: www.cambridge.org/9780521880862

The Scripture quotations contained herein are from the New Revised
Standard Version Bible, copyright © 1989 by the Division of Christian
Education of the National Council of the Churches of Christ in the
U.S.A. Used by permission. All rights reserved.

The epigraph is from "On Obstinacy in Belief" by C. S. Lewis, which first
appeared in the Autumn 1955 issue of *The Sewanee Review* and is used by
permission of *The Sewanee Review*.

First published 2008

Printed in the United States of America

A catalog record for this publication is available from the British Library.

Library of Congress Cataloging in Publication Data

Wielenberg, Erik J. (Erik Joseph), 1972–
God and the reach of reason : C. S. Lewis, David Hume, and Bertrand Russell /
Erik J. Wielenberg.
     p.   cm.
Includes bibliographical references and index.
ISBN 978-0-521-88086-2 (hardback) – ISBN 978-0-521-70710-7 (pbk.)
1. Philosophical theology.   2. Lewis, C. S. (Clive Staples), 1898–1963.
3. Hume, David.   4. Russell, Bertrand, 1872–1970.   I. Title.
BT40.W53   2007
210.92′241 – dc22   2007010036

ISBN   978-0-521-88086-2 hardback
ISBN   978-0-521-70710-7 paperback

85892373

For Jake and Henry

[T]here is evidence both for and against the Christian proposition which fully rational minds, working honestly, can assess differently.

– C. S. Lewis (1955)

CONTENTS

Contents

ACKNOWLEDGMENTS

I have acquired many debts of gratitude in writing this book and thinking about the issues discussed here. The seeds of the book were planted as I prepared to teach a first-year seminar at DePauw University in the fall of 2002. That seminar sought to introduce students to philosophy through the works of C. S. Lewis, and I selected Hume and Russell as the major figures to set in opposition to Lewis. I am grateful to the students in that course, as well as to those who took a modified version of the same course in the fall of 2004. Preliminary versions of some of the ideas in this book were presented at a Faculty Research Colloquium at DePauw on November 22, 2002, under the title "C. S. Lewis vs. the Atheists"; I am grateful to the audience for the feedback I received on that occasion. Other material was presented at a meeting of the Bertrand Russell Society at the Central APA meeting in Chicago on April 27, 2006, under the title "Bertrand Russell and C. S. Lewis: Two Peas in a Pod?" I thank the audience on that occasion for their helpful comments. The production of the initial draft of the book was done with the help of a pre-tenure leave from DePauw in the spring of 2005, and revision of the manuscript was supported by a DePauw Summer Stipend during the summer of 2006.

Many people read some or all of the various earlier versions of the book and provided helpful comments and criticism. Two anonymous readers for Cambridge University Press produced extensive and helpful reports; the final version of the book is significantly improved because of these excellent reports. One of these initially anonymous readers has subsequently been revealed to be Victor Reppert; the other remains anonymous (to me). Andy Beck, my editor at Cambridge, was extremely supportive of the project and nudged things in the right direction at crucial junctures. Daniel Story read a complete early version of the manuscript as part of an independent study course on the works of C. S. Lewis during the fall of 2005. I am also grateful to Girard Brenneman, Richard Cameron, Trent Dougherty, Jennifer Everett, Billy Lauinger, Luke Maring, Mark Murphy, James Olsen, Alexander Pruss, Karen Stohr, and William Vallicella for their comments on various parts of the manuscript. Steve Lovell was kind enough to share with me his dissertation on the philosophical works of C. S. Lewis; the debt I owe to Lovell will be obvious to the reader of my own efforts to grapple with Lewis's ideas. I am confident that nearly everyone mentioned in this paragraph disagrees with some of the material in the book; unsurprisingly, I owe the greatest debts to my most challenging critics.

DePauw University constitutes a stimulating and supportive environment in which I am free to pursue my research interests, wherever they may take me. I am grateful to my colleagues in the Philosophy Department and to the students who have taken my courses for being a big part of this environment. I am also grateful to the faculty in the Department of Philosophy at the University of Massachusetts at Amherst from 1994 to 2000, particularly my dissertation director, Fred Feldman, for the excellent training in philosophy they provided.

Finally, I thank my mother, Peggy Wielenberg, and my wife, Margaret, for various kinds of support too numerous to describe. Without their support, none of this would have been possible. As always, responsibility for the errors that this work assuredly contains resides ultimately with me.

Greencastle, Indiana
January 2007

INTRODUCTION

Plato tells us that Socrates, facing execution in 399 B.C., declared that "the one aim of those who practice philosophy in the proper manner is to practice for dying and death."[1] Writing nearly two thousand years later, Michel de Montaigne remarked that "all the wisdom and reasoning in the world boils down finally to this point: to teach us not to be afraid to die."[2]

If the measure of a philosopher is the ability to face death without fear, then Clive Staples Lewis (1898–1963), David Hume (1711–1776), and Bertrand Russell (1872–1970) were great philosophers indeed. In the penultimate paragraph of his brief autobiography, "My Own Life," David Hume relates that he has been "struck with a Disorder in my Bowels" which has "become mortal and incurable."[3] He remarks on his state of mind as follows:

> I have suffered very little pain from my Disorder; and what is more strange, have, notwithstanding the great Decline of my Person, never suffered a Moments Abatement of my Spirits: Insomuch, that were I to name the Period of my Life which I [should] most choose to pass over again I might be tempted to point to this later Period.[4]

Samuel Johnson's biographer James Boswell was simultaneously fascinated and horrified by Hume's calm acceptance of his own impending death. This was because Boswell knew that Hume did not believe in an afterlife. Boswell visited Hume repeatedly while Hume was on his deathbed, questioning him on the topic of annihilation. Hume's death on August 25, 1776, sent Boswell into "a mental crisis during

1

which he sounded the depths of moral degradation."[5] Hume's death, it seems, was harder on Boswell than it was on Hume.

C. S. Lewis also faced impending death as a result of poor health, and in one of his last letters he expressed sentiments remarkably similar to those expressed by Hume: "Yes, autumn is really the best of the seasons; and I'm not sure that old age isn't the best part of life."[6] Lewis's brother reports that Lewis faced death "bravely and calmly," at one point remarking, "I have done all I wanted to do, and I'm ready to go."[7] Lewis died peacefully on November 22, 1963; his death was overshadowed in the press by the assassination of John F. Kennedy on the same day.[8]

Bertrand Russell was by far the most politically active of the three thinkers who are the focus of this book. He wrote letters and articles, gave speeches, started a school, won the Nobel Prize for Literature, and spent time in prison, including six months in 1918 for writing an antiwar article. His activism was triggered by the outbreak of the first World War in 1914, an event that, according to Russell, shattered the "Victorian optimism" that had been taken for granted when he was a young man.[9]

In the Postscript to his autobiography, Russell reflected on his long life, remarking that "[m]y work is near its end, and the time has come when I can survey it as a whole."[10] Assessing his life, Russell noted both failures and victories. But his final remarks indicate an underlying optimism:

> I have lived in the pursuit of a vision, both personal and social. Personal: to care for what is noble, for what is beautiful, for what is gentle: to allow moments of insight to give wisdom at more mundane times. Social: to see in imagination the society that is to be created, where individuals grow freely, and where hate and greed and envy die because there is nothing to nourish them. These things I believe, and the world, for all its horrors, has left me unshaken.[11]

Russell's pursuit of a personal and social vision seems to have sustained him in his old age as death loomed, in much the way he described in an essay called "How to Grow Old":

An individual human existence should be like a river – small at first, narrowly contained within its banks, and rushing passionately past boulders and over waterfalls. Gradually the river grows wider, the banks recede, the waters flow more quietly, and in the end, without any visible break, they become merged in the sea, and painlessly lose their individual being. The man who, in old age, can see his life in this way, will not suffer from the fear of death, since the things he cares for will continue.[12]

One feature common to the deaths of Hume, Lewis, and Russell is that they were *philosophical* deaths. By this I mean that each thinker faced his death armed with a comprehensive view about the nature of human beings and their place in the universe that had been carefully developed and considered over a long period of time. Yet these worldviews were quite different from one another. Lewis's view was a fairly traditional version of Christianity, centered on a personal God who created, loves, and interacts with human beings. Hume and Russell both rejected the notion of a personal, loving God, admitting at best a distant, largely unknowable Deity that does not fiddle about in human affairs. Lewis saw our earthly lives as merely a tiny (but important) fraction of our overall existence, whereas Hume and Russell viewed such lives as all we get. Interestingly, Lewis spent many years in the Hume–Russell camp (broadly speaking) before converting to Christianity in his early thirties.

Lewis, Hume, and Russell were (among other things) philosophers, and each offered arguments for his own worldview and against competing views. This book is a philosophical examination of some of these arguments, with a particular emphasis on those of Lewis. This book is about suffering, morality, reason, joy, miracles, faith, and God. It is about the views of three great thinkers on deep and important topics.

Hume and Russell are giants in the Western philosophical tradition. Hume's work *Dialogues Concerning Natural Religion* is widely considered one of the most important works in the philosophy of religion in the Western tradition. In the introduction to a recent book devoted to examining critically Hume's views on religion, the editors observe that "from his day to ours, the vast majority of philosophical attacks against the rationality of theism have borne an unmistakable Humean aroma."[13] Russell's place in the pantheon of Western philosophers is similarly well established, though his reputation for greatness is due more to his contributions in logic and the philosophy of mathematics than to his work in the philosophy of religion. Lewis's case, however, is somewhat different; while his works of fiction and Christian apologetics are widely read and adored, his writing has been largely (but not entirely) ignored by contemporary philosophers. Or at least, his Christian writing has received relatively little attention from professional philosophers *in their professional capacity*. This is despite ample evidence that contemporary Christian philosophers are familiar with Lewis's work and, indeed, that some have been dramatically influenced by it. For instance, the prominent contemporary Christian philosopher Peter van Inwagen writes that "[l]ike many other people, I first discovered what Christianity *was* from reading Lewis."[14] He goes on to say that it was through Lewis that he first saw that "Christianity was a serious thing and intellectually at a very high level."[15] Whatever the reason for the relative neglect of Lewis in contemporary philosophy, I believe that it is a mistake, and one of my aims in this book is to show that Lewis's philosophical work is worthy of serious attention.

Here is a brief overview of what is to come. The first chapter focuses on the challenge that suffering poses for belief in God as that challenge is formulated by Hume in *Dialogues Concerning Natural Religion* and addressed by Lewis in *The Problem of Pain*. I argue that while Lewis's response to the challenge is incomplete in a certain way, that response is novel and has a richness and subtlety that has not been widely appreciated. I seek to bring out this richness by defending Lewis's solution to the problem of pain against a variety of objections.

Chapter 2 focuses on Lewis's three main arguments for the existence of a Higher Power. These arguments are grounded in human nature. Like Descartes, Lewis thinks that we can understand God by first understanding ourselves. He maintains that human beings have knowledge of objective moral truths, can reason, and have a desire that nothing on earth can satisfy. Each of these aspects of human nature constitutes the starting point of an argument for the existence of a Higher Power. Hume and Russell appear in this chapter primarily as critics of Lewis's theistic arguments. I suggest, however, that some of the most serious challenges to Lewis's arguments come from the relatively new field of evolutionary psychology, and I explain how evolutionary psychology may be drawn upon to resist Lewis's case for a Higher Power.

The third chapter is like the first in that it focuses on a challenge posed by Hume together with a direct response to that challenge from Lewis. In this case the focus is on miracles and testimony. Hume argues, roughly, that testimony (of a certain kind) never provides us with a good reason to believe that a miracle has taken place. An obvious implication of this result is that it would not be reasonable for us to believe that the Resurrection of Christ really happened on the basis of the New Testament gospels; thus, Hume's argument strikes directly at the heart of Christianity. Lewis criticizes Hume's argument and tries to show that the Resurrection has enough initial plausibility that testimony could provide sufficient evidence for its occurrence. After carefully explaining the reasoning of Hume and Lewis on these issues, I make the case that while Lewis exposes a significant weakness in Hume's argument, Lewis's own argument fails because it depends upon his case for the existence of a Higher Power, and this case is not particularly strong (as I argue in Chapter 2). The chapter concludes with a discussion of the implications of all of this for Lewis's famous "Trilemma."

Chapter 4 involves more exposition than the preceding three chapters and focuses on some perhaps surprising areas of agreement among the three thinkers. Substantial attention is devoted to determining Hume's overall views on religion, particularly in *Dialogues Concerning Natural Religion*. I argue that despite their very different positions on the status of Christianity, the three thinkers hold similar views on the importance of following the evidence and on the difficulties humans face in doing this. I further argue that all three reject the argument from design and recognize the potential for violence of organized religion. Hume and Russell favor the abandonment of traditional dogma (including Christian dogma) as the way to avoid religious violence, whereas Lewis maintains that the solution to the problem lies in a proper understanding of Christianity itself.

Lewis receives the most attention in this book, with Hume a close second and Russell a distant third. This is not because I think Lewis's conclusions are correct; as the preceding outline of the book should make clear, I think that Lewis's overall case for Christianity fails. My main goal here is to put these three great thinkers in conversation with each other, shedding light not only on the views of each but also on the quality of their various arguments. It is in part because I believe that Lewis's views have received the least serious philosophical treatment of the three that I give those views the most attention here. But this book is not just for those interested in Lewis, Hume, or Russell; it is for anyone interested in thinking seriously and thinking hard about God. We study great thinkers not just to learn about them but also to learn from them. As Lewis said in a different context: "The silly things these great men say, were as silly then as they are now: the wise ones are as wise now as they were then."[16]

We begin with suffering.

ONE

THE LOVE OF GOD AND THE SUFFERING OF HUMANITY

1.1 THE PROBLEM

On Sunday, December 26, 2004, an earthquake off the western coast of Indonesia's Sumatra Island triggered a massive tsunami that subsequently struck several countries, killing over 200,000 people. The hardest-hit countries included Indonesia, Thailand, Sri Lanka, and India. The tsunami struck with little or no warning. Entire villages were wiped from the face of the earth, and whole families were swept out to sea. The casualties were so overwhelming that little attempt was made to identify most of the corpses. Instead, they were buried as quickly as possible in mass graves.

In the aftermath of the disaster, one of the topics to which the popular media turned its attention was the problem of evil, a problem that philosophers and theologians have thought about for over two millennia. The problem of evil is often posed as a question: If there is an all-powerful, all-knowing, and perfectly good God, then why does the world contain the assorted evils that it does? The problem may be posed more aggressively as a challenge: If there *were* an all-powerful, all-knowing, and perfectly good God, then the world *wouldn't* contain the assorted evils that it does. Hence, no such God exists. A one-page article in the January 10, 2005, issue of *Newsweek* titled "Countless Souls Cry Out to God" hinted that the tsunami disaster constituted evidence that such a God does not exist, ending with these lines:

Whole families, whole communities, countless pasts and futures have been obliterated by this tsunami's roiling force. Little wonder that from Sumatra to Madagascar, innumerable voices cry out to God. The miracle, if there is one, may be that so many still believe.[1]

The 2004 tsunami is not without precedent. On November 1, 1755, an earthquake struck the Portuguese city of Lisbon, one of the largest and most beautiful cities in Europe at the time. This quake, like the one off the coast of Sumatra Island, was followed by large tsunamis as well as widespread fires that burned for days. More than 100,000 people lost their lives as a result of the Lisbon earthquake.

The earthquake was featured in Voltaire's satirical 1759 work *Candide*, which recounts the misadventures of Candide and his companion Pangloss. The latter is a philosopher who consistently maintains that ours is the best of all possible worlds, despite the various horrors the two experience.[2] The fictional Pangloss represents the actual philosopher Leibniz, who really did maintain that ours is the best of all possible worlds.[3] Voltaire means to illustrate the absurdity of this proposition in *Candide*, and the Lisbon earthquake is offered as evidence in that regard. Leibniz thought that ours must be the best of all possible worlds because a perfect God must create the best of all possible worlds. So Voltaire's ridicule of the Leibnizian claim that this is the best of all possible worlds may ultimately be seen as ridicule of the idea that a perfect God exists.

Hume and Lewis both grappled with the problem of evil.[4] Lewis's first book of Christian apologetics, *The Problem of Pain*, is devoted to dealing with the problem, and Lewis's discussion there is pretty clearly a direct response to Hume's presentation of the problem in Parts X and XI of his *Dialogues Concerning Natural Religion*. While it is Lewis's attempt to solve the problem of evil that is the focus of this chapter, it is helpful first to examine Hume's presentation of the problem.

1.2 HUME'S PRESENTATION OF THE PROBLEM

Hume worked on the *Dialogues Concerning Natural Religion* off and on over a period of almost thirty years. At the urging of his friends, many of whom read a draft of the work in the early 1750s, Hume did not publish it during his lifetime. His friends feared that because of the controversial nature of the *Dialogues*, publication would have a detrimental effect on Hume's life and reputation. Hume had good reason to take his friends' advice seriously. The writing on religion that Hume did publish during his lifetime drew the ire of many of his religious contemporaries. As a consequence of his writing on religion he was denied the chair of logic at Glasgow University in 1752, and about five years later the Church of Scotland attempted to excommunicate him.[5] Nevertheless, Hume specified in his will that the *Dialogues* be published posthumously, and it first appeared in print in 1779, three years after his death.[6]

The *Dialogues* is an extended conversation among three characters, Cleanthes, Philo, and Demea, as reported by Cleanthes's student, Pamphilus, to Pamphilus's companion Hermippus. As the title suggests, the topic of the discussion is natural religion – religion based on human reason alone, without the aid of divine revelation or other supernatural activity. Much of the conversation focuses on what human reason alone can determine about the existence and nature of God. Each of the three main characters has a distinct view on these issues, and one of them, Philo, goes so far as to question the existence of God altogether. Presumably this is at least part of what made the work so controversial in the eyes of Hume's friends.

Ascertaining Hume's own views on the basis of the *Dialogues* is a tricky business. In particular, there has been much debate over whether any one of the three characters speaks for Hume and, if so, which one. One popular view has been that Philo is Hume's mouthpiece.[7] However, even if this is correct, more work is needed to determine just what Hume's views are, because ascertaining the views of Philo is itself a less-than-straightforward matter.

In Chapter 4 we will delve into the tricky business of ascertaining Hume's own views in the *Dialogues*, but for the moment we can safely avoid this task, for the following reasons: In Parts X and XI of the *Dialogues*, the problem of evil is raised by Demea and Philo. The challenge raised here is never satisfactorily answered in the *Dialogues* nor, indeed, in any of Hume's works. This suggests at the very least that Hume considered the problem of evil to be a serious challenge, one to which he himself had no satisfactory answer. Furthermore, it is the discussion of the problem of evil in these two sections of the *Dialogues* that sets the stage for *The Problem of Pain*. Our interest, then, is in understanding the problem as it appears in the *Dialogues* and evaluating Lewis's response to that problem. The question of Hume's own view on the problem is one that we can safely set aside, at least for the moment.

In the parts of the *Dialogues* preceding Parts X and XI, two types of arguments for the existence of God are discussed. Cleanthes defends a type of design argument (dubbed "the argument *a posteriori*"), and Demea defends a cosmological argument (dubbed "the argument *a priori*"). Philo, playing the role of skeptic, criticizes both arguments, alternately joining forces with Demea or Cleanthes, depending on the topic. For the most part, Philo pretends to share the views of Demea. Although the fact that Philo's apparent agreement with Demea is mere pretense is made sufficiently clear both to Cleanthes and to the attentive reader, it is not recognized by Demea until Part XI.

Having seen his cosmological argument subjected to scathing criticism at the hands of Cleanthes and Philo in Part IX, Demea begins Part X with a new tack. He suggests that it is a "consciousness of [their own] imbecility and misery rather than . . . any reasoning" that drives people to believe in God.[8] This suggestion leads Philo to make the following ironic remark: "I am indeed persuaded . . . that the best and indeed the only method of bringing everyone to a due sense of religion is by just representation of the misery and wickedness of men."[9] While Demea and Philo agree that reflection on human suffering will lead to a "due sense of religion," they disagree on just what this "due sense" is. Demea thinks that such reflection will lead to awe and submission to God, whereas Philo thinks it will lead to doubt of the existence of a good God altogether. However, Demea does not recognize the irony of Philo's remark, instead taking it as a straightforward agreement with his own view.

Philo's remark launches an extended discussion of the assorted evils of the world. Here is Demea's colorful description of human life:

The whole earth, believe me, Philo, is cursed and polluted. A perpetual war is kindled amongst all living creatures. Necessity, hunger, want stimulate the strong and courageous: fear, anxiety, terror agitate the weak and infirm. The first entrance into human life gives anguish to the new-born infant and to its wretched parent: weakness, impotence, distress attend each stage of that life, and it is, at last, finished in agony and horror.[10]

Of particular interest is Philo's assessment of the philosophical implications of such suffering:

Is the world, considered in general and as it appears to us in this life, different from what a man or such a limited being would, *beforehand*, expect from a very powerful, wise, and benevolent Deity? It must be strange prejudice to assert the contrary. And from thence I conclude that, however consistent the world may be, allowing certain suppositions and conjectures with the idea of such a Deity, it can never afford us an inference concerning his existence. The consistency is not absolutely denied, only the inference.[11]

In this passage, Philo seems to suggest that the philosophical significance of the suffering in the world is that it provides the basis of a decisive objection to Cleanthes's design argument. Cleanthes argues that we can infer the existence of God from certain observable features of the world. But the God of traditional monotheism is omnipotent, omniscient, and morally perfect. Philo's point is that the presence of suffering in the world effectively blocks the inference from the observable universe to a morally perfect Creator. But Philo explicitly refrains from asserting that the presence of suffering is inconsistent with the existence of such a God. This might lead us to conclude that Philo's position is that we cannot infer from the suffering we observe that God does not exist. However, other passages indicate that such a conclusion would be too hasty. For instance, earlier in Part X Philo has this to say:

His power, we allow, is infinite; whatever he wills is executed: But neither man nor any other animal is happy; therefore, he does not will their happiness. His wisdom is infinite; He is never mistaken in choosing the means to any end; But the course of nature tends not to human or animal felicity: Therefore, it is not established for that

11

purpose. Through the whole compass of human knowledge there are
no inferences more certain and infallible than these. In what respect,
then, do his benevolence and mercy resemble the benevolence and
mercy of men?[12]

In these lines Philo suggests that an omnipotent and omniscient God
would surely have sufficient power and wisdom to make us happy, if
He so desired. Yet we are not happy, so God must not desire our happiness. Philo even goes so far as to remark that no human reasoning
is more certain than this. He then implicitly takes a further step: A
good God *would* desire our happiness. It follows that there is no God
who is omnipotent, omniscient, and good. It appears that Philo is
suggesting that we *can* infer the nonexistence of the traditional God
of monotheism from the presence of suffering in the world.

Some remarks Philo makes later in Part XI support this interpretation. Philo introduces *"four* hypotheses . . . concerning the first causes
of the universe."[13] The four hypotheses are (i) a perfectly good first
cause, (ii) a perfectly evil first cause, (iii) two (joint) first causes, one
perfectly good, the other perfectly evil, and (iv) a morally indifferent first cause. Only the first hypothesis is consistent with traditional
monotheism; the third hypothesis corresponds to Dualism, a view
declared heretical under Christianity and, as we will see, discussed
at some length by Lewis.[14]

Reflecting on the mixture of good and evil in the universe, Philo
rejects the first two hypotheses, suggesting that it is unlikely that
pure first causes would produce such "mixed phenomena." He rejects
the third hypothesis on the basis of the "uniformity and steadiness
of general laws" in our universe; the idea seems to be that a cosmic
struggle between good and evil first causes would produce a universe
significantly less orderly than our own. By a process of elimination,
Philo concludes that the fourth hypothesis "seems by far the most
probable."[15]

So Philo appears to maintain both (i) that as far as we can tell,
suffering is consistent with the existence of God, and (ii) that we can
infer, on the basis of suffering in the world, that God does not exist.
Does Philo thereby contradict himself? No; (i) and (ii) are compatible.

Sometimes it is reasonable to infer not-q from p even though p and q are logically consistent. Suppose, for instance, that p = tomorrow you will flip a fair coin exactly one hundred times (and you will flip no other coins tomorrow) and that q = tomorrow you will flip "heads" one hundred times. Even though p and q are compatible, I can reasonably infer not-q from p because p makes q very *unlikely*. And Philo's position seems to be that, while the presence of suffering in the world may be compatible with the existence of God, it makes God's existence unlikely. This is evident from his conclusion that the fourth hypothesis is "by far the *most probable*."

There is one other important wrinkle to Philo's position. In Part I of the *Dialogues*, Philo registers his misgivings about the feasibility of natural religion:

> [W]hen we carry our speculations into the two eternities, before and after the present state of things; into the creation and formation of the universe; the existence and properties of spirits; the powers and operations of one universal Spirit existing without beginning and without end, omnipotent, omniscient, immutable, infinite, and incomprehensible. We must be far removed from the smallest tendency to skepticism not to be apprehensive that we have here got quite beyond the reach of our faculties ... We are like foreigners in a strange country to whom everything must seem suspicious, and who are in danger every moment of transgressing against the laws and customs of the people with whom they live and converse. We know not how far we ought to trust our vulgar methods of reasoning in such a subject.[16]

These and other remarks show that Philo's discussion of human suffering in Parts X and XI is undertaken in the context of skepticism about the capacity of human reason to tell us much at all about the existence and nature of God.

To understand Philo's position in its entirety, we need to understand that his main opponent is Cleanthes. Cleanthes maintains that human reason can tell us quite a bit about the existence and nature of God, and that what it tells us is that the universe was created by a powerful, wise, and good God. Philo criticizes both aspects of Cleanthes's position, arguing that we shouldn't put much stock in the results of human reasoning when it comes to religion – but to the extent that reason is trustworthy, it tells us that the God of monotheism does not exist.[17]

The presence and interaction of these two aspects of Philo's position are perhaps clearest in the following lines:

> Why is there any misery at all in the world? Not by chance, surely. From some cause then. Is it from the intention of the Deity? But he is perfectly benevolent. Is it contrary to his intention? But he is almighty. Nothing can shake the solidity of this reasoning, so short, so clear, so decisive, except [unless] we assert that these subjects exceed all human capacity, and that our common measures of truth and falsehood are not applicable to them; a topic which I have all along insisted on.[18]

Perhaps, then, we may state Philo's version of the problem of evil this way:

The Problem of Pain

1. If God exists, then He is omnipotent, omniscient, and morally perfect.
2. If God is morally perfect, then He wants there to be no suffering in the world.
3. If God is omnipotent and omniscient, then He can bring it about that there is no suffering in the world.
4. So: If God is omnipotent, omniscient, and morally perfect, then there is no suffering in the world (from 2 and 3).
5. But there is suffering in the world.
6. Therefore, God does not exist (from 1, 4, and 5).

The first premise follows from the traditional understanding of the God of monotheism; omnipotence, omniscience, and moral perfection are central attributes of that God. The fifth premise seems beyond doubt, and the fourth is entailed (more or less) by premises two and three.[19] The substantive premises, then, seem to be two and three.

Philo has little to say in support of the second premise, but he does offer a kind of argument for the third, the claim that an all-powerful, all-knowing God would be able to create a pain-free universe. In Part XI, Philo describes *"four* circumstances on which depend all or the greatest part of the ills that molest sensible creatures." He suggests that "[n]one of them appear to human reason in the least degree necessary or unavoidable" – although, true to his two-track strategy, he cautions that "[w]e know so little beyond common life, or even of common life, that, with regard to the economy of a universe, there is no conjecture, however wild, which may not be just, nor any one, however plausible, which may not be erroneous."[20]

The four factors that Philo cautiously suggests produce all or most of the suffering in the universe and that an omnipotent, omniscient God could easily have avoided are the following: (i) pain (in addition to pleasure) functions as a motive "to excite all creatures to action"; (ii) the world is governed by general laws of nature; (iii) nature is frugal, in that each creature is endowed with just enough natural capacities to survive but not enough to avoid misery; (iv) the "inaccurate workmanship" of the world, which seems more like a rough draft than a completed project.[21] There is much to be said about each of these four circumstances, and we will return to them later, but for now it is enough to see how they are supposed to support Philo's version of the problem of pain. According to Philo, there is a workable, pain-free alternative to each of the four circumstances, an alternative that an all-powerful, all-knowing God would have known of and could have implemented. If this is correct, and the four circumstances produce all of the suffering in the world, then the third premise of the problem of pain is established.

Contemporary philosophers tend to draw a distinction between the *logical* problem of evil and the *evidential* or *probabilistic* problem of evil.[22] The logical version has it that the existence of evil is *incompatible* with the existence of the God of traditional monotheism, whereas the evidential version involves only the weaker claim that the evils of our world, while compatible with God's existence, constitute *evidence* against God's existence. Because Philo's position seems to be that suffering is compatible with but counts as evidence against God's existence, it is tempting to construe him as offering merely an evidential version of the problem of evil. However, I believe that the argument he actually gives – the argument I have just formulated – is a logical version of the problem of evil. But if this is right, why does

15

Philo not conclude that the suffering in the world *decisively proves* that God does not exist? The answer lies in Philo's two-track strategy. He presents a deductive proof of God's nonexistence based on the presence of suffering (the atheistic track) but declines to endorse the proof with certainty himself because he has serious doubts about the reliability of human reason in this area (the skeptical track). He seeks to put Cleanthes on the horns of a dilemma: Either admit that human reason is unreliable when applied to the existence and nature of God (and hence abandon your design argument), or admit that the presence of suffering proves that a perfect God does not exist (and hence abandon your theism).

Lewis's writing contains responses to both the skeptical aspect and the atheistic aspect of Philo's position. The first order of business is to examine Lewis's response to the aspect that consists of the problem of pain, the atheistic aspect. We will examine Lewis's response to the skeptical aspect in Chapters 2 and 3. To address the atheistic aspect, Lewis argues that once we properly understand God's omnipotence and goodness, and the real nature of human happiness, we will see that it is not at all surprising or improbable that God would permit (and even cause) human suffering. Making this case is the central project of *The Problem of Pain*, to which we now turn.

1.3 LEWIS'S ATTEMPT TO SOLVE THE PROBLEM

1.3.1 Introduction

Born in Belfast, Ireland, on November 29, 1898, Lewis was raised as a Christian, but shed his Christian belief during his early teens while at boarding school in England. By his own account, at school he got the impression that "religion in general, though utterly false, was a natural growth, a kind of endemic nonsense into which humanity tended to blunder."[23] At age seventeen, Lewis wrote to his close friend Arthur Greeves that "I believe in no religion" and described Christianity in particular as "one mythology among many, but the one that we happened to have been brought up in."[24] Lewis's return to Christianity was a gradual and complex process. In both his letters and the autobiographical *Surprised by Joy*, Lewis notes the influence of H. V. V. Dyson and J. R. R. Tolkien. In a 1946 letter, Lewis lists the main factors in his conversion as philosophy, increasing knowledge of medieval literature, the writers George MacDonald and G. K. Chesterton, and discussion with his friend Owen Barfield.[25] In a letter written much closer in time to the event itself (1934), Lewis describes his "route" as running "from materialism to idealism, from idealism to Pantheism, from pantheism to theism, and from theism to Christianity."[26] The process culminated with a famous trip to the zoo in late September 1931, when Lewis was thirty-two years old: "When we set out I did not believe that Jesus Christ is the Son of God, and when we reached the zoo I did."[27] About a month later, almost exactly fifteen years after he had written to Arthur Greeves that he was an atheist, Lewis described his new view of Christianity in another letter to Greeves: "[T]he story of Christ is simply a true myth: a myth working on us in the same way as the others, but with this tremendous difference that *it really happened*."[28]

The Problem of Pain, first published in 1940, was Lewis's first book-length work in Christian apologetics. I have suggested that the work was inspired by Parts X and XI of Hume's *Dialogues*. However, nowhere in *The Problem of Pain* does Lewis mention Hume or the *Dialogues*. What, then, is my evidence for the alleged connection between the two works?

There are two kinds of evidence. First, there is what we might call external evidence – evidence outside of the relevant works themselves. Lewis both studied and served as a tutor in philosophy at Oxford, and in fact planned to become a professor of philosophy before switching to English literature in 1925.[29] Hume's *Dialogues* has long been considered one of the great works in the philosophy of religion; that Lewis could have studied philosophy at an advanced level at Oxford without having read it is almost, if not actually, impossible. We know from Lewis's own words that he read at least *some* of Hume's works; in June 1924 he made the following entry in his diary: "I then began Hume: and greatly enjoyed the perfect clarity, ease, humanity, and quietness of his manner. This is the proper way to write philosophy."[30] Of course, this establishes at most that Lewis probably read the *Dialogues*, but not necessarily that *The Problem of Pain* is a response to Hume's work. To establish this further claim, we must consider the works themselves. As we will see, *The Problem of Pain* contains responses to many of the specific points that arise in the *Dialogues*. Moreover, the presentations of the problem of pain itself in the two works are strikingly similar. For instance, in Part XI of the *Dialogues*, Philo says:

> Look round this universe. What an immense profusion of beings, animated and organized, sensible and active! ... But inspect a little more narrowly these living existences, the only beings worth regarding. How hostile and destructive to each other! How insufficient all of them for their own happiness! How contemptible or odious to the spectator! The whole presents nothing but the idea of a blind nature, impregnated by a great vivifying principle, and pouring forth from her lap, without discernment or parental care, her maimed and abortive children![31]

Shortly after these remarks, Philo reaches his conclusion that the hypothesis that the first causes of the universe are morally indifferent is "by far the most probable."[32]

The opening chapter of *The Problem of Pain* begins as follows: "Not many years ago when I was an atheist, if anyone had asked me, 'Why do you not believe in God?' my reply would have run something like this...."[33] Note the parallels between Lewis's explanation of his past atheism and Philo's speech just quoted:

> Look at the universe we live in.... [W]hat is [life] like while it lasts? It is so arranged that all the forms of it can live only by preying upon one another. In the lower forms this process entails only death, but in the higher there appears a new quality called consciousness which enables it to be attended by pain. The creatures cause pain by being born, and live by inflicting pain, and in pain they mostly die.... If you ask me to believe that this is the work of a benevolent and omnipotent spirit, I reply that all the evidence points in the opposite direction. Either there is no spirit behind the universe, or else a spirit indifferent to good and evil, or else an evil spirit.[34]

Finally, consider Lewis's own account of the problem of pain, and note its similarity to Philo's description of the problem, which I quoted in the previous section:

> 'If God were good, He would wish to make His creatures perfectly happy, and if God were almighty He would be able to do what He wished. But the creatures are not happy. Therefore God either lacks goodness, or power, or both.' This is the problem of pain, in its simplest form.[35]

Lewis observes that there are three key concepts that lie at the heart of the problem: divine omnipotence, divine goodness, and human happiness. According to Lewis, there are popular but false ways of understanding each of these three concepts as well as less popular but correct ways of understanding them. The problem of pain rests upon the popular conceptions. Since these conceptions are flawed, the problem of pain fails, and once we have an accurate understanding of the three concepts, we will see how the problem can be solved. The reason that most people find the problem of pain convincing (at least initially) is that they accept (at least implicitly) the popular but false understandings of omnipotence, goodness, and happiness. In unraveling Lewis's solution to the problem of pain, therefore, it is essential that we distinguish the true and false ways of understanding each concept. We will begin, as Lewis does, with divine omnipotence.

1.3.2 Divine Omnipotence

Most people, when asked to define omnipotence for the first time, come up with something like this: Omnipotence is the ability to do anything. This view has a scriptural basis: "[F]or God, all things are possible."[36] There is, however, a long and glorious tradition according to which this definition must be qualified somewhat, and Lewis is part of this tradition. The tradition goes back at least as far as the great thirteenth-century theologian Thomas Aquinas, who maintained that "there does not fall under the scope of God's omnipotence anything that implies a contradiction."[37]

A popular example of something that lies beyond the bounds of omnipotence is the creation of a round square. Since round shapes have exactly zero corners, and square shapes have exactly four corners, a round square would have precisely zero corners and also precisely four corners. This seems to be just plain impossible. Not even God could create such a shape. However – and this is crucial – God's inability to create such a shape does not indicate a lack of power on God's part; rather, the notion of creating a round square just doesn't make sense. Lewis classifies things like round squares as "intrinsically impossible" and puts the point about omnipotence this way:

> His Omnipotence means power to do all that is intrinsically possible, not to do the intrinsically impossible. You may attribute miracles to Him, but not nonsense. This is no limit to His power. . . . It remains true that all *things* are possible with God: the intrinsic impossibilities are not things but nonentities.[38]

It is important to avoid a certain kind of confusion here. Sometimes it is suggested that God could make a round square simply by changing the meanings of the terms "round" and "square." For instance, if God were to change the meaning of "round" so that it meant what the word "green" currently means, then making a round square would be a straightforward matter.

However, making the *sentence* "There is a round square" true is not quite the same as actually making a round square. When we consider whether God could make a round square, we are considering whether God could make a shape that would be round (given the actual meaning of "round") and also square (given the actual meaning of "square"). And, given the actual meanings of these terms, it seems clear that God couldn't make a round square. He could fiddle about with language in such a way as to make the sentence "There is a round square" come out true, but He would still have failed to create any round squares.[39]

Sometimes it is suggested that round squares are impossible only given the actual laws of logic, and that since God is the creator of those laws, He could alter them in such a way that round squares would be possible. My own view is that this suggestion really doesn't make sense and is rooted in the mistake of taking the expression "laws of logic" too literally. More importantly, the proposal seems to have some practical implications that theists might find problematic. Consider, for instance, divine promise making. Theists typically think they can count on God's promises in the following sense: If God has promised that some situation p will not occur, then we can be darn sure that p will not occur. However, if God can alter the very rules of logic as He sees fit, then God's promises guarantee nothing, since He could simply change the rules of logic so that, for instance, bringing about p is perfectly consistent with keeping one's promise not to bring about p. So theists who think we can count on God to keep His promises ought to reject the view that God can modify logic as He sees fit.

Here, then, we have the first distinction between a popular but false understanding of a concept and the true understanding of that concept. The popular but false understanding of omnipotence is that omnipotence is the ability to bring about absolutely any situation, including situations that are intrinsically impossible. The correct understanding of omnipotence, according to Lewis, is that it is the ability to bring about any situation that is intrinsically possible.[40]

With this understanding of omnipotence in hand, Lewis seeks to make the case that the class of intrinsically impossible situations includes the following: that there is a society of free souls in which no soul can inflict pain on another soul. Lewis's argument for this claim can be construed as consisting of two main steps. Each of the steps is an alleged entailment or necessary connection between two situations, p and q, where p entails or necessitates q in such a way that it is intrinsically impossible for p to obtain without q also obtaining. The two necessary connections are these:

Necessary Connection 1: If there is a society of free souls, then there *must* also be a relatively independent, law-governed environment containing that society of free souls.

Necessary Connection 2: If there is a relatively independent, law-governed environment containing a society of free souls, then the free souls that belong to the society *must* be capable of inflicting pain on each other.

The two necessary connections together entail Lewis's desired conclusion:

Conclusion: If there is a society of free souls, then the free souls that belong to the society *must* be capable of inflicting pain on each other.

A society of free souls is a group of souls with certain properties. Each soul has the capacity to act freely, recognizes the distinction between itself and other souls, and is capable of interacting with other souls to some extent. A relatively independent and law-governed environment is an environment shared by the various free souls that is not under the complete control of any one of them and instead behaves according to some set of exceptionless (or nearly exceptionless) laws that cannot be modified by the souls.

Two questions arise concerning the first necessary connection: Why does a society of free souls require an *environment* at all? And why must the shared environment be independent and law-governed? Lewis's answer to the first question is that without a shared environment the souls could interact with each other only if it were possible for "naked minds to 'meet' or become aware of each other."[41] However, this is not possible, argues Lewis, because such a meeting could transpire only if one soul were to become directly aware of the thoughts of another soul. The problem is that this would leave each soul with no way of distinguishing thoughts originating in itself from thoughts originating in other souls. Each soul would find itself confronted with a host of thoughts but would have no way of knowing which ones (if any) were produced by other free agents.[42] Therefore, no soul would be in a position to know that there *were* free agents distinct from itself.

With respect to the second question, Lewis argues that the only alternative to a "neutral field" with a "fixed nature of its own" is an environment that is entirely under the control of a single free agent.[43] Under such circumstances, only the controlling agent would have the ability to act freely, because no other agent would be able to influence the environment at all. So a fixed environment is required if *all* the souls in the society are to have the capacity for free action.

In support of the second necessary connection (that free souls in a stable environment must be able to inflict pain on each other), Lewis argues that an independent, law-governed environment makes conflict between the various free souls possible, and that this in turn leads to the possibility that they will inflict pain on each other:

> If a man travelling in one direction is having a journey down a hill, a man going in the opposite direction must be going up hill. If even a pebble lies where I want it to lie, it cannot, except by a coincidence, be where you want it to lie. And this...leaves the way open to a great evil, that of competition and hostility. And if souls are free, they cannot be prevented from dealing with the problem by competition instead of courtesy. And once they have advanced to actual hostility, they can then exploit the fixed nature of matter to hurt one another. The permanent nature of wood which enables us to use it as a beam also enables us to use it for hitting our neighbour on the head.[44]

With this, we arrive at one of those advertised occasions upon which Lewis directly responds to a point from Hume's *Dialogues*. In the previous section I briefly described four circumstances that, according to Philo, account for most or all of the suffering in the world *and* that an omnipotent God could have avoided. The second of these circumstances is that the world is governed by general laws of nature. Philo claims that rather than setting up the world so that it follows general laws of nature, God might have created a world "conducted by particular volitions."[45] The suggestion here is that God might interfere in some undetectable fashion whenever He sees that events are unfolding in a way that, if unchecked, would lead to suffering. Philo says:

> A being...who knows the secret springs of the universe might easily, by particular volitions, turn all these accidents to the good of mankind, and render the whole world happy, without discovering himself in any operation. A fleet whose purposes were salutary to society might always meet with a fair wind: Good princes enjoy sound health and long life: Persons born to power and authority be framed with good tempers and virtuous dispositions.[46]

Lewis's response to Philo's suggestion is that if God interfered often enough to prevent *any* agent from causing another to suffer, the freedom to choose between right and wrong would vanish entirely:

> [S]uch a world would be one in which wrong actions were impossible, and in which, therefore, freedom of the will would be void; nay, if the principle were carried out to its logical conclusion, evil thoughts would be impossible, for the cerebral matter which we use in thinking would refuse its task when we attempted to frame them. All matter in the neighborhood of a wicked man would be liable to undergo unpredictable alterations.[47]

What Lewis has offered, to this point, is a version of the free will defense, one of the most ancient and popular proposed solutions to the problem of evil.[48] A key tenet of Lewis's approach is that a society of free souls who cannot inflict pain on each other is an intrinsic impossibility. Thus, it is no more within God's power to create such a society than it is to create a round square. If God brings into being a society of free agents, He thereby makes suffering possible.

At this stage, I would like to point out two shortcomings in what Lewis has said so far as well as a question that remains to be answered. Neither of the shortcomings is fatal, and Lewis does provide an answer to the question in due course. I mention these things now so that we can see that Lewis has more work to do, at least if he wants to account for *all* of the human suffering in the world.[49]

A distinction is often drawn between *moral* and *natural* evil. As our focus is on suffering, we may distinguish between moral suffering (suffering that is the result of free human actions) and natural suffering (suffering that is not the result of such free actions; this would include suffering caused by natural disasters like the 1755 Lisbon earthquake and the 2004 Indonesian tsunami). This distinction allows us to see the first shortcoming in what Lewis has said so far: He has addressed only moral suffering. He has said nothing yet that would explain why God would permit natural suffering.

The second shortcoming is that what Lewis has said so far does not seem sufficient even to account for all of the moral suffering we find in our world. To see this point, consider the recent phenomenon of the internet chat room. A chat room is a shared, neutral environment that allows various free agents to recognize the existence of other free agents and interact with them. Agents interacting in such an environment can inflict some types of pain on each other: They can frustrate each other's desires, insult each other, induce various kinds of emotional pain in each other. But no free agent in such an environment can, for example, cause electrical shocks to be emitted from the keyboard of another user, or whirling blades to pop out of another user's screen, or another user to burst into flame. But in the actual world, free agents can (and sometimes do) electrocute, stab, and incinerate each other. The point is that it is possible for there to be a society of free souls without it being possible for them to inflict *these* kinds of suffering on each other. So these more extreme types of suffering seem to remain unaccounted for at this point.

Finally, here is a question for Lewis: If a society of free souls does require the possibility of the sort of suffering we find in our world, why would God not simply skip the society of free souls altogether? Another way of putting this question is this: What is so great about a society of free souls that makes it *worth* all the suffering?

To see how Lewis might address these various concerns, we must examine the rest of his solution to the problem of pain. Two of the three key concepts involved in the problem remain to be discussed: divine goodness and human happiness. Following the order of Lewis's presentation once again, let us turn to his analysis of divine goodness.

1.3.3 Divine Goodness and Human Happiness

Lewis's discussion of divine goodness in *The Problem of Pain* focuses on God's love for humanity. Though Lewis does not think that love is the only aspect of God's goodness, it is the one that is most relevant to the problem of pain. What makes human suffering so puzzling is that God is supposed to *love* us. To explain God's love for humanity, Lewis first draws a distinction between genuine love and mere kindness. The primary goal of kindness, as Lewis understands it, is a pleasant existence. To be kind to someone is to reduce her suffering or increase her pleasure. The popular way of thinking of divine goodness is as kindness. This false conception of divine goodness has it that God's goodness amounts to nothing more than His wanting humans to live comfortable, pleasant earthly lives. Comfort and pleasure, then, constitute the popular but false conception of human happiness:

> We want...not so much a Father in Heaven as a grandfather in heaven – a senile benevolence who, as they say, 'liked to see young people enjoying themselves' and whose plan for the universe was simply that it might be truly said at the end of each day, 'a good time was had by all'. Not many people, I admit, would formulate a theology in precisely those terms; but a conception not very different lurks at the back of many minds.[50]

To say that God is good is to say that He loves us, which is to say that his overriding goal for us is that we live pleasurable, comfortable earthly lives: "Kindness...cares not whether its object becomes good or bad, provided only that it escapes suffering."[51]

But, says Lewis, genuine divine goodness involves love rather than kindness. To explain the nature of divine goodness, Lewis examines four kinds of love. Although none of the four kinds corresponds perfectly to God's love for humanity, the idea is that these imperfect approximations have certain features that can shed some light on the nature of God's love for humanity. The four kinds of love are (i) an artist's love for his creation, (ii) a person's love for a beast (e.g., the love of a man for his dog), (iii) a father's love for his son, and (iv) a man's love for a woman.

One element common to all four is that the lover in each case wants the object of his love to be a certain way. Specifically, the lover wants the beloved to be perfect: "Love...demands the perfecting of the beloved."[52] It is important to note that the love is *not* conditional upon the perfection of the beloved; instead, the love precedes the perfection of the beloved object, and the love persists even if (as is often or perhaps always the case) the beloved object never becomes perfect. A consequence of this aspect of love is that if the beloved object is not perfect, the lover will want the beloved to approach as near to perfection as possible. Accordingly, the lover may attempt to transform the object of his love.

Two aspects of this process of transformation are worth noting. The first is that the beloved object may well fail to understand the point of the process of transformation imposed upon it. The second (and related) aspect is that the transformation may require suffering on the part of the beloved:

> [O]ver the great picture of his life – the work which he loves ... [the artist] will take endless trouble – and would, doubtless, thereby *give* endless trouble to the picture if it were sentient. One can imagine a sentient picture, after being rubbed and scraped and recommenced for the tenth time, wishing that it were only a thumbnail sketch whose making was over in a minute.[53]

Similarly, because God loves us, He wants us to approach as near to perfection as possible. This means that each of us needs to be transformed, and, like Lewis's imagined sentient painting, we find the transformation painful. The painting example may be misleading in an important way: It might convey the impression that the transformation is entirely for the sake of the lover. After all, a great painting primarily benefits its artist; the painting itself seems to get little out of the deal! Has the happiness of the beloved dropped out of Lewis's account of love altogether?

The answer is no. Lewis writes that "when we are such as He can love without impediment, we shall in fact be happy."[54] But what does it take to become the sort of being that God can love without impediment? An important difference between us and a painting is precisely that we are capable of entering into a personal relationship with our Creator. Unlike the painting, we can love the Artist back – and I believe that Lewis's view is that it is precisely love for God that renders us worthy of God's love: "God wills our good, and our good is to love Him."[55] Loving God entails striving to become like God (in certain respects): "We are bidden to 'put on Christ', to become like God.... To be God – to be like God and to share His goodness in creaturely response – to be miserable – these are the only three alternatives."[56] The final wrinkle is that we must love God *freely*. God does not want coerced love but rather freely given love. Freely loving God *is* true human happiness. The devil Screwtape explains some of these ideas to his nephew Wormwood in Lewis's fictional work *The Screwtape Letters* as follows:

> He really *does* want to fill the universe with a lot of loathsome little replicas of Himself – creatures whose life, on its miniature scale, will be qualitatively like His own, not because He has absorbed them but because their wills freely conform to His....But you now see that the Irresistible and the Indisputable are the two weapons which the very nature of His scheme forbids Him to use. Merely to override a human will...would be for Him useless. He cannot ravish. He can only woo.[57]

This completes Lewis's analysis of the three key concepts involved in the problem of pain. The following chart summarizes Lewis's views on these concepts:

	False Conception	True Conception
Divine omnipotence	Ability to do absolutely anything	Ability to do anything that is intrinsically possible
Divine goodness	Desire that humans have false happiness	Desire that humans have true happiness[58]
Human happiness	Comfortable, pleasant earthly lives	Freely loving God and striving to become "Christlike"

We are now in a position to see Lewis's answer to the question that I posed at the end of the previous section: What is so great about a society of free souls that makes it *worth* all the suffering? The answer is that only *free* souls are capable of achieving genuine happiness. This is the great good that makes a society of free souls

worthwhile, even if it brings along tremendous suffering as a consequence.[59]

We are also now ready to see Lewis's explanation of natural suffering. The essence of that explanation is that natural suffering is one
of the tools God uses to transform us, to nudge us toward genuine
human happiness while leaving our freedom intact. Natural suffering
plays a "remedial or corrective" role.[60] Lewis's discussion of the four
kinds of love hints at the fact that the transformation of the beloved
by the lover may be painful, but we still need to know exactly why
making human beings more "Christlike" sometimes requires that
they suffer. As Lewis observes: "Not all medicine tastes nasty: or if it
did, that is itself one of the unpleasant facts for which we should like
to know the reason."[61] The role of suffering in our transformation is
the topic of the next section.

1.3.4   God's Three Uses of Pain

Lewis writes:

> When souls become wicked they will certainly...hurt one another;
> and this, perhaps, accounts for four-fifths of the sufferings of
> men....But there remains, none the less, much suffering which can-
> not be traced to ourselves. Even if all suffering were man-made, we
> should like to know the reason for the enormous permission to torture
> their fellows which God gives to the worst of men.[62]

In these lines, Lewis implicitly acknowledges the distinction between
moral and natural suffering. To account for natural suffering, Lewis
describes three ways that God might use pain to nudge us toward
genuine happiness.

The first use to which God sometimes puts pain is to get us to
recognize our moral shortcomings. Part of loving God is obeying
the moral laws that God has laid down for humanity. But a person
who doesn't realize that he is violating the rules of morality will
never even attempt to obey them. Among the components of moral
corruption is blindness to one's own corruption: "[E]rror and sin
both have this property, that the deeper they are the less their victim

suspects their existence."[63] Pain can function as a kind of wake-up call, stimulating the corrupt person to engage in self-examination, which may lead him to recognize his corruption:

> [P]ain insists upon being attended to. God whispers to us in our plea-
> sures, speaks in our conscience, but shouts in our pain: it is His mega-
> phone to rouse a deaf world. A bad man, happy, is a man without
> the least inkling that his actions do not 'answer', that they are not in
> accord with the [moral] laws of the universe.[64]

The passage indicates that pain is just one of the tools in God's tool-box, but in some cases it may be the only effective one: "No doubt pain as God's megaphone is a terrible instrument.... But it gives the only opportunity the bad man can have for amendment."[65]

Lewis describes a second use of pain in these lines:

> God, who has made us, knows what we are and that our happiness
> lies in Him. Yet we will not seek it in Him as long as He leaves us any
> other resort where it can even plausibly be looked for. While what we
> call 'our own life' remains agreeable we will not surrender it to Him.
> What then can God do in our interests but make 'our own life' less
> agreeable to us, and take away the plausible source of false happiness?

Imagine that you have a child who loves to play video games. Your child loves video games so much that he thinks of nothing else; he is perfectly happy to play video games until, as they say, the cows come home. Suppose also that you know that your child would be happier, would lead a fuller life, if he were to put aside his video games and devote his energies elsewhere. One way to get him to do this would be to ruin video game playing for him. If you could somehow make the video games boring or unpleasant for him, this would motivate him to look elsewhere for fulfillment.

Lewis's idea is that humans are somewhat like this video-game-playing child. We tend to look for happiness and fulfillment in earthly things and do not look for happiness in God. One of the dangers of free will is that we might misuse it: "From the moment a creature becomes aware of God as God and of itself as self, the terrible alter-native of choosing God or self for the centre is opened to it."[66] God knows that our true happiness lies in Him but sees that we will never turn to Him if we remain content with earthly things. He needs a way to nudge us away from earthly things without eliminating our free will. Lewis's idea is that God can accomplish this by using pain to spoil the earthly things for us. This frees us of the illusion that the earthly things hold real happiness and inclines us to look elsewhere. The contemporary philosopher Peter van Inwagen, who has developed this particular strand of Lewis's thought powerfully and at some length, puts the point this way:

> An essential and important component of God's plan of Atonement...is to make us *dissatisfied* with our state of separation from Him...by simply allowing us to "live with" the natural consequences of this separation, and by making it as difficult as possible for us to delude ourselves about the kind of world we live in: a hideous world.[67]

Unlike the first use of pain, this second use is not applicable only to the thoroughly corrupt: "[T]his illusion of self-sufficiency may be at its strongest in some very honest, kindly, and temperate people, and on such people, therefore, misfortune must fall."[68] If this claim is plausible, it makes Lewis's view quite powerful, because it allows Lewis to account for the suffering of those who seem least to deserve it. And this is surely one of the most problematic kinds of suffering:

> We are perplexed to see misfortune falling upon decent, inoffensive, worthy people.... How can I say with sufficient tenderness what here needs to be said?... The life to themselves and their families stands between them and the recognition of their need; He makes that life less sweet to them.[69]

This idea meshes with Jesus' warning to the rich young man that "it will be hard for a rich person to enter the kingdom of heaven.... [I]t is easier for a camel to go through the eye of a needle than for someone who is rich to enter the kingdom of God."[70] Wealth tends to produce contentedness with one's earthly life, and thus is one of the main obstacles to seeking happiness in God. As Screwtape advises Wormwood: "Prosperity knits a man to the World. He feels that he is 'finding his place in it,' while really it is finding its place in him."[71]

Lewis also suggests that understanding this function of pain may help us to understand the particular mixture of pleasure and pain that we find in this world:

> We are never safe, but we have plenty of fun, and some ecstasy. It is not hard to see why. The security we crave would teach us to rest our hearts in this world and oppose an obstacle to our return to God: a few moments of happy love, a landscape, a symphony, a merry meeting with our friends, a bathe or a football match, have no such tendency. Our Father refreshes us on the journey with some pleasant inns, but will not encourage us to mistake them for home.[72]

The third role of pain is the most complex of the three. In explaining it, Lewis appeals to the principle that "to choose involves knowing that you choose." More precisely, Lewis's principle seems to be that a person *freely* chooses x for reason r only if she *knows* that she chooses x for reason r. Lewis applies this principle as follows:

> We cannot therefore know that we are acting at all, or primarily, for God's sake, unless the material of the action is contrary to our inclinations, or (in other words) painful, and what we cannot know that we are choosing, we cannot choose. The full acting out of the self's surrender to God therefore demands pain.[73]

The idea here is perhaps best explained by way of an example. I will use an example peculiar to my own pleasures, but I am confident that the reader can adapt the example in accordance with her own pleasures. Suppose that God commanded me to spend the day playing the X-Box video game Halo 2 while drinking Whiskey and Coke. Suppose I obey. Can I be confident that I performed the commanded act *because* it was commanded by God? (In this example, x = playing Halo 2, and r = God commanded me to play Halo 2). I suspect that Lewis would say that the answer is no, for the following reason: The thing I have been commanded to do is something I find quite pleasurable and so am inclined to do regardless of whether I think it has been commanded by God. Therefore, even if I obey, I cannot know that I did not perform the action because it was pleasurable rather than because it was commanded by God. And so it follows from Lewis's principle that it is not the case that I freely performed the act because it was commanded by God.[74] It would therefore be misleading to describe this as a case in which I surrendered myself to God, despite the fact that I did what God commanded.

To illustrate how pain can enable us to know that we are performing an action because it is commanded by God, Lewis discusses the Old Testament account of the binding of Isaac, in which God commands Abraham to kill his only son. This is surely a command that it would bring Abraham tremendous pain and no pleasure to obey; nevertheless, he goes about obeying the command, until God stops the proceedings at the last moment.[75] In this example, Abraham can be confident that he performed the action because it was commanded by God, for there is no other plausible motive. That the action is one that is so painful to carry out therefore makes this a case in which Abraham can freely perform the action because it is commanded by God.[76]

This completes Lewis's solution to the problem of pain.[77] Accordingly, let us consider again our initial formulation of the problem:

The Problem of Pain

1. If God exists, then He is omnipotent, omniscient, and morally perfect.
2. If God is morally perfect, then He wants there to be no suffering in the world.
3. If God is omnipotent and omniscient, then He can bring it about that there is no suffering in the world.
4. So: If God is omnipotent, omniscient, and morally perfect, then there is no suffering in the world (from 2 and 3).
5. But there is suffering in the world.
6. Therefore, God does not exist (from 1, 4, and 5).

What would Lewis say about this argument? The answer to this question depends on how we construe the second premise. Specifically, we need to know whether, according to the premise, God's moral perfection entails that he desires a world devoid of suffering *more than He desires anything else.* If the premise is construed in this strong fashion, then Lewis would reject it. Lewis's position is that there is at least one good that is more important than a pain-free world, a good that might in fact require that the world contain suffering. This great good is, of course, genuine human happiness, and we have seen why even an omnipotent God may be unable to bring about this good without also permitting human suffering. Because the good is *so* good, God will strive to bring it about even if He must use suffering as a means to attain it. Of course, Lewis can allow that God desires that there be as *little* suffering in the world as is consistent with promoting genuine human happiness. If the second premise is construed as claiming that this is all that moral perfection requires, then Lewis can accept it. However, if the premise is construed in this way, it is not strong enough to support the fourth premise. So, in Lewis's eyes, the second premise is either false or too weak to support the fourth premise; either way, the argument fails.[78]

One loose string remains: At the end of the earlier section on omnipotence, I mentioned the problem posed by the internet chat room. The problem for Lewis's view was that it seems possible for there to be a society of free souls in which the souls cannot inflict upon each other the kinds of extreme suffering that they can inflict upon each other in our world. How, then, can Lewis account for this feature of our world?[79]

Perhaps Lewis could draw upon his explanation of natural suffering to answer this question. It may be that there are cases that require extreme kinds of natural suffering. For instance, perhaps there are people who will turn to God (and hence toward genuine happiness) only if they undergo extreme pain. Let's call such people "hard cases."

We have seen why, according to Lewis, a society of free souls requires the existence of a law-governed environment. Since it is (typically) via these laws that God inflicts natural suffering, if God is to handle the hard cases adequately, the laws that govern the environment must permit the occurrence of extreme pain. But if the laws permit such pain, this opens up the possibility that some of the free agents within the environment will exploit those laws to inflict extreme pain upon others. Here is a simple example that illustrates this point: If God can use fire to inflict pain by way of volcanic eruptions and forest fires, then humans can master the laws relating to fire and exploit those laws to burn other humans. Perhaps the existence of hard cases explains why we don't live in an environment similar to an internet chat room: Such an environment would not permit God to deal with the hard cases while also leaving the free will of the agents in that environment intact.

If Lewis's solution to the problem of pain is to be entirely successful, all human natural suffering must be explicable in terms of the three roles described in this section. Whether this is so is the main topic of the penultimate section of this chapter, in which we will consider some objections to Lewis's solution to the problem of pain. Before turning to that task, however, it will be useful to consider a literary illustration of some of Lewis's ideas. Doing this will both bring Lewis's ideas to life and help to sharpen our comprehension of the difference between how human suffering appears when viewed in light of false understandings of omnipotence, goodness, and happiness and how it appears when viewed in light of correct understandings of these concepts.

1.4 THE CASE OF IVAN ILYICH

Leo Tolstoy's great novella *The Death of Ivan Ilyich* presents a case study of at least two of the three roles that Lewis says natural suffering can play. The story recounts the life and death of Ivan Ilyich. Tolstoy writes that Ivan lived a life that was "most simple and commonplace – and most horrifying."[80] For most of his adult life, Ivan is concerned primarily with advancing his legal career, achieving financial success, and arranging his life in such a way as to fill it with his favorite pleasures. Foremost among these is the pleasure of a good game of whist.[81] Tolstoy makes it clear that along the way Ivan engages in some morally questionable behavior. This is a consequence of a certain lack of reflection on the part of Ivan. He simply adopts the beliefs and values of the social class to which he wishes to belong.

He has some inkling that what he is doing is not quite right, but manages to push these feelings of unease aside:

> As a student he had done things which, at the time, seemed to him extremely vile and made him feel disgusted with himself; but later, seeing that people of high standing had no qualms about doing these things, he was not quite able to consider them good but managed to dismiss them and not feel the least perturbed when he recalled them.[82]

One of the best illustrations of Ivan's approach to life is his decision to marry:

> Ivan Ilyich had no clear and definite intention of marrying, but when the girl fell in love with him, he asked himself: "Really, why shouldn't I get married?" ... Ivan Ilyich married for both reasons: in acquiring such a wife he did something that gave him pleasure and, at the same time, did what people of the highest standing considered correct.
>   And so Ivan Ilyich got married.[83]

Ivan is, in a nutshell, a "bad man, happy ... without the least inkling that his actions do not 'answer', that they are not in accord with the laws of the universe."[84] Just when everything has fallen into place for Ivan, he injures himself in a fall from a ladder, and as time passes it becomes clear that he is suffering from a chronic and ultimately fatal illness. One of the first consequences of the illness is that it ruins Ivan's greatest pleasure – the pleasure of whist. Tolstoy describes Ivan's despondency at the end of an evening of card playing ruined by his illness: "After supper his friends went home, leaving Ivan Ilyich alone with the knowledge that his life had been poisoned and was poisoning the lives of others, and that far from diminishing, that poison was penetrating deeper and deeper into his entire being."[85]

As Ivan's illness progresses, it strips him of his ability to experience pleasure altogether and leaves him isolated and alone. For the first time in his life, Ivan reflects on his life. Eventually he reaches an awful conclusion:

> "What if my entire life, my entire conscious life, simply was *not the real thing*?" It occurred to him that what had seemed utterly inconceivable before – that he had not lived the kind of life he should have – might in

fact be true. It occurred to him that those scarcely perceptible impulses of his to protest what people of high rank considered good, vague impulses which he had always suppressed, might have been precisely what mattered, and all the rest had not been the real thing. His official duties, his manner of life, his family, the values adhered to by people in society and in his profession – all these might not have been the real thing. He tried to come up with a defense of these things and suddenly became aware of the insubstantiality of them all.[86]

In this passage Ivan discovers the moral defects in his character. Elsewhere we find an account of Ivan's discovery of the amount of true happiness his life has contained:

[I]n his imagination he called to mind the best moments of his pleasant life. Yet, strangely enough, all the best moments of his pleasant life now seemed entirely different than they had in the past – all except the earliest memories of childhood.... As soon as he got to the period that had produced the present Ivan Ilyich, all the seeming joys of his life vanished before his sight and turned into something trivial and often nasty. And the farther he moved from childhood, the closer he came to the present, the more trivial and questionable these joyful experiences appeared.[87]

Ivan's illness and suffering play two of the roles described by Lewis. Ivan discovers that throughout his adult life he has been spiraling downward into immorality and misery. In his last few hours of life, Ivan grapples with these discoveries: "Yes, all of it was simply *not the real thing*. But no matter. I can still make it *the real thing* – I can. But what *is* the real thing?"[88] He realizes that his prolonged illness and suffering is torturing his family (he spends the last three days of his life screaming). At the very end it dawns on him that there is a way to redeem himself and his wasted life – a way to make his life "the real thing":

And suddenly it became clear to him that what had been oppressing him and would not leave him suddenly was vanishing all at once – from two sides, ten sides, all sides. He felt sorry for them, he had to do something to keep from hurting them. To deliver them and himself from this suffering. "How good and simple!" he thought.[89]

And so Ivan performs the first genuinely altruistic action of his adult life: He lets go and permits himself to die in order to end his family's suffering. With this act Ivan finds redemption.[90] There is also the suggestion that he discovers that real happiness does not lie in earthly things at all. Throughout his illness Ivan is plagued by an overwhelming fear of death. But at the very end, after he decides to allow himself to die in order to spare his family from further suffering, he no longer fears death: "He searched for his accustomed fear of death and could not find it. Where was death? What death? There was no fear because there was no death. Instead of death there was light."[91] I suggest that Ivan no longer fears death because he has realized that true happiness does not lie in earthly things, but elsewhere, beyond this life.[92]

Let us consider for a moment how someone who accepts the popular but false conceptions of omnipotence, divine goodness, and human happiness might view Ivan's ordeal. Just when Ivan finally achieves happiness (a comfortable, pleasant life), he is stricken by an incurable illness that slowly sucks all the pleasure out of his life. What sort of God would let this happen? An omnipotent God can do anything, and a God who loved Ivan wouldn't let such a thing happen to him. So God must either be a bumbling fool, or he must not like Ivan very much. When Ivan thinks about God for the first time in the story, after his illness has struck, he reaches the latter conclusion:

> He cried about his helplessness, about his terrible loneliness, about the cruelty of people, about the cruelty of God, about the absence of God. "Why hast Thou done all this? Why hast Thou brought me to this? Why dost Thou torture me so? For what? . . . Go on then! Hit me again! But what for! What have I done to Thee?"[93]

When seen through the eyes of someone in the grips of mistaken conceptions of omnipotence, goodness, and happiness, Ivan's suffering can seem like overwhelming evidence against the existence of God. But for someone with a correct understanding of these concepts (and of Ivan's character), Ivan's suffering is no evidence against the existence of God at all. In fact, Lewis would maintain that once we understand these concepts correctly, we will see that it is precisely *because* God loves Ivan that He permits him to suffer. Lewis's solution to the problem of pain, if successful, does more than reconcile God's love with human suffering; it illustrates how human suffering actually flows from divine love. God's goodness is not the senile grandfatherly goodness that is concerned only with making you *feel* good. Rather, it's the real, terrible goodness that is concerned with making you *become* good. Perhaps this is why Lewis repeatedly describes God's love for humanity as an "intolerable compliment."[94]

What is true of Ivan's suffering is, according to Lewis, true of all human suffering. Philo sees the distribution of pleasure and pain in the world as evidence against God's existence; Lewis sees it as just what we would expect once we correctly understand the key concepts. To Philo's rhetorical question, "Is the world, considered in general and as it appears to us in this life, different from what a man or such a limited being would, *beforehand*, expect from a very powerful, wise, and benevolent Deity?," Lewis's response would be: Well, no, actually.[95]

In the discussion of Hume's *Dialogues* earlier in this chapter, I briefly mentioned Philo's "four circumstances" – the four avoidable sources of suffering in the world. We have already discussed Lewis's views concerning the second of these features, "the conducting of the world by general laws."[96] The remaining three circumstances are these: (i) pain (in addition to pleasure) functions as a motive "to excite all creatures to action"; (iii) nature is frugal, in that each creature is endowed with just enough natural capacities to survive, but not enough to avoid misery; and (iv) the "inaccurate workmanship" of the world, which seems more like a rough draft than a final project.[97]

I think we can see now how Lewis would respond to Philo's suggestion that an omnipotent, good God would have avoided these three circumstances. With respect to the first circumstance, Philo seems to assume that the only way pain can be beneficial is by functioning as a motive to perform an action that contributes to one's comfort or safety (e.g., by motivating you to pull your hand away from a flame). Lewis has taken great pains to describe the other beneficial functions of pain; if Lewis is right, Philo's assumption is simply mistaken. With respect to the third circumstance, we have seen why, according to Lewis, a God who loves us would not want us to get too comfortable in this world. What Philo sees as unnecessary frugality that needlessly prevents us from achieving lasting security and comfort Lewis sees as one of God's tools for nudging us toward genuine happiness. Finally, with respect to the fourth circumstance, we may observe that in order to evaluate the quality of the workmanship of the world accurately, one must know what the main purpose of the world is.[98] Assuming that the point of the world is to produce comfortable, pleasure-filled lives for its inhabitants, Philo marvels at its shoddy workmanship. Lewis would suggest that once we comprehend that the point of the world is to provide an environment in which free souls can work toward genuine happiness, what seem like marks of shoddy workmanship will be recognized as masterful touches on the part of the Artist.

1.5 THE INCOMPLETENESS OF LEWIS'S SOLUTION

Perhaps the most extended critical discussion of Lewis's work in Christian apologetics is John Beversluis's book *C. S. Lewis and the Search for Rational Religion*. Beversluis devotes a chapter to *The Problem of Pain*, and we will begin our critical examination of Lewis's solution to the problem of pain by considering some of the more interesting objections Beversluis offers in that chapter.

I have emphasized that an important part of Lewis's account is that genuine human happiness involves *freely* loving God. In the words of Screwtape, God "cannot ravish. He can only woo."[99] But Beversluis suggests that God's use of severe pain to lead humans to surrender themselves to Him would amount to ravishing rather than mere wooing:

> Consider the case of truly hard-core sinners who will not turn to God except in response to pain – prolonged and excruciating pain. What if they finally do turn to God as a result? Will they have done so freely? No. An analogy may help. I ask you for information that I know you possess. You refuse. So I inflict pain on you until you tell me everything

I want to know. Have you imparted this information freely? No you have not. It was the pain that brought you to terms. The same is true of the pain-racked sinners who finally turn to God as a result of their pain.... In such cases, we have been reduced to a single alternative, and one alternative is not an alternative at all.[100]

The objection here is that Lewis's account is internally incoherent. On the one hand, Lewis claims that genuine human happiness involves freely turning toward God. On the other hand, Lewis claims that God uses pain as a tool to produce genuine human happiness. The problem, according to Beversluis, is that the use of pain to get us to turn toward God entails that such turning is not done freely. Therefore, using pain to produce genuine human happiness is intrinsically impossible, and hence God cannot do it.

This objection fails because the way God uses pain in Lewis's model is quite different from the way pain is used in Beversluis's example. In short, Beversluis's analogy is not very analogous. In Beversluis's case, it is clear to the sufferer that there are just two options: reveal the information or suffer extreme pain. I agree with Beversluis that someone who reveals information under these circumstances has not done so freely. The "choice" such a person faces is much like the "choice" a person faces when confronted by an armed mugger who says "your money or your life": it is no choice at all.

However, the case of the sinful human who experiences natural suffering is not like this at all. This is so because (typically) it is not at all clear to such a human that the only two options are to surrender oneself to the Christian God or to suffer extreme pain. God is not directly present to the sufferer in the way that the torturer is directly present to the person from whom he intends to extract information in Beversluis's example. The situation the sinful human faces is far more ambiguous, and consequently there are many options available to him. Surrendering himself to the God of Christianity is just one of them; there are a host of other putative Gods to whom he might turn. Another option is simply to maintain that there is no God; the universe is governed by blind forces, life tends to be painful – and that's just the way things are, tough luck. Another option is to conclude that there is a God, but He's not particularly good.[101]

Remember Screwtape's remark that "the Irresistible and the Indisputable are the two weapons which the very nature of His scheme forbids Him to use"; because God's presence is not indisputable, He can use pain in the way described by Lewis without making surrender to Him irresistible.[102]

In Beversluis's example, the use of pain by the torturer marks the *end* of the sufferer's deliberation about what to do. The pain makes it clear that there is really just one available option. God's use of pain, by contrast, often marks the *beginning* of the sufferer's deliberation.[103] We can see this by recalling the case of Ivan Ilyich. Ivan moves through life unreflectively until he becomes ill. The illness stimulates reflection on his life and how he might change it – reflection that would not otherwise have occurred. We might even go so far as to say that Ivan's suffering *increases* his level of freedom, since the life he lived before the suffering was one lived without much deliberation at all. In any case, Ivan's suffering begins a process of self-examination without limiting that process to a single possible outcome. Although Ivan does eventually turn to God, his suffering does not *compel* him to do so.

A more challenging objection posed by Beversluis has it that Lewis's view conflicts with our knowledge of the actual distribution of pleasure and pain:

> Some people who do not suffer seem far from God while others who do suffer seem close to him. There are flourishing atheists and terminally ill believers. . . . the more you suffer, the further from God you are; and the less you suffer, the closer you are. Finally, the more you suffer, the more God loves you, and the less you suffer, the less God loves you, since it is those we love that we punish and those to whom we are indifferent that we allow to be happy in contemptible and estranging modes.[104]

There are actually a number of objections posed in this passage; I will focus on just one of them.[105] Consider Beversluis's remark about "flourishing atheists." It certainly seems to be the case that there are plenty of people in the world who have turned their backs not only on God but also on morality and who nevertheless live out their lives in relative comfort and ease without ever facing the kind of suffering that Ivan (or Lewis, for that matter) faced. In the final sentence of the passage just quoted, Beversluis reminds us of Lewis's remark that "[i]t is for people whom we care nothing about that we demand happiness on any terms."[106] What, then, are we to make of the vicious yet happy (in the popular sense) among us? God seems to be permitting them to wallow in false happiness, presumably at the cost of genuine happiness. As Beversluis hints and Lewis's own words suggest, this seems to indicate that God does not love them; if He did, wouldn't He use His megaphone of pain to rouse them? If this reasoning is correct, it follows that God doesn't love all humans, and this is hard to reconcile with Lewis's understanding of God's goodness.[107] Ironically, Lewis's solution to the problem of pain may generate a problem of *not enough* pain.

The problem of not enough pain is challenging. In order to develop a Lewisian response to it, we will need to take something of a detour. We will examine two other objections to Lewis's view and consider how Lewis might respond to them. The ideas developed in the course of this discussion will provide us with the materials we need to deal with the problem of not enough pain. Here is the first of the two other objections to Lewis's view.

According to Lewis, God sometimes uses pain to nudge His creatures toward true happiness. This suggests that "suffering is good" and consequently ought "to be pursued rather than avoided."[108] Specifically, the suffering of *others* is good for *them*. Aren't we commanded to love our neighbors?[109] And doesn't loving them entail seeking their good? Therefore, we ought to inflict suffering on our neighbors, particularly the vicious among us who live in comfort.[110] In doing this, we would be doing "God's good work."

In *The Problem of Pain*, Lewis points out that "suffering is not good in itself."[111] Pain is *intrinsically* evil (evil in its own nature); Lewis's view commits him only to the claim that pain is sometimes *instrumentally* good (good because of what it leads to). Specifically, it sometimes leads to genuine happiness; nevertheless, it remains intrinsically evil. In *A Grief Observed*, Lewis writes that "[i]f there is a good God, then these tortures are necessary. For no even moderately good Being could possibly inflict or permit them if they weren't."[112] Because pain is intrinsically evil, it should be imposed on another only when there is a very good reason to do so – for instance, when doing so will lead to the other person's genuine happiness. This means that there are certain restrictions on when it is permissible to cause another person to suffer; in particular, if you are not sufficiently confident that some good would result from causing someone else to suffer, then you ought not to cause the other person to suffer.[113]

In *Mere Christianity*, Lewis claims that "[w]hen a man makes a moral choice two things are involved. One is the act of choosing. The other is the various feelings, impulses and so on which his psychological outfit presents him with, and which are the raw material of his choice."[114] We may not have much say in the "raw material" with which we must contend, and, according to Lewis, "bad psychological material is not a sin but a disease."[115] Of course, we do not all have the same raw material, and this generates difficulty when it comes to assessing the character of others:

> Human beings judge one another by their external actions. God judges them by their moral choices. . . . When a man who has been perverted from his youth and taught that cruelty is the right thing, does some tiny little kindness, or refrains from some cruelty he might have committed, and thereby, perhaps, risks being sneered at by his companions, he may, in God's eyes, be doing more than you and I would do if we gave up life itself for a friend. . . . That is why Christians are told not to judge. We see only the results which a man's choices make out of the raw material. But God does not judge him on the raw material at all, but on what he has done with it.[116]

The upshot of this is that there is a gap between the knowledge a human can have of another person's character and the knowledge that God can have of that person's character. In fact, Lewis's position seems to be that *only* God can have a complete and accurate understanding of another person's character. And this means that only God can know exactly what effect suffering would have on a given person's character at a given time. In particular, only God can know whether the suffering would nudge the person toward genuine happiness. This gap between our knowledge and God's knowledge, together with the principle that it is morally permissible to cause another person to suffer only if you are reasonably confident that doing so would have good consequences, implies that it is never morally permissible for a human to cause another human to suffer in order to nudge her toward genuine happiness. James Petrik makes a point along these lines by likening God to a surgeon:

> A surgical procedure that a trained surgeon may benevolently perform would be regarded as a moral abomination were I (a surgically inept professor of philosophy) to undertake the procedure in my basement. . . . In the same vein, it can be said that the reason that it would be abhorrent for human beings to routinely allow the kind of suffering that is, according to Lewis, permissible for God to allow is that an individual's spiritual and moral development is an extremely complex affair. . . . Thus, to allow intense suffering in order to effect a moral or spiritual transformation is to act in reckless ignorance. Of course, God operates under no such ignorance; therefore, it may well be permissible for God to allow intense suffering to effect character transformations when it is not permissible for human beings to do so.[117]

When it comes to using pain as a tool for the promotion of genuine happiness, God knows what He is doing; we don't. This is why it is permissible for God to use pain in ways in which it is not permissible for us to use it. So Lewis's solution to the problem of pain does not commit him to the view that it is permissible for us to inflict suffering on our neighbors in order to turn them toward God.

This response provides us with some but not all of the ideas we will need to deal with the problem of not enough pain. To get the rest of the ideas we will need, we must consider Lewis's response to a certain objection to the doctrine of hell. Consider the following passage:

> A simpler form of the same objection consists in saying that death ought not to be final, that there ought to be a second chance. I believe that if a million chances were likely to do good, they would be given. But a master often knows, when boys and parents do not, that it is really useless to send a boy in for a certain examination again. Finality must come some time, and it does not require a very robust faith to believe that omniscience knows when.[118]

We have already discussed those "truly hard-core sinners" who will turn to God only if they undergo extreme suffering. But there is another category of sinners that must be considered. This category contains those who would not *freely* surrender themselves to God under any circumstances. At one point Lewis remarks that "[p]ain as God's megaphone is a terrible instrument; it may lead to final and unrepented rebellion."[119] If there are such incorrigibles, God would recognize them and would know that inflicting suffering on them would be useless. Because pain is intrinsically evil, God refrains from inflicting it on those whom He knows it will not help. This could explain why He allows some people to wallow in false happiness. He knows that there is nothing He can do for them.

Suppose you knew next to nothing about medicine or even human biology and physiology. You might be quite mystified by the actions of a doctor working in a triage unit; why does he ignore some patients and treat others? What accounts for the different treatments he provides to different patients? The answers to these questions would be beyond you. Now suppose that you *thought* you knew something about medicine but had lots of false beliefs in this area. Under these circumstances you might come to doubt the goodness or competence of the doctor: Why does he ignore that patient altogether when he could have helped him? Why does he waste his time on that one who is clearly a goner? Such doubts would be based on misunderstandings of the situation.

One thing that human beings are remarkably bad at is assessing character, and not just others' character but their own character as well. Our inability to assess the nature of our own character and motivation is a central theme of Lewis's novel *Till We Have Faces*, in which we find the following passage:

> When the time comes to you at which you will be forced at last to utter the speech which has lain at the center of your soul for years, which you have, all that time, idiot-like, been saying over and over, you'll not talk about the joy of words. I saw well why the gods do not speak to us openly, nor let us answer. Till that word can be dug out of us, *why should they hear the babble that we think we mean?* How can they meet us face to face till we have faces?[120]

Our inadequate understanding of ourselves and others has been insisted on by assorted philosophers and is amply supported by contemporary work in psychology.[121] Despite this, forming judgments about the character of others is something we cannot seem to stop ourselves from doing. It seems to be part of human nature to form significantly inadequate beliefs about the character of those around us. This can help explain why we might find natural suffering mystifying and consider it to be evidence against the existence of a good God – *even if we have an accurate understanding of divine omnipotence, divine goodness, and human happiness*. Like the medical ignoramus who thinks he knows something about medicine and consequently doubts the goodness or competence of the triage doctor, we are ignoramuses when it comes to human character and consequently tend to doubt the goodness or competence of God. Because this doubt is rooted in ignorance, it is unwarranted. More precisely, the existence of incorrigibles, together with our inability to identify them, can lead us (mistakenly) to doubt the existence (or goodness) of God. God applies the awful treatment of pain to those cases where it will be effective, and foregoes it in those cases where it will not. Because we are poor judges of character, we are ill-equipped to distinguish the two kinds of cases, even when it comes to ourselves. This seems to me to be Lewis's best available response to the problem of not enough pain.[122]

Let us return to the event that was discussed at the beginning of this chapter – the 2004 Indonesian tsunami. Can Lewis's solution to the problem of pain adequately explain events of this sort? In answering this question, we should focus exclusively on the *suffering* caused by this event rather than on the deaths it caused, as Lewis's main project in *The Problem of Pain* is to explain suffering rather than death itself.[123] Can the suffering caused by the 2004 tsunami be plausibly construed as God nudging humanity toward genuine happiness?

The sheer scale of the event makes an affirmative answer to this question seem unlikely. Hundreds of thousands, perhaps millions of people suffered as a result of the tsunami. The extent and nature of this suffering seemed to depend on an incredibly large number of variables. Are we really to believe that all this suffering was distributed in such a way that each person who suffered received precisely the right amount of pain required for the promotion of genuine happiness?[124] Frankly, this is hard to swallow.[125]

On the other hand, I have offered an explanation of why such a claim might strike us as implausible even if it were true – namely, our incompetence when it comes to assessing character. How might we go about investigating such a claim? The task would be stupendous; it would require examining the long-term (presumably lifelong) impact of the suffering of each individual affected by the tsunami. To establish that Lewis's view cannot explain all this suffering, we would need to find at least one instance of suffering that did not promote genuine happiness in some way. Given the difficulty of assessing the character of others, it is hard to see how we could be confident that we had found such an instance. So while the claim that the suffering caused by the tsunami was the work of a master Surgeon and that not an iota of that suffering failed to promote genuine happiness strikes me as implausible, I do not know how to turn this sense of implausibility into a decisive objection to Lewis's solution to the problem of pain.

However, there is another kind of suffering that merits consideration: the suffering of children. One of the most famous philosophical discussions of this sort of suffering is found in an oft-anthologized chapter of Fyodor Dostoevsky's 1880 novel *The Brothers Karamazov* entitled "Rebellion." The chapter consists of a discussion between two of the Karamazov brothers, Ivan and Alyosha. Ivan describes a series of horrendous examples of the suffering of children. One of the most powerful examples appears in the following passage:

> And so these refined parents subjected their five-year-old girl to all kinds of torture. They beat her, kicked her, flogged her, for no reason that they themselves knew of. The child's whole body was covered with bruises. Eventually they devised a new refinement. Under the pretext that the child dirtied her bed . . . they forced her to eat excrement, smearing it all over her face. And it was the mother who did it! And then that woman would lock her little daughter up in the

outhouse until morning and she did so even on the coldest nights, when it was freezing. . . . Imagine the little creature, unable even to understand what is happening to her, beating her sore little chest with her tiny fist, weeping hot, unresentful, meek tears, and begging 'gentle Jesus' to help her, and all this happening in that icy, dark, stinking place! Do you understand this nonsensical thing. . . . Tell me, do you understand the purpose of that absurdity? Who needs it and why was it created?[126]

In each of Ivan's examples, children suffer at the hands of adults. Perhaps this suffering could be explained by the free will defense. However, there is plenty of *natural* child suffering – suffering that is the result not of free human action but rather of disease or natural disaster. Consider, for example, late infantile metachromatic leukodystrophy. This is a genetic disorder that affects the development of the myelin sheath, the fatty covering that acts as an insulator around nerve fiber. Children with this disease have difficulty walking after the first year of life. As the disease progresses, the symptoms typically include blindness, muscle rigidity, convulsions, impaired swallowing, paralysis, and dementia. Eventually afflicted children become bedridden, blind, and enter a vegetative state, typically dying by age ten.[127] Childhood diseases like this, which mercilessly strike the most innocent and helpless among us, seem to constitute one of the most horrific kinds of natural evil. Can Lewis's solution to the problem of pain account for this kind of suffering?

The case that it cannot begins with the observation that in sufficiently young children, suffering cannot play any of the three roles described by Lewis in his attempt to explain natural suffering. This is so for the straightforward reason that pain can play those three roles only in individuals who have a suitable grasp of certain key concepts (e.g., God, moral rightness and wrongness), and sufficiently young children are incapable of grasping such concepts. Very young children cannot freely surrender themselves to God for the same reason they cannot play chess: They simply lack the requisite cognitive equipment. Therefore, it is hard to see how suffering could nudge them toward genuine happiness.

It might be suggested that there could be a substantial temporal gap between the suffering and the turn toward God. Perhaps suffering as a child, even unremembered suffering, can lead to a surrender to God later in life. This is an interesting suggestion. However, even if we grant it, it will not completely solve the problem. This is because there are some children who suffer and then die without ever acquiring the cognitive equipment required to surrender to God. It seems clear that this sort of suffering cannot possibly contribute to the genuine happiness of its young victims.

In his defense of Lewis's account of divine goodness against the objections of Beversluis, Petrik suggests that "some suffering may be for the sake of the spiritual development of a person other than the sufferer."[128] The fifth-century theologian Augustine applies this idea to the suffering of children, remarking that "[s]ince God achieves some good by correcting adults through the suffering and death of children who are dear to them, why shouldn't those things take place?"[129] Although Lewis never explicitly makes this sort of point, there are hints of it in his writing. Recall his remark concerning apparently undeserved suffering: "The life to themselves and their families stands between them and the recognition of their need; He makes that life less sweet to them."[130] Lewis specifically mentions the family as something that can function as an obstacle to genuine happiness. Children would obviously fall into the category of family, and it is hard to imagine a more effective way of removing the sweetness from a person's life than allowing her children to suffer and die.

Can the pain-filled life of a child who lives in agony for a few years and then dies without the slightest glimmer of understanding of what is happening to him be justified by the benefits that such a life (eventually) produces for those affected by the child's suffering? That it can is a bitter pill to swallow indeed. Toward the end of "Rebellion," Ivan presents Alyosha with a challenge:

> "[L]et's assume that you were called upon to build the edifice of human destiny so that men would finally be happy and would find peace and tranquility. If you knew that, in order to attain this, you would have

to torture just one single creature, let's say the little girl who beat her chest so desperately in the outhouse, and that on her unavenged tears you could build that edifice, would you agreed to do it? Tell me and don't lie!"

"No, I would not," Alyosha said softly.

"And do you find acceptable the idea that those for whom you are building that edifice should gratefully receive a happiness that rests on the blood of a tortured child and, having received it, should continue to enjoy it eternally?"

"No, I do not find that acceptable" Alyosha said. . . . [131]

Ivan's point is that it is not morally permissible to permit the suffering of children, even if doing so is the only means of attaining genuine happiness for the rest of humanity.[132] This is a case where the end fails to justify the means because of the severity of the evil involved in the means.

Suppose there is a person who will acquire genuine happiness if, and only if, a child lives a pain-filled life for a few years and then dies in agony. Would a good God attain the good of genuine happiness for such a person at the cost of the suffering of the child?[133] To answer this question we must weigh the child's suffering against the adult's genuine happiness. Augustine's answer to the question is yes. After all, genuine happiness lasts forever, whereas the child's suffering is only temporary: "Once the suffering is past, it will be for the children as if they had never suffered."[134] My own view is that the answer to the question is no. I believe that even if the happiness outweighs the child's suffering, justice requires that the happiness be withheld because it is not the child who gets the great good of happiness but someone else.[135] A person whose genuine happiness can be acquired only through the horrific suffering of a child should not receive genuine happiness.[136]

The reader must draw her own conclusion on the issue. If I am correct, then Lewis's solution to the problem of pain is incomplete because it cannot account for all cases of child suffering. This point can be put a bit more precisely: If the explanations of human suffering proposed by Lewis in *The Problem of Pain* were the *only* explanations for human suffering, then our world would not contain the sort of suffering by children that I have described. On the other hand, if Augustine is correct, then Lewis's view can account for this sort of suffering. If Augustine is right then God's love for us might lead Him to permit our children to suffer and die. And this realization brings new significance to the following lines from Lewis's work *A Grief Observed*:

> The more we believe that God hurts only to heal, the less we can believe that there is any use in begging for tenderness. A cruel man might be bribed – might grow tired of his vile sport – might have a temporary fit of mercy, as alcoholics have fits of sobriety. But suppose that what you are up against is a surgeon whose intentions are good. The kinder and more conscientious he is, the more inexorably he will go on cutting.[137]

1.6 CONCLUSION

Suppose that my claim that Lewis's theory in *The Problem of Pain* cannot account for certain kinds of suffering experienced by children is correct; how damaging is this to Lewis's overall project? In thinking about this question, it is useful to distinguish more and less ambitious projects that a theist might undertake. One kind of project could be called a *defense*; this is the task of showing that the existence of evil (or of a particular kind of evil) is *compatible* with the existence of God.[138] A more ambitious project is that of providing a *theodicy*; this is the task of providing an actual (or at least plausible) explanation for why God would permit evil (or a particular kind of evil). A still more ambitious project is that of providing a *complete theodicy* – providing actual (or at least plausible) explanations for *all* the evils of the world.

Some of Lewis's remarks suggest that he is engaged only in a defense against the problem of pain. At one point he says that his project is "to discover how, perceiving a suffering world, and being assured, on quite different grounds, that God is good, we are to conceive that goodness and that suffering without contradiction."[139] However, there is good evidence that Lewis in fact has aims that are more ambitious than that passage suggests. For instance, when turning from the topic of moral evil to natural evil, he says that "[e]ven if all suffering were man-made, we should like to *know the reason* for the enormous permission to torture their fellows which God gives to the worst of men."[140] The passage makes it clear that Lewis intends to offer a suggestion about the *actual explanation* of certain kinds of suffering. Moreover, the very nature of Lewis's solution to the problem of pain suggests that he aims for at least a partial theodicy; he is clearly concerned to offer a plausible account of why God might permit the kind of suffering we actually find in the world. There is some indication that Lewis strives even for a theodicy that covers *all* suffering. For example, he offers distinct treatments of the suffering of those in hell as well as animal suffering, recognizing that these kinds of suffering cannot be explained in the same fashion as earthly human suffering.[141]

My charge of incompleteness, if sound, shows that Lewis has not presented a theodicy that covers all suffering; the correctness of my criticism is compatible with Lewis having provided a successful defense as well as a theodicy that accounts for some of the suffering we find in the world. The charge of incompleteness does, however, suggest a revised version of the problem of pain that has been the focus of this chapter. Let us define *non-victim-improving natural child suffering* as suffering experienced by a child that is not the result of human free action and does not contribute at all to the genuine happiness of the child who experiences the suffering. (As noted previously, such suffering may contribute to the genuine happiness of someone else).

The Problem of Child Suffering

1. If God exists, then He is omnipotent, omniscient, and morally perfect.
2. If God is morally perfect, then He wants there to be no non-victim-improving natural child suffering in the world.
3. If God is omnipotent and omniscient, then He can bring it about that there is no non-victim-improving natural child suffering in the world.

4. So: If God is omnipotent, omniscient, and morally perfect, then there is no non-victim-improving natural child suffering in the world (from 2 and 3).
5. But there is non-victim-improving natural child suffering in the world.
6. Therefore, God does not exist (from 1, 4, and 5).

As before, (2) and (3) are substantive premises. In this argument, premise (5) also seems to be substantive in the sense that it is not beyond question in the way that the original version of the premise was. What are we to make of this argument?

We would be well advised to remember Philo's warning that "[w]e know so little beyond common life, or even of common life, that, with regard to the economy of a universe, there is no conjecture, however wild, which may not be just, nor any one, however plausible, which may not be erroneous."[142] Perhaps for some unknown (by us) reason not even an omnipotent and omniscient God can prevent all non-victim-improving natural child suffering. Lewis warns us that we often make mistakes when it comes to determining which things are intrinsically impossible.[143] Perhaps what appears to be non-victim-improving natural child suffering somehow, in some fashion not conceived of by Lewis, does contribute to the child's genuine happiness after all.[144] Or perhaps such suffering is connected up with some great good in a way we cannot fathom – a good so great that, contrary to Ivan Karamazov's position, it justifies the existence of the suffering.[145]

These days, the heady dream of providing a decisive proof or disproof of God's existence – an argument that would compel acceptance by any rational person who could understand it – is widely regarded as a *mere* dream. Increasingly, theists and atheists alike are turning instead to cumulative-case arguments – arguments that draw on a large body of evidence and aim at showing that, all things considered, their favored position is the more reasonable one. Let us therefore consider traditional Christianity as one position and Philo's atheistic hypothesis of a morally indifferent cause of the universe as another. It seems to me that the existence of non-victim-improving natural child suffering, while *compatible* with both positions, is less surprising on the supposition that Philo's atheistic hypothesis is correct than it is on the supposition that traditional Christianity is correct. I think, therefore, that such suffering counts as evidence for the atheistic hypothesis and against traditional Christianity.[146]

Of course, in the context of cumulative-case arguments, this hardly settles the issue. It may be that there is evidence that supports traditional Christianity that is sufficient to outweigh the evidence against it. In order to investigate this possibility we must consider the positive arguments Lewis offers in support of Christianity. These arguments are the focus of the next two chapters.

TWO

BEYOND NATURE

2.1 INTRODUCTION

According to Lewis, "a sane man accepts or rejects any statement, not because he wants to or does not want to, but because the evidence seems to him good or bad."[1] This statement encapsulates Lewis's approach to religion: Follow the evidence. The overarching project of Lewis's Christian writings is to make the case that the evidence leads to Christianity. In the previous chapter, we examined Lewis's attempt to show that the suffering we find in the universe does not constitute decisive evidence against the existence of God. In this chapter and the next, we turn our attention to Lewis's positive case *for* the truth of Christianity.

It is helpful to view this case as having two main components. The first component consists of arguments for the claim that there is, in addition to the natural, physical universe that we perceive with our senses, some transcendent being, a Higher Power that created the natural universe and is "more like a mind than it is like anything else we know."[2] Lewis's writings suggest three main arguments for this conclusion or something like it. As Lewis is well aware, establishing such a conclusion does not establish the truth of Christianity, which adds to this claim a particular conception of the nature of this Higher Power as well as a host of additional theological and historical claims. The second component of Lewis's positive case for Christianity is intended to go at least part of the way toward establishing the further conclusion that the Higher Power is indeed the God of Christianity and that the most important historical episode of Christianity, the Resurrection of Christ, really occurred. The topic of the present chapter is the first component of Lewis's case for Christianity. We will examine the second component in the next chapter.

Before we consider Lewis's arguments for a Higher Power, we should briefly consider his explicit rejection of a particular kind of argument for such a Power. The type of argument Lewis rejects is one of the oldest, most popular, and most enduring types of theistic arguments on the market: the argument from design. Many have thought that this type of argument is endorsed by Paul the Apostle in these lines:

> For the wrath of God is revealed from heaven against all ungodliness and wickedness of those who by their wickedness suppress the truth. For what can be known about God is plain to them, because God has shown it to them. Ever since the creation of the world his eternal power and divine nature, invisible though they are, have been understood and seen through the things he has made.[3]

A key element of the argument from design is the idea that the observable universe has certain features that indicate intelligent design at work in its formation. This argument comes in many varieties and has had many defenders. As I mentioned in Chapter 1, Hume has the character Cleanthes defend a version of the design argument in the *Dialogues Concerning Natural Religion*, and that argument is subjected to scathing criticism by Philo and Demea. Lewis, interestingly, is no friend of the design argument either. In the early stages of *Mere Christianity*, he writes:

> We want to know whether the universe simply happens to be what it is for no reason or whether there is a power behind it that makes it what it is. Since that power, if it exists, would not be one of the observed facts but a reality which makes them, no mere observation of the facts can find it. . . . If there was a controlling power outside the universe, it could not show itself to us as one of the facts inside the universe – no more than the architect of a house could actually be a wall or staircase or fireplace in that house.[4]

This rejection of the design argument is fairly crude; the idea at work in the design argument is not that the creator of the universe *is* some component or aspect of the universe. Rather, the idea is that certain components or aspects of the universe point beyond themselves and toward a creator; they are *indicators* of a creator. The reasons Lewis provides here for rejecting the argument from design may not be particularly convincing, but the passage makes it clear that Lewis does in fact reject that argument. He claims that a creator *couldn't* reveal itself to us by way of any observable feature of the universe, which seems directly at odds with Paul's claim that God's existence and nature can be "seen through the things he has made."

A more reasonable concern about the design argument appears in the opening chapter of *The Problem of Pain*:

> If the universe is so bad . . . how on earth did human beings ever come to attribute it to the activity of a wise and good Creator? Men are fools, perhaps; but hardly so foolish as that. . . . The spectacle of the universe as revealed by experience can never have been the ground of religion: it must always have been something in spite of which religion, acquired from a different source, was held.[5]

Here, Lewis appears to endorse Philo's claim that "however consistent the world may be, allowing certain suppositions and conjectures with the idea of such a Deity, it can never afford us an inference concerning his existence."[6] Lewis realizes that the design argument could never lead to a *good* Higher Power; in fact, insofar as it tells us anything about the moral attributes of the Higher Power at all, it points *away* from a good Power. Similar ideas can be found in a letter Lewis wrote in 1946:

> The early loss of my mother, great unhappiness at school, and the shadow of the last war and presently the experience of it, had given me a very pessimistic view of existence. My atheism was based on it: and it still seems to me that *far* the strongest card in our enemies' hand is the actual course of the world. . . . I still think the argument from design the weakest possible ground for Theism, and what may be called the argument from un-design the strongest for Atheism.[7]

Lewis thinks that to find evidence of a Higher Power we should look not to the physical universe but rather to ourselves. The following slogan captures the general thrust of Lewis's approach: Human nature cannot be explained by Nature alone. Lewis identifies three features of human nature that point to a Higher Power: human morality, our capacity to reason, and a kind of desire he labels "Joy." Each of these aspects of human nature constitutes the starting point of a theistic argument. In thinking about these arguments, it will be helpful to keep in mind the concept of a cumulative-case argument that I introduced at the end of the previous chapter. None of Lewis's arguments is intended to be a decisive proof that there is a Higher Power; instead, Lewis strives to present a cumulative case for the existence of a Higher Power through the combined force of the three arguments. Robert Holyer describes Lewis's overall strategy this way:

> On their most common construction his arguments are all attempts to show that the theistic explanation of a certain human phenomenon makes better sense of it than do non-theistic rivals. It is this general argument that Lewis prosecutes in the specific cases of romantic longing, morality, and human reason.... Lewis would seem to be arguing that these three human phenomena are most at home in the Christian vision of things.[8]

We begin with the argument from morality.

2.2 THE MORAL ARGUMENT

2.2.1 Lewis's Presentation of the Argument

Book One of *Mere Christianity* is devoted to expounding the first of Lewis's main arguments for a Higher Power. Some brief background about *Mere Christianity* will be useful before we consider the argument. The book was developed from a series of radio talks by Lewis that the BBC broadcast from 1942 to 1944. In the Foreword to my edition of *Mere Christianity*, Kathleen Norris aptly describes the book as "a work of oral literature, addressed to people at war."[9] One consequence of this is that Lewis's presentation is sometimes compressed or oversimplified. We should keep this in mind when considering Lewis's moral argument. To provide the most charitable interpretation of that argument we may need to fill in some gaps in Lewis's presentation.

The moral argument is based on the existence of certain moral phenomena. The first of these is what Lewis calls "the Law of Nature." When Lewis talks about the Law of Nature in this context he intends to speak of what I call universal, objective moral truths. Consider, for instance, the claim that it is morally wrong to torture innocent children purely for entertainment. To label this moral claim "universal" is to say that it applies to all normal human beings whether they know it or not. To label this claim "objective" is to say that its truth is independent of human emotions, beliefs, and conventions in a certain way. For instance, the claim is not *made true* by the facts (if they are facts) that (a) all or most normal humans have a certain emotional reaction when they reflect on torturing children just for fun, (b) all or most normal humans think such torture is wrong, or reprehensible, or (c) torturing children just for fun is at odds with the established customs or practices of some or all cultures. The sort of objectivity I have in mind here might roughly be characterized as follows: Just as it is a fact that the earth's moon is 2,160 miles in diameter, regardless of what anyone may think of it, similarly, child torture just for fun is morally wrong, regardless of what anyone may think of it.

Lewis suggests not only that there are universal, objective ethical facts, but also that most of us know at least some of these.[10] This phenomenon of moral knowledge has at least two components in addition to the ethical facts themselves. There is a psychological component (our moral beliefs) and a normative component (the warrant or justification possessed by at least some of these beliefs).

In light of Lewis's earlier claim in connection with the design argument that a Higher Power could not reveal itself through any observable facts, we can infer that Lewis thinks that at least some ethical facts are not known on the basis of observation. This is certainly plausible; it seems unlikely, for instance, that we learn that torturing innocent babies just for fun is wrong by observing such torture and perceiving the wrongness of the act by way of sense perception.

Indeed, it seems clear that we do not need to observe this sort of torture at all in order to know that it is wrong. This knowledge seems to be an instance of a priori knowledge (knowledge that does not depend on experience). Lewis says that "people thought that every one knew [the Law of Nature] by nature and did not need to be taught it.... And I believe they were right."[11] What does it mean to know something "by nature"? One possibility is that Lewis means that moral knowledge is *innate* knowledge, knowledge that normal human beings possess when they are born. But a more likely possibility is that Lewis means that each normal human, once she understands concepts like innocence, torture, and moral wrongness, can come to know that baby torture just for fun is wrong simply by reflecting on the relevant concepts.[12] Lewis appears to endorse this second option in his later work *Miracles: A Preliminary Study*: "I believe that the primary moral principles on which all others depend are rationally perceived.... Their intrinsic reasonableness shines by its own light."[13]

Finally, there is a cluster of moral emotions associated with our knowledge of these moral facts. Lewis speaks of "a Something which is directing the universe, and which appears in me as a law urging me to do right and making me feel responsible and uncomfortable when I do wrong."[14] Lewis alludes to two feelings here, one of which is pretty clearly guilt, and the other of which we might call a sense of obligation – the feeling that one *must* (morally speaking) perform a certain action.

If we grant that the phenomena just described are real, how do we move from their existence to the existence of a Higher Power? Lewis explains the crucial transition this way:

> If there was a controlling power outside the universe, it could not show itself to us as one of the facts inside the universe.... The only way in which we could expect it to show itself would be inside ourselves as an influence or a command trying to get us to behave in a certain way. And that is just what we do find inside ourselves. Surely this ought to arouse our suspicions?... I find that I do not exist on my own, that I am under a law; that somebody or something wants me to behave in a certain way.[15]

This is one of those places where we need to fill in some gaps in Lewis's presentation. It is tempting to put an uncharitable interpretation on Lewis's remarks here, as I think John Beversluis does in *C. S. Lewis and the Search for Rational Religion*. Beversluis construes Lewis's argument as having the following structure: (i) If there were a Higher Power, then it would manifest itself as an internal command urging us to behave morally; (ii) we find within ourselves such a command; (iii) therefore, there is a Higher Power.[16] As Beversluis notes, formulated this way the argument is formally invalid, committing the fallacy of affirming the consequent.[17]

Now, intelligent people rarely commit simple logical fallacies of this sort. Such a mistake would be particularly surprising coming from Lewis, who received substantial training in philosophy. This suggests to me that Beversuis probably has not formulated Lewis's argument correctly and that we should look for a better interpretation. And, indeed, a better interpretation is available. To see the better interpretation, consider for a moment how scientific theories come to be verified. Suppose we have some scientific theory, T, which makes predictions P1, P2, and P3. Through observation, P1 is confirmed. This is taken as evidence for the truth of T. But what sort of reasoning is being employed here? Superficially, the reasoning seems to commit the fallacy of affirming the consequent: (i) If T were true, then P1 would be true; (ii) P1 is true; (iii) therefore, T is true. Are we to conclude, then, that this commonly employed method of confirming scientific theories is in fact based on a logical fallacy?

The answer, fortunately, is no, because there is a better way of understanding what is going on here. The implicit reasoning that is used in such cases relies on abduction, or inference to the best explanation. The reasoning is more happily formulated this way: (i) P1 is true; (ii) the best explanation of the truth of P1 is the truth of T; (iii) therefore, T is true. This is a perfectly respectable and fallacy-free form of reasoning.

With this in mind, let us return to Lewis's argument. Let us call the three moral phenomena upon which the argument is based "Lewisian moral phenomena." In light of the lesson we just learned, it seems likely that Lewis's moral argument relies on the following reasoning: (i) Lewisian moral phenomena exist; (ii) the best explanation of such phenomena is a Higher Power; (iii) therefore, a Higher Power exists. Lewis also thinks that we can know some important facts about the nature of this Higher Power. Because the Higher Power gives us instructions via the Law of Nature, we can infer that the Power "is more like a mind than it is like anything else we know."[18] Furthermore, the kind of instructions the Power gives us reveals something about its character:

> [T]he Being behind the universe is intensely interested in right conduct – in fair play, unselfishness, courage, good faith, honesty and truthfulness. In that sense we should agree with the account given by Christianity and some other religions, that God is 'good'.[19]

In light of all this, I think that Lewis's argument is best formulated as follows:

Lewis's Moral Argument

1. Lewisian moral phenomena exist.
2. The best explanation of the existence of Lewisian moral phenomena is the existence of a Higher Power that created the universe.
3. So: There is a Higher Power that created the universe (from 1 and 2).
4. The Higher Power issues instructions and wants us to engage in morally right conduct.
5. If (4), then there is a good, mindlike Higher Power that created the universe.
6. Therefore, there is a good, mindlike Higher Power that created the universe (from 4 and 5).

After giving this argument, Lewis notes that "[w]e have not yet got as far as the God of any actual religion, still less the God of that particular religion called Christianity."[20] He also makes the following comment about his method: "We are not taking anything from the Bible or the Churches, we are trying to see what we can find out about this [Higher Power] on our own steam."[21] Thus, Lewis is engaged in an exercise in natural religion.

In the previous chapter we saw that in Hume's *Dialogues,* Philo's criticism of Cleanthes's position has two aspects or "tracks." One of these is the skeptical track, according to which human reason is impotent when it comes to understanding God. In advancing a philosophical argument for the existence of a good, mindlike Higher Power, Lewis is implicitly attacking Philo's skeptical track. But how convincing is Lewis's argument? Our discussion of this question begins with an objection from Russell.

2.2.2   Russell's Objection

Bertrand Russell lived for nearly one hundred years. Born in Wales in 1872, he was twenty-six years Lewis's senior, yet outlived Lewis by nearly a decade, dying in Wales in 1970. Russell was an often-harsh critic of religion in general and of Christianity in particular. Consider, for instance, the opening lines of his 1929 essay "Has Religion Made Useful Contributions to Civilization?": "My own view on religion is that of Lucretius. I regard it as a disease born of fear and as a source of untold misery to the human race."[22] Like Hume, Russell drew the ire of the religious establishment as a result of his criticism of religion. In the previous chapter I mentioned Hume's being denied a professorship at Glasgow University in 1752; Russell was similarly denied a position at City College in New York City in 1940. One of Russell's more infamous essays on religion is the 1927 piece "Why I Am Not a Christian." There, Russell considers and rejects a number of arguments for the existence of God, including one he calls the moral argument. Though Russell's essay precedes the talks upon which *Mere Christianity* is based by over a decade, the moral argument Russell considers is quite similar to Lewis's moral argument. Russell has this to say about the argument:

> One form is to say that there would be no right or wrong unless God existed.... The point I am concerned with is that, if you are quite sure there is a difference between right and wrong, you are then in this situation: Is that difference due to God's fiat [command] or is it not? If it is due to God's fiat, then for God Himself there is no difference

between right and wrong, and it is no longer a significant statement to say that God is good. If you are going to say, as theologians do, that God is good, you must then say that right and wrong have some meaning which is independent of God's fiat, because God's fiats are good and not bad independently of the mere fact that He made them. If you are going to say that, you will then have to say that it is not only through God that right and wrong come into being, but that they are in their essence logically anterior to God.[23]

A key element of Russell's argument here is a certain view about what it takes for God to be good. Russell claims that God is good only if "for God Himself" there is a difference between right and wrong. The idea is that God's goodness requires that He be subject to morality in the sense that there are certain moral principles of which God is not the author and which govern His actions. Russell's claim is:

(RC)   The only way a being (even God) can be good is by conforming its actions to a moral law of which it is not the author.

In *Mere Christianity*, Lewis maintains that God is good *and* is the ultimate source of objective rightness and wrongness. But (RC) implies that God cannot be both of these things together. Hence, Russell's objection strikes at the heart of the view about God's relationship to objective morality that Lewis puts forth in *Mere Christianity*.

In his 1943 essay "The Poison of Subjectivism," Lewis considers an objection that bears a striking similarity to the one presented by Russell in the passage just quoted.[24] There, he describes the view that God is "the mere executor of a law somehow external and antecedent to His own being" as "intolerable."[25] Thus, Lewis rejects (RC). But this means that it is incumbent upon Lewis to provide an alternative account of the nature of God's goodness: How can God be good if not by conforming to a moral law of which He is not the author?

I believe that Lewis's writings suggest three distinct answers to this question. We shall consider each in turn. The first answer is suggested by Lewis's response to the Russell-style objection in "The Poison of Subjectivism." The central question of that discussion is: "[H]ow is the relation between God and the moral law to be represented?"[26] Before providing his own answer to this question, Lewis rejects two other possible answers, declaring that "God neither *obeys* nor *creates* the moral law. The good is uncreated; it never could have been otherwise; it has in it no shadow of contingency; it lies, as Plato said, on the other side of existence."[27] This passage is important for two reasons. First, it helps us determine Lewis's own view on the relationship between God and the moral law by telling us what, in Lewis's eyes, that relationship is not. Second, it indicates that in this context Lewis uses "the good" and "the moral law" interchangeably, a piece of information that is crucial in deciphering Lewis's position here. That position is stated in the following tricky passage:

> [W]hat lies beyond existence, what admits no contingency, what lends divinity to all else, what is the ground of all existence, is not simply a law but also a begetting love, a love begotten.... God is not merely good, but goodness; goodness is not merely divine, but God.[28]

Commenting on this passage in his doctoral dissertation on Lewis's philosophical writings, Steve Lovell interprets Lewis as claiming that "God = (His?) Goodness" and remarks: "I must confess to not having much idea about what [this thesis] could mean. It appears to assert an identity relation between God and an abstract object, indeed between God and a property."[29] I too have trouble grasping the claim that a mindlike Higher Power is identical to the property of goodness.[30]

I am not sure, however, that Lovell's interpretation of the crucial passage is quite right. In light of my suggestion that in this context the good = the moral law, a more likely interpretation is that Lewis is suggesting that God is identical to the moral law. This interpretation makes sense of the discussion as a whole: Lewis begins with the question of how God is related to the moral law, says that God neither obeys it nor creates it, and concludes that God simply *is* the moral law. If this proposal makes sense, it gives Lewis a way of rejecting (RC) by suggesting a way God might be good other than by conforming to an independent moral law:

(LA1) Being *identical to* the moral law is a way of being good.

I find the proposal that God is the moral law roughly as puzzling as the proposal that God is the property of goodness. Insofar as I can understand the claim that God is the moral law, it seems to be the claim that God is identical to a conjunction of ethical facts, facts like: It is morally wrong to torture the innocent just for fun. It is hard to see how a conjunction of such facts could be a mindlike Higher Power, much less the personal God of Christianity. The obscurity of Lewis's proposal here seems to me to be a serious strike against it; however, I will leave the proposal on the table for the sake of examining its implications for Lewis's moral argument.[31] Before considering such implications we must examine two other accounts of divine goodness that I think are suggested by Lewis's writing.

In *Mere Christianity*, Lewis appears to conceive of the relationship between God and the moral law in a way that is incompatible with the position he takes in "The Poison of Subjectivism." For instance, in *Mere Christianity* he says that "there is a real Moral Law, *and* a Power *behind* the law."[32] The language here suggests that the Moral Law and the Higher Power are distinct, and a natural interpretation of the overall discussion in *Mere Christianity* is that the Higher Power is the author or creator of the Moral Law, one of the two options explicitly rejected in "The Poison of Subjectivism."

This suggests that in *Mere Christianity* Lewis is working with a conception of divine goodness distinct from the one he proposes in "The Poison of Subjectivism." But what is this other conception? The following passage sheds some light: "God is quite definitely 'good' or 'righteous', a God who takes sides, who loves love and hates hatred, who wants us to behave in one way and not in another."[33] We should also recall Lewis's remark that the Higher Power is "intensely interested . . . in fair play, unselfishness, courage, good faith, honesty and truthfulness."[34] These passages suggest the view that one way of being good is by loving certain things (and perhaps hating certain other things).[35] If this is right, we have another alternative to (RC):

(LA2) Loving love, fair play, unselfishness, courage, good faith, honesty, and truthfulness is a way of being good.

A third way of thinking of divine goodness is the conception of divine goodness that Lewis employs in *The Problem of Pain*:

(LA3)   Desiring that human beings attain genuine happiness (that they freely love God and strive to become Christlike) is a way of being good.

At this point I would like to review the discussion so far and say a bit about what is to come. We started with an exposition of Lewis's moral argument from *Mere Christianity*. Against that kind of argument, Russell raises a puzzle about the nature of God's goodness. Russell's puzzle appears to rely on (RC), the claim that there is only one way a being can be good: by conforming to a moral law not authored by the being in question. Russell and Lewis rightly agree that such a view makes it impossible for God to be good *and* to be the author of the moral law. Russell concludes from this that moral arguments like Lewis's fail. Lewis, on the other hand, concludes that (RC) is false. I have suggested that Lewis's writings suggest three alternatives to (RC): God can be good by being identical to the moral law (LA1), by loving certain things (LA2), or by desiring that humans attain genuine happiness (LA3).[36] The next order of business is to examine the implications for Lewis's moral argument of each of the alternatives.

In *Mere Christianity*, Lewis not only appeals to morality to argue for the existence of a Higher Power; he also argues against a view he calls Dualism. I think it is no mere coincidence that Lewis undertakes both projects in the same work. I believe that if Dualism is a tenable view, this fact constitutes the basis of a powerful objection to Lewis's moral argument. I will argue that if either (LA2) or (LA3) is true, then Lewis fails to refute Dualism, and hence his moral argument fails. If this is right, it means that Lewis's moral argument can succeed only if (LA2) and (LA3) are false. On the other hand, if (LA1) is true, then Lewis's objection to Dualism goes through. However, (LA1) leads to two other problems for Lewis's moral argument. The first is that the argument depends on an account of the relationship between God and the moral law that is at best obscure and at worst incoherent. The second is that (LA1) points in the direction of a plausible atheistic explanation of Lewisian moral phenomena. The existence of such an explanation renders Lewis's moral argument toothless. If all of this is correct, the upshot is that Lewis has no understanding of the nature of divine goodness that enables his moral argument to succeed – and, to the extent that the atheistic account of Lewisian moral phenomena that I will sketch is plausible, Lewis's argument fails in any case. I turn now to the task of making this case.

Let us begin with Lewis's case against Dualism. My main goal in the upcoming section is to establish two claims: first, that the truth of either (LA2) or (LA3) ruins Lewis's argument against Dualism, and second, that the failure of the argument against Dualism entails the failure of the moral argument as well.

2.2.3   Lewis's Attack on Dualism

The view that Lewis calls Dualism is common to a number of religious alternatives to Christianity, including Zoroastrianism and Manicheanism.[37] It is the view that "there are two equal and independent powers at the back of everything, one of them good and the other bad, and that this universe is the battlefield in which they fight out an endless war."[38] Zoroastrianism is an ancient Persian religion that still has adherents in Iran and southern Asia. Manicheanism, on the other hand, seems to have pretty much died out, but it was at one time one of the main rivals of Christianity, particularly in the early days of Christianity. Saint Augustine adhered to the view for some time, and in the thirteenth century Pope Innocent III launched a crusade against the Cathars in southern France, who held a version of Manicheanism.[39] In *Mere Christianity*, Lewis describes Dualism as "next to Christianity . . . the manliest and most sensible creed on the market."[40] In a 1942 letter, however, he offers a more blunt explanation for taking on Dualism: "You wouldn't be surprised at the space I give to Dualism if you knew how attractive it is to some simple minds."[41]

Despite its manliness and attractiveness to simple minds, the view has difficulties, says Lewis. One alleged problem stems from the claim that the two Highest Powers have opposite moral qualities, one being good, the other evil. This claim entails that there is

> a third thing in addition to the two Powers: some law or standard or rule of good which one of the powers conforms to and the other fails to conform to. But since the two powers are judged by this standard, then this standard, or the Being who made this standard, is farther back and higher up than either of them, and He will be the real God.[42]

The crucial premise here is that the existence of equal, independent Powers, one good, one evil, entails the existence of a third Power superior to both of the first two. Since Dualism is incompatible with the existence of such a third Power, Lewis aims to show that Dualism is internally inconsistent.

The truth of either (LA2) or (LA3) seems to undermine this crucial premise. Let us first consider the implications of (LA2) in this regard:

(LA2) Loving love, fair play, unselfishness, courage, good faith, honesty, and truthfulness is a way of being good.

Given (LA2), it is natural to suppose that *hating* love, fair play, and so on is a way of being evil. But if this is right, then it is hard to see why Dualism would require a third Higher Power. The existence of two equal and opposite Powers, one of which loves love, fair play, and the rest, the other of which hates these things, without a third Higher Power superior to these two, seems perfectly coherent. Similar considerations apply to Lewis's third alternative to (RC):

(LA3) Desiring that human beings attain genuine happiness (that they freely love God and strive to become Christlike) is a way of being good.

Like (LA2), (LA3) suggests a corresponding account of evil – in this case, that desiring that human beings fail to attain (or attain the opposite of) genuine happiness is a way of being evil. And, again, it is hard to see why, under this understanding of good and evil, the existence of a good Power and an evil Power would require the existence of a third Even Higher Power.

Finally, consider the principle suggested by Lewis's discussion in "The Poison of Subjectivism":

(LA1) Being *identical to* the moral law is a way of being good.

Suppose that this is true *and* that there are only two ways of being good – either (i) by obeying a moral law not of one's own creation or (ii) by being identical to the moral law. It follows that the good Power of Dualism is either subject to a moral law it did not create or is itself the moral law. Under the first alternative, Lewis's claim that we must posit a third Higher Power superior to the other two Powers seems reasonable; in any case, I will assume that the Dualist cannot consistently say that the good Power of Dualism is subject to a moral law it did not create. This means that the Dualist must identify the good Higher Power with the moral law. This in turn implies that the evil Power is subordinate to the good Power, since presumably what makes the evil Power evil is that it violates a moral law to which it is subject. But since we are supposing that the good Power *is* the moral law, it follows that the evil Power is subject to the good Power – and that conclusion also conflicts with Dualism. Therefore, given the supposition put forth at the start of this paragraph, Lewis's first argument against Dualism goes through, but if either (LA2) or (LA3) is true, the argument fails. Thus we may (tentatively) conclude that Lewis's objection to Dualism succeeds only if both (LA2) and (LA3) are false.

However, matters are complicated by the fact that Lewis presents a second objection to Dualism in *Mere Christianity*. If this other objection succeeds, then the limitations of the first objection to Dualism are irrelevant. To support my contention that Lewis can refute Dualism only if (LA2) and (LA3) are false, I will make the case that this second objection to Dualism simply fails. Here is the essence of the second objection:

> If Dualism is true, then the bad Power must be a being who likes badness for its own sake. But in reality we have no experience of anyone liking badness just because it is bad.... [W]ickedness, when you examine it, turns out to be the pursuit of some good in the wrong

way. You can be good for the mere sake of goodness: you cannot be bad for the mere sake of badness.[43]

The central premise of this objection is that loving evil for its own sake is impossible. Yet Dualism requires that this be possible. Hence, Dualism is false. To support the central premise, Lewis appeals to experience: We never encounter people who love evil for its own sake.

This argument is unconvincing. One problem is that from the fact that we have no experience of beings who love evil for its own sake it hardly follows that such beings are impossible.[44] Indeed, it is somewhat surprising to find this sort of argument coming from someone like Lewis, who believes in supernatural, transcendent beings remarkably unlike any we experience. Furthermore, it is far from clear that beings who love evil for its own sake have not actually existed. For instance, if we take Saint Augustine at his word, the youthful Augustine was just such a being:

> I stole things which I already had in plenty and of better quality. Nor had I any desire to enjoy the things I stole, but only the stealing of them and the sin. . . . Such was my heart, O God, such was my heart. . . . Let that heart now tell You what it sought when I was thus evil for no object, having no cause for wrongdoing save my wrongness. The malice of the act was base and I loved it – that is to say I loved my own undoing, I loved the evil in me – not the thing for which I did the evil, simply the evil: my soul was depraved, and hurled itself down from security in You into utter destruction, seeking no profit from wickedness but only to be wicked.[45]

Notice in particular Augustine's remark that he loved "not the thing for which [he] did the evil" but loved "*simply the evil.*" Surely the most natural interpretation of this remark is that Augustine is claiming to have loved evil *for its own sake* – precisely the thing that Lewis claims is impossible. Intriguingly, the younger, atheistic Lewis maintained that the kind of desire Augustine describes is not only possible but widespread. In a 1923 diary entry Lewis endorses the view that "most of us could find positive Satanic badness down there somewhere, the desire for evil not because it was pleasant but because it was evil."[46]

If the psychological claims of Augustine and young Lewis are correct, then the elder Lewis's argument fails. At the very least, it is hard to resist the conclusion that the kind of motivation Augustine describes is *possible*, and this seems to be enough to save Dualism from Lewis's attack.

Against this criticism of Lewis's argument it might be suggested that even though Lewis appeals to experience to establish his crucial premise, an a priori argument (one that does not rely on experience) for the same conclusion is available. That argument runs as follows: Every action must aim at a goal that the agent regards as good or worthwhile in some respect. But no goal can be regarded as good or worthwhile merely on the grounds that it is wicked or evil; hence, no action can be directed at evil purely for its own sake. With respect to the case of Augustine, a defender of this argument might suggest an alternative interpretation of Augustine's remarks. This alternative interpretation is based on the fact that Augustine says that he got a pleasurable thrill from doing the things he knew he should not do. It was at least partially for the sake of this pleasure that he did these things, and pleasure, after all, is a good – a good that Augustine pursued in ways he should not have.[47]

My response to this line of reasoning is that the question of what kinds of considerations can motivate agents is an empirical question about human psychology. The a priori argument simply assumes a certain answer to this question – that agents can pursue only goals that they take to be good. But I do not see why such a claim should be accepted a priori.[48] It is true that Augustine says that he experienced pleasure *as a result of* performing evil actions. But it does not follow from this that he performed the wicked actions (even partially) *for the sake of* that pleasure. In general, from the fact that action A had a particular *consequence* C, it does not follow that the agent who performed A did so *for the sake of* C. A simple example illustrates this point: Every physical action I have performed has among its consequences the displacement of some oxygen molecules, but I have never once performed an action for the sake of displacing oxygen molecules. That Augustine performed evil actions for the sake of pleasure is one possibility; another possibility is that he performed evil actions *purely because they were evil* and that when he did so he experienced a thrill *as a consequence of* doing evil *for its own sake*. The case of Augustine presents prima facie evidence against the view that agents cannot pursue evil for its own sake. The case can be construed in such a way as to be consistent with this view, but such a construal is not the only plausible one.

It seems to me that the proposed a priori argument begs the question against the Dualist by assuming that evil cannot be pursued simply because it is evil. Lewis himself tries to establish this premise by relying on the empirical claim that people in fact never pursue evil for it own sake. This empirical claim is questionable and, even if true, fails to establish the crucial premise of Lewis's argument. I conclude that Lewis's second objection to Dualism fails.

If everything I have said in this section so far is correct, then Lewis can refute Dualism only by rejecting both (LA2) and (LA3). To refute Dualism, he must insist that there are just two ways a being can be good – either by *being* the moral law, or by *obeying* a moral law the being did not create. The importance of this result lies in the fact that if Lewis cannot rule out Dualism, then his moral argument is in trouble, as I shall now argue.

Consider the Apostle Paul's famous remarks on his own efforts to do the right thing: "I can will what is right, but I cannot do it. For I do not do the good I want, but the evil I do not want is what I do."[49] Charles Freeman remarks: "No one reading Paul can ignore the powerful emotional force of this message: human beings live at the centre of a cosmic drama that reaches to the core of each personality as the forces of good and evil battle within the individual."[50] We find within ourselves not just promptings inclining us toward goodness, but also promptings inclining us toward evil, and the conflict between the two can produce internal turmoil. Indeed, this inner struggle is one of the central features of human moral experience and has been discussed by every important moral philosopher in the Western tradition. This brief remark by Immanuel Kant captures the phenomenon nicely: "Be a man ever so virtuous, there are in him promptings of evil, and he must constantly contend with these."[51] Is not Dualism a perfectly reasonable explanation of this phenomenon?

Among the data Lewis draws on in developing his moral argument are certain moral emotions, including guilt and a sense of obligation. Lewis suggests that these phenomena point toward a good Higher Power. But we also find within ourselves temptations and evil inclinations. If it is reasonable to suppose that positive moral emotions are indicative of a good Higher Power, is it not equally reasonable to suppose that negative moral emotions are indicative of an evil Higher Power?

Lewis notes that traditional Christianity includes the belief that there is a "Dark Power" who was "created by God, and was good when he was created, and went wrong."[52] This Dark Power is "behind death and disease, and *sin*."[53] Perhaps our internal struggle mirrors the struggle between the two Powers of Dualism. These considerations suggest an argument for Dualism that is structurally parallel to Lewis's moral argument:

A Moral Argument for Dualism

1. Positive and negative moral phenomena exist.
2. The best explanation of the existence of such moral phenomena is the existence of a Higher Power (or Powers) that created the universe.
3. So: There is a Higher Power (or Powers) that created the universe (from 1 and 2).
4. The Higher Power(s) issue instructions and want us to engage in morally right conduct but also tempt us and want us to engage in morally wrong conduct.
5. If (4), then there are two Higher Powers that created the universe, one good, one evil.
6. Therefore, there are two Higher Powers that created the universe, one good, one evil (from 4 and 5).

We have, then, parallel arguments for incompatible conclusions. Unless there is an independent reason to prefer one argument to the other, we arrive at the following stand-off: It is reasonable to endorse one argument only if it is also reasonable to endorse the other. But it is not reasonable to endorse both; hence, it is not reasonable to endorse either. Of course, Dualism is not a live option for most people, but this is beside the point. The issue at hand is whether it is reasonable to believe in a single good Higher Power on the basis of Lewis's moral argument; the fact that there are few Dualists around today does not constitute a good reason to prefer Lewis's argument to the moral argument for Dualism. If Dualism could be refuted directly, this of course would break the stand-off. I suspect that this is at least part of the reason why Lewis attempts such a refutation in *Mere Christianity*. Without the refutation, Lewis has not given us a good reason to prefer his moral argument to the moral argument for Dualism.[54]

In this section I have argued for two main claims. First, I've argued that Lewis's attack on Dualism in *Mere Christianity* succeeds only if there are only two ways a being can be good – either by *being* the moral law, or by *obeying* a moral law the being did not create. Second, I've argued that Lewis's moral argument succeeds only if Lewis's attack on Dualism succeeds. It follows from these two claims that Lewis's moral argument succeeds only if there are just two ways a being can be good – either by *being* the moral law, or by *obeying* a moral law the being did not create. Given the obscurity and possible incoherence of the notion that God *is* the moral law, this result makes serious trouble for Lewis's moral argument. In the next section I will examine a different kind of objection to Lewis's moral argument. The essence of this other objection is that Lewisian moral phenomena are perfectly at home in a universe devoid of Higher Powers altogether.

2.2.4   Godless Objective Morality

Here again is Lewis's moral argument:

Lewis's Moral Argument

1. Lewisian moral phenomena exist.
2. The best explanation of the existence of Lewisian moral phenomena is the existence of a Higher Power that created the universe.
3. So: There is a Higher Power that created the universe (from 1 and 2).

4. The Higher Power issues instructions and wants us to engage in morally right conduct.
5. If (4), then there is a good, mindlike Higher Power that created the universe.
6. Therefore, there is a good, mindlike Higher Power that created the universe (from 4 and 5).

I suggested earlier that Lewis's argument relies on an inference to the best explanation. This suggests two strategies for attacking the argument. One strategy is to deny the existence of Lewisian moral phenomena and reject the first premise. For example, some resist arguments like Lewis's moral argument by denying the existence of objective morality altogether. I will not consider this approach here for the simple reason that I find it implausible. A second strategy is to find explanations for Lewisian moral phenomena that do not involve Higher Powers and reject the second premise. Both Russell and Hume pursue the second strategy with respect to at least some of the Lewisian moral phenomena.

Let us remind ourselves of the nature of Lewisian moral phenomena. There are three such phenomena: (i) that humans have certain moral obligations (moral facts), (ii) that most humans know what at least some of these obligations are (moral knowledge), and (iii) that most humans experience various emotions related to these obligations, such as guilt and a sense of obligation (moral emotions).

The faculty that is commonly thought to be responsible for components (ii) and (iii) is conscience, which is typically thought to be possessed by all or nearly all humans. Some passages indicate that Lewis thinks that conscience has a divine origin. For example, in *Mere Christianity*, he describes the Higher Power as something that "appears in me as a law urging me to do right," and he describes the moral law as something "which He has put into our minds."[55] In *The Problem of Pain*, he remarks that God "speaks in our conscience."[56]

We have already considered Russell's criticism of the moral argument from his 1927 essay "Why I Am Not a Christian." Several years later, Russell seemed to favor a different kind of response to the moral argument. This other response is based on the alleged variation in the deliverances of conscience from one person to the next. For instance, in his 1939 essay "The Existence and Nature of God," Russell writes:

> [C]onscience varies with different people in different instances.... Take such a thing as human sacrifice. It has existed in pretty nearly all races. It is the normal phase of a certain stage in the development of the race. To those who practiced it, it was an essential part of their religion.... You will find that what your conscience tells you varies according to the age and place....[57]

In 1948, the BBC broadcast a debate on the existence of God between Russell and the Jesuit philosopher F. C. Copleston. In that debate Copleston suggested that "the consciousness of moral law and obligation [is] best explained through the hypothesis of... an author of the moral law."[58] Russell's immediate response was that "the moral law... is always changing. At one period in the development of the human race, almost everybody thought cannibalism was a duty."[59]

Let us grant Russell's claim that the deliverances of conscience vary widely from person to person. What, exactly, is the significance of this supposed to be? Russell's idea is that this variation is evidence that conscience has not a divine origin but rather an earthly one: "[C]onscience is the stored up discomfort due to disapproval experienced or imagined in the past, particularly in early youth. So far from having a divine origin, it is a product of education, and can be trained to approve or disapprove as educators see fit."[60] In the debate with Copleston, Russell remarked that "the feeling that one has about 'ought' is an echo of what has been told one by one's parents or one's nurses."[61]

Russell's argument, then, seems to be that the variation in the deliverances of conscience from one person to the next indicates that conscience is entirely a product of the education (or, more pejoratively, the conditioning) that one receives while very young. The moral precepts ingrained during youth persist into adulthood, and they "come up as if they had an external source and seem like the voice of God," but this is merely an illusion.[62] In fact, which precepts one is instilled with is often a matter of chance, since it is often a matter of chance who is responsible for one's education while one is young, and consequently the precepts one finds instilled in oneself may turn out to be false. Russell had some personal experience with this phenomenon, and this may have influenced his views on the issue. In his autobiography, Russell has this to say concerning his first wife, Alys:

> She had been brought up, as American women always were in those days, to think that sex was beastly, that all women hated it, and that men's brutal lusts were the chief obstacle to happiness in marriage. She therefore thought that intercourse should only take place when children were desired.[63]

Russell's argument is not intended to show, nor does it in fact show, that there are no universal, objective moral truths. The mere fact that we can be indoctrinated with false beliefs in a given area does not imply that there are no truths in this area; if it did, nearly all truths would vanish. The point of the argument, rather, is to establish that the explanation for our moral beliefs and emotional dispositions lies not in divine activity but instead in our upbringing.

In reflecting on this argument, it is important to distinguish the claim (a) that there is significant variation in the moral precepts held by different people from the claim (b) that there are no moral precepts that are held by everyone (or almost everyone). Russell offers various examples of variation in the deliverances of conscience, but of course such examples at best support the weaker claim (a), whereas it seems that his argument requires the stronger claim (b). From (a) the most that would follow is that conscience can be corrupted through a bad upbringing, but it is hard to see how we can reasonably move from this claim to the desired conclusion that conscience is *entirely* a product of one's upbringing. There is no indication that Lewis maintains that conscience is entirely incorruptible or that any old moral belief or feeling a person has is produced by that person's uncorrupted conscience. The presence of some moral beliefs and emotions that have an earthly origin is perfectly consistent with the presence of others that have a divine origin.

It seems, therefore, that Russell's argument fails to establish its intended conclusion. The fundamental problem with the argument is that establishing the presence of disagreement is not the same as establishing the absence of agreement. Russell has accomplished at most the first thing, but his argument requires that he accomplish the second thing. Moreover, in the Appendix to *The Abolition of Man*, Lewis presents a host of moral precepts that he claims to be universally (or nearly universally) recognized, together with textual evidence from various traditions indicating recognition of the relevant precept within each tradition.[64] To give his argument legs, Russell would need to discuss such alleged universal precepts and show that they are not so widely held after all, and this is something that he does not do.

Of course, even if there are moral precepts held by just about everyone, it *could* be the case that such shared precepts are a result of education; the common precepts could be a result of common elements of education. But Russell is trying to establish that conscience *is* entirely a product of education, not merely that it *might* be.

Perhaps more problematic for Lewis's argument than *variation* in the deliverances of conscience is the fact that some people apparently lack a conscience altogether. Psychopathy (sometimes called "sociopathy") is a personality disorder characterized by, among other things, the absence of the capacity to experience various emotions, including empathy, love, and guilt.[65] Psychopaths know the difference between right and wrong in some sense; at least, they recognize that other people view certain acts as being right or wrong and are able to apply the terms "right" and "wrong" appropriately. But rightness and wrongness are of no significance to psychopaths, who literally do not care about morality. Robert Hare, a psychologist who has studied psychopathy for over a quarter of a century, puts it this way:

> [T]hey *know* the rules but follow only those they choose to follow, no matter what the repercussions for others. They have little resistance to temptation, and their transgressions elicit no guilt.

Without the shackles of a nagging conscience, they feel free to satisfy their needs and wants and do whatever they think they can get away with.[66]

Lewis acknowledges that there may be "an odd individual here and there" who does not know the Law of Nature, "just as you find a few people who are colour-blind or have no ear for a tune."[67] Interestingly, those who study psychopaths have used similar analogies to describe psychopathy. Hare quotes two researchers who declare that when it comes to emotion, a psychopath "knows the words but not the music."[68] Hare himself uses color-blindness to explain psychopathy as follows:

> The psychopath is like a color-blind person who sees the world in shades of gray but who has learned how to function in a colored world. He has learned that the light signal for "stop" is at the top of the traffic light. When the color-blind person tells you he stopped at the *red* light, he really means he stopped at the *top* light.... Like the color-blind person, the psychopath lacks an important element of experience – in this case, emotional experience – but may have learned the words that others use to describe or mimic experiences that he cannot really understand.[69]

Recall the "problem of not enough pain" discussed in the previous chapter. It seems that the phenomenon of psychopathy may pose a similar problem for Lewis's view. The problem stems from Lewis's idea that the human conscience is a tool that God uses to communicate with us. More precisely, conscience is a tool that God uses to get us to recognize our need for Him. Lewis says: "Christianity tells people to repent and promises them forgiveness. It therefore has nothing (as far as I know) to say to people who do not know they have done anything to repent of and who do not feel that they need any forgiveness."[70]

Psychopaths are incapable of feeling that they need forgiveness. Has God abandoned them? Psychologists estimate that about 4 percent of human beings are psychopaths (at least in the West).[71] In light of Lewis's views on divine goodness and human happiness described in the previous chapter and his idea that conscience is an important tool that God uses to lead human beings to genuine happiness, what are we to make of the fact that roughly one in twenty-five human beings is a psychopath? Recall the fourth premise of Lewis's moral argument:

4. The Higher Power issues instructions and wants us to engage in morally right conduct.

The phenomenon of psychopathy seems to undermine this premise to some extent. If the Higher Power wants us to engage in morally right conduct, why does He permit so many of us to lack the emotional equipment essential to doing so? I am not sure that this objection is decisive, primarily because of the possibility of a justification for psychopathy that lies beyond our understanding, but it seems to me that psychopathy joins non-victim-improving natural child suffering as a phenomenon that does not fit very well with Lewis's overall view of things.

In any case, let us put aside psychopathy and focus on the vast majority of human beings who do have the basic elements of a complete conscience. In particular, let us suppose that Lewis is correct that there are certain universally (or nearly universally) held moral precepts. Is there any way such universality could be explained other than as a result of divine activity?

Enter Hume. Hume agrees with Lewis that certain moral beliefs are widely shared but, like Russell, seeks a naturalistic explanation for our moral beliefs. He seeks to explain the universality of certain moral judgments by appealing to certain emotions (or, more precisely, dispositions to feel certain emotions) that he thinks are part of human nature. The most important of these is what Hume calls "benevolence" or "humanity," which he characterizes as "friendship for human kind."[72] Humanity is universal in two ways. First, it is universal in its distribution. The tendency to feel sympathy for others is common to all human beings. Second, it is universal in its object. We feel this friendship even toward those who have nothing to do with us. As Hume puts it, this type of friendship is "so universal and comprehensive as to extend to all mankind, and render the actions and conduct, even of the persons the most remote, an object of applause or censure, according as they agree or disagree with that rule of right which is established."[73] In Hume's eyes, moral judgments are rooted in the emotions, and the emotional disposition he calls "humanity" explains why certain moral judgements are also universal:

> [I]f you represent a tyrannical, insolent, or barbarous behavior, in any country or in any age of the world, I soon carry my eye to the pernicious tendency of such a conduct, and feel the sentiment of repugnance and displeasure towards it. No character can be so remote as to be, in this light, wholly indifferent to me.[74]

Hume's tyrant is universally condemned, Hume thinks, because he invokes the same emotional response from all who reflect on him. Because "the humanity of one man is the humanity of every one," all who reflect on the tyrant feel repugnance and displeasure. This repugnance in turn produces a (negative) moral judgment of the tyrant's character. Thus, the universal moral judgment is ultimately rooted in the humanity common to all human beings.

A second important universal emotional disposition, in Hume's eyes, is what he calls "the love of fame."[75] Hume maintains that a concern to be well regarded by others tends to produce virtue:

> By our continual and earnest pursuit of a character, a name, a reputation in the world, we bring our own deportment and conduct frequently in review, and consider how they appear in the eyes of those who approach and regard us. This constant habit of surveying ourselves, as it were, in reflection, keeps alive all the sentiments of right and wrong, and begets, in noble natures, a certain reverence for themselves as well as others, which is the surest guardian of every virtue.[76]

The passage indicates that the love of fame, working in conjunction with humanity, plays an important role in producing the moral judgments we make about ourselves. Our love of fame leads us to engage in frequent self-scrutiny in which we consider ourselves from the outside, as we appear to others. Once we take this standpoint with respect to ourselves, our humanity generates moral judgments about ourselves in much the same way that it generates such judgments about others.

Hume's remarks are insightful and plausible; but do they make trouble for Lewis's moral argument? In the end, I think they do not, for the following reason. We started out wondering if there might be an alternative explanation for certain Lewisian moral phenomena other than activity on the part of a Higher Power. Hume tries to explain why certain moral judgements and emotions are universal by appealing to the existence of universal emotional dispositions. But this just seems to push the question back one step: Why, after all, are the emotional dispositions Hume identifies part of human nature? What accounts for *their* universality? Specifically, can the emotional dispositions universal to human beings be explained other than as a product of a Higher Power?[77]

Some contemporary writers have suggested that the relatively new field of evolutionary psychology might provide just such an explanation.[78] To understand the basic elements of such an explanation, we must first understand what is required to provide an evolutionary explanation for the widespread presence of a given trait.

Suppose we observe that all the members of a given species or population possesses a given trait T. A crucial element of an evolutionary explanation of the widespread presence of T in the population is support for the claim that, everything else being equal, individual organisms that possess T are more likely to survive and reproduce than are individual organisms that lack T.[79] The simplest and most intuitive examples of this sort of explanation involve physical traits. For instance, imagine a species of birds that subsists on a certain kind of seed. Suppose that birds of the species in question live in an environment in which the seeds are found only at the bottom of relatively deep and narrow holes in the ground. Everything else being equal, birds with longer and narrower beaks will be more likely to survive and reproduce because they will be better able to reach the seeds than will birds with shorter or fatter beaks. Birds with shorter or fatter beaks would be at a disadvantage in the struggle for limited resources and hence would tend to die out. This sheds light on why all the birds in the species have long, narrow beaks.

The central idea of evolutionary psychology is that this type of explanation can be applied not just to physical traits but also to psychological traits. The most interesting (and controversial) application of evolutionary psychology is to human beings. It has been suggested that certain apparently universal human psychological dispositions or tendencies can be explained in evolutionary terms. The contemporary evolutionary psychologist David Buss offers the following illustration:

> Consider a common observation that has been documented by scientific research: A woman's physical appearance is a significant part of her desirability to men.... The most widely advocated evolutionary hypothesis is that a woman's appearance provides a wealth of clues to her fertility.... Over evolutionary time, men who were drawn to women showing these fertility cues would have outreproduced men who were drawn to women lacking fertility clues, or who were indifferent to a woman's physical appearance altogether.[80]

Some have suggested that dispositions to form certain moral beliefs or to experience certain moral emotions can be explained in this way, and evolutionary psychologists have devoted much attention to such topics. Consider, for example, the disposition to feel gratitude and warmth toward those who have treated us kindly or fairly and the disposition to feel outrage and anger toward those who have treated us unkindly or unfairly. If someone keeps a promise made to us, we are likely to feel positively about that person and hence to be more likely to trust her in the future; similarly, we are likely to feel negatively about those who break promises and to be less likely to trust them. The actions of others produce emotional responses within us, and these emotional responses in turn influence our behavior. For example, the emotional tendencies I have just described incline us to engage in "reciprocal altruism" – cooperation with those who have proven to be trustworthy partners in the past. More precisely, these emotional dispositions incline us to follow the "TIT FOR TAT" strategy (named after a computer program written by Anatol Rapaport). The essence of this strategy is to cooperate with those who have cooperated with us in the past and to refrain from cooperating with those who have cheated us in the past.[81]

The emotional dispositions I have described can seem so natural and obvious as not to need any explanation; of course we get mad when others cheat us! But the apparent naturalness and obvious-ness of such reactions supports the claim that they are part of human nature and therefore good candidates for evolutionary explanation. Imagine a person who never gets mad when others cheat him. Such a person will be much easier to take advantage of than someone who experiences the normal human response to being cheated. Thus, everything else being equal, a person with the normal emotional disposition will be more likely to survive and reproduce than the person incapable of moral outrage. Similarly, a person who remains indifferent to those who prove to be trustworthy attains fewer of the benefits of cooperation than a person who experiences the normal positive feelings of warmth toward those who are trustworthy. Again, the normal emotional response provides an evolutionary advantage. Thus, we can see why the normal human emotional dis-positions would have been selected for by evolution.[82]

Another moral emotion, closely related to conscience, is guilt. If those around us tend to follow the TIT FOR TAT strategy, then it may be in our own best interest to keep our promises and not cheat others. The emotion of guilt may motivate us to do precisely this; if we feel guilty (an unpleasant experience) when we cheat, we will be less likely to do so. And this may make us more likely to attain the benefits of cooperation. Robert Wright suggests that guilt may also play a second role:

> [G]uilt, which may originally have had the simple role of prompting payment of overdue debts, could begin to serve a second function: prompting the preemptive confession of cheating that seems on the verge of discovery. (Ever notice how guilt does bear a certain correla-tion with the likelihood of getting caught?)[83]

Confessing before we are caught will probably be better for us than merely getting caught; as La Rochefoucauld observes, "[o]ur repen-tance is less a regret for ills we have caused than a fear of ills we may encounter."[84] This illustrates another way in which the disposition to feel guilty in certain situations, while sometimes unpleasant for the person who has it, can also be advantageous for that person.

Thus, we can see why the disposition to feel guilt under the right circumstances might have been selected for.[85]

This brief discussion of evolutionary psychology is intended to provide nothing more than a sketch of how some Lewisian moral phenomena might be explained in a nontheistic fashion. To the extent that this sort of explanation is plausible, Lewis's moral argument is weakened. It is important to note, however, that this kind of explanation does nothing to account for the existence of moral facts. In Lewis's terminology, evolutionary explanations *may* account for our beliefs and emotions regarding the Law of Nature, but they shed no light whatsoever on the origin of the Law itself. In general, explaining why everyone (or almost everyone) believes p is quite different from explaining why p is true, and this is so when it comes to moral facts. Explaining why most or all people have certain moral beliefs does not suffice to explain why the corresponding moral facts are true. For instance, explaining why most people *believe* torturing innocent children just for fun is wrong is one thing; explaining why torturing innocent children just for fun really *is* wrong is something else altogether.

This distinction is of crucial importance and is often overlooked, so it is worth pausing a moment to emphasize it. Whenever someone tells you that she is going to "explain morality," listen carefully with an ear toward determining just what it is she is trying to explain. Is she trying to explain why people have certain moral *beliefs and attitudes*? Or is she trying to explain why certain moral claims are *true*? Evolutionary psychology may provide a plausible nontheistic explanation of human moral beliefs and emotions.[86] But such an account by itself does not provide a complete nontheistic explanation of Lewisian moral phenomena. It must be supplemented by a discussion of the possibility of objective moral truth without a theistic foundation.

Can objective moral facts exist in a godless universe? I believe that they can; moreover, I believe that Lewis's remarks in "The Poison of Subjectivism" point us toward a plausible atheistic ethical realism. Recall Lewis's claim in that essay that "[t]he good is uncreated; it never could have been otherwise; it has in it no shadow of contingency."[87] I suggested earlier that in this context the good $=$ the moral law. If this is right, then Lewis's claim is that the moral law is uncreated and could not have been otherwise than it is.

Contemporary philosophers tend to distinguish between two kinds of truths: On the one hand there are contingent truths – truths that are true but could have been false. On the other hand there are necessary truths – truths that are true and *must* be true. Necessary truths are truths that simply could not have been false. In the passage just quoted, Lewis appears to be claiming that at least some ethical truths are necessary truths; they have, as Lovell puts it, *strong modal status*.[88]

The notion that some ethical truths are necessarily true provides the foundation for one kind of atheistic ethical realism.[89] This is because necessary truths do not require an explanation of their truth. Indeed, theists routinely exploit this fact to respond to the question of God's origin. A common theistic view is that God did not come from anywhere; God exists necessarily, and hence His existence requires no explanation. If some ethical truths are necessarily true, then the atheist can make a similar claim about them: Their truth does not need an explanation. Recall that Lewis's moral argument relies on an inference to the best explanation; if ethical truths require no explanation, this inference is undercut, and Lewis's argument loses much of its bite. I think that arguments like Lewis's derive much of their force from the sense that moral obligations must have some source, that they cannot "just exist." But if the idea that some moral obligations are grounded in necessary truths is plausible, then obligations can indeed "just exist."

Of course, Lewis claims not only that the moral law exists necessarily but that it is identical to God. My claim here is not that Lewis himself endorsed the idea that the moral law could exist independently of God; rather, what I am suggesting is that Lewis's claim that the moral law exists necessarily opens the door to such a proposal. By my lights, the notion of ethical truths that are necessarily true and are *not* identical to God is more plausible than the notion that such truths *are* identical to God, because the former view lacks the obscurity and possible incoherence of the second view.

One final Lewisian moral phenomenon remains unaccounted for: moral *knowledge*. Suppose the atheistic alternative to Lewis's view sketched so far is plausible; nevertheless, nothing has yet been said that directly addresses the question of how humans living in a godless universe could come to *know* objective ethical truths. This is a complicated topic, but here again we can turn to Lewis himself for some assistance.[90] Recall Lewis's suggestion that "the primary moral principles on which all others depend are rationally perceived. . . . Their intrinsic reasonableness shines by its own light."[91] The atheist can appeal to this idea as well: At least some moral truths are self-evident in that they can be known to be true in a direct way without being inferred from other things that one knows. For instance, I have no idea how to *prove* that torturing the innocent just for fun is wrong, yet I know it. Once I understand what the claim says, I can simply see that it is true.[92] The idea of "just seeing" certain things to be true can seem mysterious. However, it is hard to see how we could know anything at all unless at least some things can be seen to be true even though we cannot prove that they are true. As we will see, this point is recognized by Lewis, Hume, and Russell.[93]

One worry that might arise here is that this view conflicts with the notion that the human mind is a product of evolutionary processes. After all, evolutionary processes would tend to select for cognitive mechanisms that produce moral beliefs that make those who have them more likely to pass on their genes (fitness-enhancing cognitive mechanisms) rather than mechanisms that produce moral beliefs that are true. So, if our minds are products of evolution, does this not give us reason to believe that the moral claims that we "just see" to be true are more likely to be advantageous for us to believe than actually true?[94]

This worry can be put to rest, I think, by expanding on the following remark by Peter Singer:

Human beings lack the strength of the gorilla, the sharp teeth of the lion, the speed of the cheetah. Brain power is our specialty. The brain is a tool for reasoning, and a capacity to reason helps us to survive, to feed ourselves, and to safeguard our children. . . . But the ability to reason is a peculiar ability. Unlike strong arms, sharp teeth or flashing legs, it can take us to conclusions that we had no desire to reach. For reason is like an escalator, leading upwards and out of sight.... We have evolved a capacity to reason because it helps us to survive and reproduce. But if reason is an escalator, then although the first part of the journey may help us to survive and reproduce, we may go further than we needed to go for this purpose alone.[95]

Allow me to illustrate the sort of thing I think Singer has in mind here. Each of the following two cognitive capacities seems likely to be sufficiently fitness-enhancing to be the sort of mechanism that would be selected for by evolution. The first is the capacity to recognize oneself as a bearer of certain fundamental rights – for example, the right not to be killed for no reason and the right not to be exploited by others. Beings that recognize that they have such rights are more likely to resist treatment that would render them less likely to pass on their genes to the next generation and hence, everything else being equal, are more likely in fact to pass on their genes to the next generation than are beings that fail to recognize that they have such rights. The second fitness-enhancing cognitive capacity is the tendency to recognize that things that are similar to each other with respect to their observed properties are likely to be similar with respect to their unobserved properties (or at least the capacity to *reason in accordance* with such a principle, even if one does not consciously recognize the principle). This capacity is advantageous because the principle it is centered around is true, and failure to reason in accordance with this principle can be deadly. Failure to infer that *these* round, shiny, bright red berries are likely to be poisonous from the fact that *those other* round, shiny, bright red berries produced frothing at the mouth and then death in one's companion yesterday may well lead to trouble for oneself today.

Things get interesting when we notice that these two cognitive capacities together may lead one to infer that all those beings one encounters that are similar to oneself with respect to their observable properties have the same fundamental rights as oneself. In this way, cognitive faculties that *in general* lead us to beliefs that enhance our fitness may nevertheless *in particular cases* lead us to conclusions that are not fitness-enhancing. Recognizing the rights of beings similar to oneself can put quite a damper on things when it comes to passing one's genes on to the next generation; for instance, one cannot help but realize that taking advantage of that oh-so-exploitable being similar to oneself would be morally wrong. Thus, the claim that minds produced by evolution would inevitably form only moral beliefs that enhance the fitness of those who hold them is simply false; the escalator of reason can lead us to moral beliefs that may actually make those who hold them *less* likely to pass on their genes than they would be if they did not hold such beliefs. And, as in the case just described, evolution-produced minds may also be "wired" to zero in on moral *truths*.

Singer's escalator analogy also suggests an evolutionary explanation for the internal moral conflict that pervades human life. Our minds can reason, and hence can lead us to moral beliefs that conflict with our genetic fitness. Yet those same minds (for obvious evolutionary reasons) also produce desires that are fitness-enhancing. And thus arises the interminable struggle between doing what is right and doing what we want to do.[96] The human struggle to do what we see to be right is not necessarily a reflection of a cosmic struggle between a Good Power and an Evil Power, or of a disastrous Fall away from God. It may instead be a consequence of the evolutionary processes that shaped our minds.

Combining the various ideas discussed in this section affords the atheist the following response to Lewis's moral argument: There is an atheistic explanation for Lewisian moral phenomena that is at least as good as Lewis's preferred Higher Power-based explanation. The atheistic explanation is as follows: Some ethical facts are necessarily true and hence require no explanation; the remaining ethical facts are contingent and follow from the necessarily true ethical facts together with certain contingent truths. (For example: Suppose that it is necessarily true that torturing the innocent just for fun is morally wrong, and that it is contingently true that by pushing a certain button, Bob would be torturing the innocent just for fun; from this follows the (contingent) ethical truth that it would be wrong for Bob to push the button). Human moral beliefs, knowledge, and emotions are products of the complex, sophisticated human mind, the basic capacities of which can be accounted for in terms of evolutionary processes. Even without God, there is real meaning, value, and morality in the universe, and our imperfect, evolutionarily shaped minds are able to provide us with at least partial knowledge of the moral structure of the godless universe. The "escalator of reason" may even give us knowledge of moral truths that, from the standpoint of fitness, we would be better off not knowing. Hence, there is no need to posit a Higher Power to account for Lewisian moral phenomena.[97]

The ultimate conclusion of our discussion of Lewis's moral argument is as follows: In order to avoid Russell's (first) objection, Lewis must reject this principle:

(RC)   The only way a being (even God) can be good is by conforming its actions to a moral law of which it is not the author.

Lewis's writings suggest three alternatives to (RC):

(LA1)   Being *identical to* the moral law is a way of being good.
(LA2)   Loving love, fair play, unselfishness, courage, good faith, honesty, and truthfulness is a way of being good.
(LA3)   Desiring that human beings attain genuine happiness (that they freely love God and strive to become Christlike) is a way of being good.

Two of these, (LA2) and (LA3), render Lewis's attack on Dualism ineffective, and this in turn renders his moral argument vulnerable to the problem posed by Dualism described in the previous section. On the other hand, the ideas that underlie (LA1) point toward another objection to the moral argument, one rooted not in Dualism but in atheism. The atheistic moral realism sketched in this section, if plausible, casts serious doubt on the second premise of Lewis's moral argument:

2.   The best explanation of the existence of Lewisian moral phenomena is the existence of a Higher Power that created the universe.

My own view is that the contribution of Lewisian moral phenomena to Lewis's cumulative case for a Higher Power is weak; I believe that objective morality is not the thorn in the side of atheism that it is often thought to be. We have also seen that the phenomenon of psychopathy does not fit particularly well with Lewis's overall view of things. While the existence of psychopaths is not decisive evidence against Lewis's position, it is one significant factor that must be taken into account when weighing the evidence for and against various worldviews. Of course, there is undoubtedly more to be said here, and readers must draw their own conclusions. In any case, we now turn our attention to a second aspect of human nature that Lewis believes points toward the existence of a Higher Power: our ability to reason.

2.3 THE ARGUMENT FROM REASON

In Part IX of Hume's *Dialogues*, Philo tentatively suggests the following hypothesis:

> Is it not probable ... that the whole economy of the universe is conducted by ... necessity, though no human algebra can furnish a key which solves the difficulty? And instead of admiring the order of natural beings, may it not happen that, could we penetrate into the intimate nature of bodies, we should clearly see why it was absolutely impossible they could ever admit of any other disposition?[98]

In *Miracles*, Lewis's third and final book-length work in Christian apologetics, he seeks to refute precisely this hypothesis, which he labels "Naturalism":

> [B]y Naturalism we mean the doctrine that only Nature – the whole interlocked system – exists. And if that were true, every thing and event would, if we knew enough, be explicable without remainder ... as a necessary product of the system. The whole system being what it is, it ought to be a contradiction in terms if you were not reading this book at the moment.[99]

The ultimate conclusion of Lewis's argument against Naturalism is that there is, in addition to Nature, "an eternal, self-existent, rational

Being, whom we call God."[100] The heart of this argument is developed in the third chapter of *Miracles*. It is widely known among Lewis scholars that Lewis wrote two versions of this chapter. Lewis revised the chapter after a famous encounter with the philosopher G. E. M. Anscombe on February 2, 1948, at a meeting of the Oxford Socratic Club.[101] On that occasion, Anscombe criticized the first version of Chapter 3 of *Miracles*. Although varying opinions about how damaging Anscombe's criticisms were to Lewis's original argument have been put forth, it is clear that Lewis made significant revisions to the chapter after the debate with Anscombe.[102] Anscombe herself says of the revised version of the chapter that "[t]he last five pages of the old chapter have been replaced by ten pages of the new . . . the rewritten version is much less slick and avoids some of the mistakes of the earlier one: it is much more of a serious investigation."[103] I will focus on the revised version of the chapter, since presumably Lewis took this to be the strongest presentation of the argument.[104] In my view, the revised chapter is among the most difficult of Lewis's philosophical writings to understand, so we will need to do some work to get clear on exactly how the argument in question is supposed to work.

Before turning to my analysis of Lewis's argument, I must point out that there is already an entire book devoted to Lewis's argument from reason. This book is Victor Reppert's *C. S. Lewis's Dangerous Idea*. In that work, Reppert develops six distinct versions of the argument from reason that he claims are at least suggested by things Lewis says in various places. I will not undertake a discussion of Reppert's six arguments. Instead, I will focus on Lewis's discussion of the argument from reason in *Miracles*, which is his most extended and developed presentation of the argument. Readers who are interested in other ways the argument could be developed are encouraged to read Reppert's book, which is quite well done.[105]

Let us begin our examination of the argument from reason by considering a distinction that is crucial to the argument. Lewis distinguishes two ways that a pair of things can be related to each other. One relation that can hold between two things is causation (which Lewis labels "Cause and Effect"). To illustrate this relation, Lewis uses the sentence "Grandfather is ill today *because* he ate lobster yesterday."[106] Here, "because" indicates causation; grandfather's eating the lobster makes him feel ill. A second relation that can hold between two things is entailment (which Lewis labels "Ground and Consequent"). To illustrate this relation, Lewis uses the sentence "Grandfather must be ill today *because* he hasn't gotten up yet (and we know he is an invariably early riser when he is well)."[107] Here, "because" indicates entailment. The claim (a) whenever grandfather is not ill he gets up early, and he hasn't gotten up early today entails (b) Grandfather is ill today.

With the distinction between causation and entailment in hand, Lewis argues that if Naturalism is true, "valid" reasoning (by which Lewis means reasoning that yields knowledge) can occur only if these two quite different relations can hold between the very same pair of beliefs.[108] To clarify this point and how Lewis arrives at it, it will be useful to consider an example.

Imagine me, sitting at my desk, struggling to write this exposition of Lewis's argument. To give myself a bit of a break, and to verify that I can still reason properly, imagine that I run through a very simple argument in my mind. First, I reflect on (and endorse) the proposition that (i) all humans are mortal, and I am human. Next, I reflect on (and endorse) the proposition that (ii) I am mortal. Let us refer to my conscious endorsement of proposition (i) as Thought A, and my conscious endorsement of proposition (ii) as Thought C.

What is required for this simple series of thoughts to constitute successful reasoning that leads to knowledge? According to Lewis, one requirement is that the final thought in the sequence be entailed by the earlier thought (or, more precisely, that the proposition that is the object of the final thought be entailed by the proposition that is the object of the earlier thought).[109] This requirement is met in our imagined example.

However, Naturalism allegedly imposes an additional requirement on the series of thoughts under discussion. As Lewis understands Naturalism, it includes the thesis that every event has a *natural* cause, a cause that is itself part of nature. Thus, if Naturalism is true, then Thought C (which itself must be a part of nature) must have some cause that is also part of Nature. What could this cause be? The most likely candidate seems to be Thought A. Thus, Naturalism seems to imply that the series consisting of Thought A and Thought C constitutes reasoning that yields knowledge only if the two very different relations of causation and entailment both hold between the two thoughts. As Lewis puts it, "in order for a train of thought to have any value, these two systems of connection [causation and entailment] must apply simultaneously to the same series of mental acts."[110] This gives us the first premise of Lewis's argument:

1. If Naturalism is true, then valid reasoning occurs only if one thought can both *entail* and *cause* another thought.

Lewis's next important move is found in this passage:

> We know by experience that a thought does not necessarily cause all, or even any, of the thoughts which logically stand to it as Consequents to Ground. We should be in a pretty pickle if we could never think 'This is glass' without drawing all the inferences which could be drawn. It is impossible to draw them all; quite often we draw none.... One thought can cause another not by *being*, but by being *seen to be*, a ground for it.[111]

Lewis's point here reveals that the story I just told about concluding that I am mortal is incomplete. I left out an important part of the story, namely, the moment when I realized that proposition (i) (all humans are mortal, and I am human) entails proposition (ii) (I am mortal). We can label this realization Thought B. If, as Naturalism allegedly requires, Thought A causes Thought C, then Thought B must occur. Lewis's claim in the final sentence of the passage I just quoted implies that it is only through the occurrence of Thought B that Thought A can cause Thought C. He apparently made much the same point during the discussion at the meeting of the Oxford Socratic Club mentioned earlier. On that occasion, Lewis claimed that "the recognition of a ground could be the cause of assent, and that assent was only rational when such was its cause."[112] This gives us a second crucial premise:

2. One thought can both entail and cause another thought only if the first thought can be *known* to entail the second.

At this point, Lewis proceeds to argue that Naturalism does not permit the occurrence of thoughts like Thought B. Indeed, Lewis maintains that Naturalism does not permit knowledge of any sort. Lewis's argument for this claim relies on a certain principle about knowledge: "An act of knowing must be determined . . . solely by what is known; we must know it to be thus solely because it *is* thus."[113] Here, Lewis endorses a causal principle about knowledge: A person, S, knows a proposition, p, only if (i) S believes p, and (ii) the complete cause of S's belief that p is the truth of p itself. With this principle in hand, Lewis argues as follows:

> If there is nothing but Nature . . . reason must have come into existence by a historical process. And of course, for the Naturalist, this process was not designed to produce a mental behaviour that can find truth. . . . The type of mental behaviour we now call rational thinking or inference must therefore have been 'evolved' by natural selection, by the gradual weeding out of types less fitted to survive.
>
> Once, then, our thoughts were not rational. . . . Those which had a cause external to ourselves at all were (like our pains) responses to stimuli. Now natural selection could operate only by eliminating responses that were biologically hurtful and multiplying those which tended to survival. But it is not conceivable that any improvement of responses could ever turn them into acts of insight, or even remotely tend to do so. The relation between stimulus and response is utterly different from that between knowledge and the truth known.[114]

Strictly speaking, evolutionary theory is not part of Naturalism as Lewis has defined it, but presumably Lewis's (reasonable) supposition is that those who are inclined to accept Naturalism will also be inclined to accept evolutionary theory. Thus, Lewis supposes that the Naturalist will likely be committed to the claim that the capacity for knowledge arose by way of the processes posited by evolutionary theory, one of which is natural selection. However, Lewis argues, evolutionary theory has it that the creatures upon which natural selection initially operated were incapable of knowledge. At best, they were capable of giving certain responses when certain stimuli were present. But responding to stimuli is not the same thing as having knowledge.

For instance, imagine a simple creature that feels pain when poked with a stick. The experience of pain causes the creature to recoil from the stick. But the creature never forms the belief that it is being poked by a stick. (Indeed, it forms no belief at all.) There is a mental state here – pain – but no knowledge. The reason there is no knowledge is that the pain is not *about* anything. It has no object or content – it is not what contemporary philosophers of mind call an *intentional state*. Instead, it is a subjective feeling that causes a certain action (recoiling) to occur.

Let us add another mental state to our example. Suppose that the pain produces a belief that it would be good to recoil, and this belief in turn produces the act of recoiling. This belief still fails to constitute knowledge. To see why, recall Lewis's principle about knowledge: S knows p only if (i) S believes p, and (ii) the complete cause of S's belief that p is the truth of p itself. In the case at hand, the belief that it would be good to recoil is caused by the truth of the proposition that the creature is being poked by a stick, not by the truth of the proposition that it would be good to recoil. Hence the second condition specified by Lewis's principle about knowledge is not met. Again, the point Lewis is trying to make here is that a creature can have mental states and respond to stimuli in fairly sophisticated ways without possessing *knowledge* at all.

This point is essential for Lewis's argument because an important part of his argument is the claim that natural selection is incapable of somehow turning the capacity to respond to certain stimuli into a capacity for genuine knowledge. If the capacity to respond to stimuli *entailed* the capacity for knowledge, then Lewis's argument would lose its bite. The naturalist could simply point out that by conceding that natural selection could produce creatures capable of responding to stimuli, Lewis would have implicitly conceded that natural selection could produce creatures capable of knowledge.

In the passage quoted earlier, Lewis claims that the transformation of (mere) stimuli-responders into genuine knowers by way of natural selection is "not conceivable." Therefore, if Naturalism were true, we might be capable of responding to stimuli, but we would be incapable of genuine knowledge. This yields another pair of premises:

3. If Naturalism is true, then knowledge exists only if natural selection could produce a capacity for knowledge starting with creatures with no such capacity.
4. But natural selection could not produce a capacity for knowledge starting with creatures with no such capacity.

Adding these premises to the first two and making some additional inferences yields what I take to be Lewis's main argument in Chapter 3 of *Miracles*:

1. If Naturalism is true, then valid reasoning occurs only if one thought can both *entail* and *cause* another thought.
2. One thought can both entail and cause another thought only if the first thought can be *known* to entail the second.
3. If Naturalism is true, then knowledge exists only if natural selection could produce a capacity for knowledge starting with creatures with no such capacity.
4. But natural selection could not produce a capacity for knowledge starting with creatures with no such capacity.
5. So: If Naturalism is true, then knowledge does not exist (from 3 and 4).
6. If knowledge does not exist, then no thought be known to entail a second thought.
7. Therefore, if Naturalism is true, then valid reasoning does not occur (from 1, 2, 5, and 6).

Before considering how the argument progresses from here, it is worth pausing for a moment to note something odd about the argument so far. Lewis's goal in Chapter 3 of *Miracles* seems to be to show that Naturalism is self-defeating in the following sense: If it were true, it could not be known to be true, because there would be no knowledge at all. Given this, the early stages of the argument (represented in the formulation presented here by the first two premises) are entirely superfluous. This is because premises 3 and 4 by themselves yield the desired conclusion that Naturalism implies that there is no knowledge.

What is going on here? One hypothesis is that the first two premises are what remain of the original argument of Chapter 3 of *Miracles*, the argument that was criticized by Anscombe at the meeting of the Oxford Socratic Club in 1948. In order to respond to Anscombe's criticism and patch up his argument, Lewis introduced some additional reasoning, represented by premises 3–5. The new reasoning, if successful, would indeed patch up the original argument – but would also render the original argument entirely unnecessary. It may be that Lewis simply failed to notice the latter point.[115]

In any case, by the end of Chapter 3, Lewis thinks he has established that nature alone cannot produce genuine knowledge. Since knowledge plainly exists, there must be something in addition to nature that is responsible for knowledge. Since Naturalism entails that nothing outside of nature exists, Naturalism apparently stands refuted: "Naturalism ... offers what professes to be a full account of our mental behaviour; but this account, on inspection, leaves no room for the acts of knowing or insight on which the whole value of our thinking, as a means to truth, depends."[116]

In the subsequent chapter of *Miracles*, Lewis suggests that each of us possesses a supernatural capacity, reason, which enables us to have genuine knowledge. Human reason must have some source, and since it has already been established that human reason cannot have been produced by nature, it must have a supernatural source. This supernatural source turns out to be God:

> Human minds, then, are not the only supernatural entities that exist. They do not come from nowhere. Each has come into Nature from Supernature: each has its tap-root in an eternal, self-existent, rational Being, whom we call God. ... [H]uman thought is ... God-kindled.[117]

Incorporating this idea, and putting aside the superfluous early stages of the Chapter 3 argument, it seems to me that Lewis's argument from reason, as it appears in the revised version of *Miracles*, amounts to the following:

Lewis's Argument from Reason

1. If Naturalism is true, then knowledge exists only if natural selection could produce a capacity for knowledge starting with creatures with no such capacity.
2. But natural selection could not produce a capacity for knowledge starting with creatures with no such capacity.
3. So: If Naturalism is true, then knowledge does not exist (from 1 and 2).
4. But knowledge does exist.
5. So: Naturalism is false (from 3 and 4).
6. If knowledge exists and Naturalism is false, then there is a supernatural, eternal, self-existent, rational Being that is the ultimate source of all knowledge.
7. Therefore, there is a supernatural, eternal, self-existent, rational Being that is the ultimate source of all knowledge (from 4, 5, and 6).

How might this argument be resisted? The second premise is one that many contemporary nontheists would be inclined to reject. Let us take a closer look at how Lewis supports this crucial premise.

Lewis claims that it is "not conceivable" that evolutionary processes could produce creatures capable of knowledge from creatures incapable of knowledge.[118] To evaluate this claim, we must distinguish two ways of understanding it. One interpretation has it that Lewis is claiming that he (and perhaps the reader as well – perhaps *everyone*) cannot conceive of any way in which evolutionary processes could produce beings capable of knowledge. Let us say that when something is inconceivable in this sense, it is *weakly* inconceivable. Consider, for example, the process by which the letters inscribed on the keys on my computer keyboard appear on the screen when I press down the keys. This process is weakly inconceivable (by me).

Another interpretation has it that Lewis is claiming that he can see that it is impossible for evolutionary processes to yield beings capable of knowledge. Let us say that when something is inconceivable in this sense, it is *strongly* inconceivable. Consider, for example, the concept of a round square, discussed in the previous chapter. Such a shape is inconceivable, not merely in that I cannot conceive of a process that would produce such a shape (although that is true), but also in that I can see in a rather direct way that no such shape could exist. Indeed, I can give a proof that such a shape is impossible. Here it is: A square must have exactly four corners, and a circle must have exactly zero corners. So a round square must have exactly four corners and simultaneously have exactly zero corners. But this is plainly impossible; hence there cannot be a round square.

When Lewis claims that the production of beings capable of knowledge by way of evolutionary processes is inconceivable, does he mean to say that it is weakly inconceivable or strongly inconceivable? The former claim seems too weak for his purposes. This is because the fact that a given process is weakly inconceivable is perfectly consistent with the occurrence of the process in question. I cannot conceive of the process by which the letters I type appear on the screen; nevertheless, it is happening right now! Even if everyone who understood the process were to forget how it works so that no one at all could conceive of the process, it would not follow that the process is impossible. It seems, therefore, that Lewis must be claiming that he can see that the production of beings capable of knowledge by evolutionary processes is impossible. What support does Lewis offer for such a claim?

Lewis remarks that if Naturalism is true, then "all our thoughts once were ... merely subjective events, not apprehensions of objective truth."[119] What exactly is the contrast Lewis is attempting to highlight with this distinction between merely subjective thoughts and thoughts that are apprehensions of truth? An earlier passage sheds some light on this question: "Acts of thinking ... are a very special sort of events. They are 'about' something other than themselves and can be true or false."[120] The later passage suggests that Lewis's view is that not all mental states have intentionality (are about something). Some mental states do have intentionality; for example, mental states that are apprehensions of objective truth.

There are other mental states, purely subjective mental states (e.g., pain), that are not about anything.

It is shortly after the passage about subjective and objective thoughts that Lewis claims that "[t]he relation between response and stimulus is utterly different from that between knowledge and the truth known."[121] It seems that when Lewis speaks of stimulus and response in this context, he has in mind a very specific type of response – specifically, responses involving mental states that are not about anything (lack intentionality). Immediately after the sentence I just quoted, Lewis provides the following example to illustrate his point:

> Our physical vision is a far more useful response to light than that of the cruder organisms which have only a photo-sensitive spot. But neither this improvement nor any possible improvements we can suppose could bring it an inch nearer to being knowledge of light.[122]

I think that what Lewis has in mind here is that the human visual system is capable of producing a much broader range of visual experiences than is a photosensitive spot. Despite this difference, however, neither system produces mental states that are *about* anything. Visual experiences are not intentional states (according to Lewis, at any rate). Furthermore, no increase in the range of experiences a given visual system can produce can ever render the system capable of producing intentional mental states. The mere addition of more and more nonintentional mental states will never somehow "add up" to intentionality. This means that no increase in the range of experiences a given visual system can produce can ever turn it into a system capable of producing knowledge. This is because knowledge requires intentionality.

It seems to me, therefore, that the fundamental problem Lewis sees with the notion that knowledge could arise via evolutionary processes is that he thinks it is impossible that intentional mental states could be created by evolutionary processes. Nature alone cannot produce intentionality; for this, you need something outside of nature, something that Lewis calls "reason." Without supernatural reason, there could be no thinkers capable of thinking *about* the natural universe:

> [A]cts of reasoning are not interlocked with the total interlocking system of Nature as all its other items are interlocked with one another. They are connected with it in a different way; as the understanding of a machine is certainly connected with the machine but not in the way the parts of the machine are connected with each other. The knowledge of a thing is not one of the thing's parts. In this sense something beyond Nature operates whenever we reason.[123]

Lewis presents a complicated and challenging argument. Let us consider how a naturalist might defend her position against the argument. One potential weakness in the argument lies in Lewis's attempt to establish the impossibility of the production of intentional states by evolutionary processes. The attempted proof runs roughly as follows: If evolutionary processes could produce intentional states at all, they could do so only by increasing the variety of nonintentional mental states produced by an already-existing response system. But such increases can never generate intentional states; hence, evolutionary processes cannot produce intentional states. The weakness in this argument is in the first premise. Why should the naturalist accept that if evolutionary processes can produce intentional states at all, they would have to do so in the specific way described by Lewis? From the fact that evolutionary forces couldn't accomplish the task *in that particular way*, it does not follow that they couldn't accomplish it *at all*.

Despite this weakness, the argument highlights a real puzzle for naturalism, and drawing attention to this puzzle is among Lewis's most important contributions to contemporary philosophy.[124] By Lewis's own account, doubt about the compatibility of naturalism and knowledge was one of the main intellectual components of his abandonment of naturalism and eventual conversion to Christianity. Lewis credits his friend Owen Barfield with drawing his attention to the difficulty. He writes that Barfield "convinced me that the positions we had hitherto held left no room for any satisfactory theory of knowledge."[125] Questions about the compatibility of naturalism and human knowledge are also prominent in the contemporary debate between theists and naturalists; the Christian philosopher Alvin Plantinga has proposed a much-discussed argument that owes much to Lewis's argument in *Miracles*.[126]

In the previous chapter I suggested that a certain kind of suffering, while compatible with the existence of the Christian God, constitutes evidence against such a God because the presence of such suffering is less surprising on the hypothesis that atheism is true than it is on the hypothesis that the Christian God exists. While Lewis's argument from reason fails to establish that intentionality is incompatible with naturalism, it may show that the existence of intentionality constitutes evidence against naturalism in much the same way that certain kinds of suffering constitute evidence against the existence of the Christian God: The presence of intentionality is, perhaps, less surprising on the hypothesis that an eternal Reasoner exists than it is on the hypothesis that naturalism is true.

How might a naturalist address this sort of challenge? One obvious strategy is to find a plausible explanation of the emergence of intentionality in the context of naturalism. Tellingly, explaining how natural forces alone might produce intentional states is one of the central projects of contemporary philosophy of mind. The literature on this topic is vast, indicating that contemporary naturalists are keenly aware of the problem that bothered Lewis.[127]

Another strategy is available. This other strategy involves the claim that naturalism actually predicts that it will be difficult or impossible for us to understand how intentionality could be produced by evolution. The idea underlying this strategy is that if a given theory predicts a certain fact, that fact cannot constitute evidence against the theory in question. This kind of strategy has been pursued by some theists in connection with the following line of reasoning:

1. The world contains evil for which we can discern no justification (inscrutable evil).

2. Inscrutable evil is probably evil that has no justification (pointless evil).

3. Therefore, the world probably contains pointless evil (and hence God probably does not exist).[128]

In response to this kind of argument, some theists point out that given the large gap between the cognitive abilities of God and those of human beings, it is not at all surprising that we cannot find an explanation for every instance of suffering, and hence that the second premise of the argument just given – the inference from inscrutable to pointless evil – is no good.[129] Indeed, Lewis himself pursues this kind of strategy, as we will see in Chapter 4. Now consider the following line of reasoning:

1. The world contains mental phenomena (e.g., intentionality) such that we can discern no evolutionary process that could produce such phenomena (evolutionarily challenged mental phenomena).
2. Evolutionarily challenged mental phenomena are probably mental phenomena that were not produced by evolution (nonevolved mental phenomena).
3. Therefore, the world probably contains nonevolved mental phenomena (and hence naturalism is probably false).

Can the naturalist respond to this kind of argument in a way that parallels the theistic response to the previous argument? I believe so. Colin McGinn has taken such an approach with respect to consciousness. Although consciousness as understood by McGinn is importantly different from intentionality, consideration of McGinn's approach can give us a sense of the kind of strategy I have in mind. According to McGinn, the human mind is structured in such a way that it is incapable of grasping the connection between the brain and conscious experience. Furthermore, the fact that the human mind is so constituted is to be explained at least in part by evolutionary theory. The following passage summarizes this aspect of McGinn's view:

> I maintain that the perennial puzzlement surrounding consciousness and its relation to the body is an indication that we are on the edge of what we can make comprehensible to ourselves. Human

intelligence . . . is an evolutionary contrivance, designed with purposes far removed from the solution of profound philosophical problems, and it is not terribly surprising if it lacks the tools to crack every problem. . . . There is no product warranty inscribed on our brains reading, "This device is guaranteed to solve any problem it can formulate. If not completely satisfied, please return to Philosophical Products Inc. for a sincere apology and your money back."[130]

A central theme of McGinn's approach is that contemporary evolutionary theory predicts that in general, human beings will tend not to be very good at solving philosophical problems.[131] McGinn does not stop here; he proceeds to offer a fairly developed account of the specific capacities of the human brain and why these capacities fail to provide us with tools sufficient to understand the brain-consciousness relationship. His theory ("New Mysterianism") depends on certain properties peculiar to conscious experience and so cannot be straightforwardly applied to intentionality, but McGinn's more general theme can: Understanding how evolutionary processes could produce intentional states is (at least in part) a philosophical problem, just the sort of problem evolutionary theory predicts our brains will be bad at solving. So, just as the presence of evil for which we can discern no justification should not lead us to infer that such evil has no justification, the presence of mental phenomena for which we can discern no evolutionary explanation should not lead us to infer that such phenomena have no evolutionary explanation.

Christianity and contemporary naturalism both predict that human beings will have certain significant cognitive limitations. In Christianity, this prediction is grounded in the gap between the cognitive abilities of human beings and those of God. In contemporary naturalism, this prediction is grounded in the nature of the processes that produced the human mind. This feature of the two worldviews provides them with similar strategies for dealing with certain objections. If these strategies are successful, each side seems to have a philosophical card that can be used to evade challenges from the other side – like this: The naturalist says, "Look, there's this evil for which we can discern no justification. This kind of evil is evidence against your view." The Christian replies, "Ah, but my view predicts that there will be evil for which we can discern no justification (even though such evil is justified). After all, finite, limited, and flawed beings such as ourselves cannot be expected to have complete comprehension of the ways of an infinite, perfect God. So such evil is not evidence against my view after all." Or the Christian says: "Look, there's this mental phenomenon for which we can discern no evolutionary explanation. This kind of phenomenon is evidence against your view." The naturalist replies, "Ah, but my view predicts that there will be phenomena for which can discern no evolutionary explanation (even though such an explanation exists). After all, finite, limited, glorified monkeys cannot be expected to be able to solve every philosophical problem; our brains were selected for other purposes. So such phenomena are not evidence against my view after all."

Both sides seem to recognize that this second kind of strategy (our worldview predicts this kind of puzzle) is far less satisfying than the first kind of strategy (here is a solution to the puzzle); theists continue to propose theodicies, and naturalists continue to seek accounts of how intentionality could arise by way of evolution. This means that even if pointing to such puzzles fails to settle the issue of which worldview is correct, it does stimulate thinkers on both sides to investigate further. Lewis's argument from reason and related arguments, while not deserving of the rarely achieved title of "proof," should at least provoke reflective naturalists to engage in some serious thought. As Victor Reppert observes, "[g]reat thinkers are always the ones that make us think harder for ourselves, not thinkers who do our thinking for us. And the same is true for Lewis."[132]

2.4   THE ARGUMENT FROM DESIRE

In his autobiography, Lewis credits a state of mind he labels "Joy" with playing an important role in his conversion to Christianity. The importance of Joy in his conversion is indicated by the title of his autobiography, *Surprised by Joy*. Early in that work Lewis remarks that "in a sense the central story of my life is about nothing else."[133] He describes Joy as "an unsatisfied desire which is itself more desirable than any other satisfaction."[134] Lewis encountered Joy periodically throughout his life, but apparently found the experience fleeting and devoted much effort to recapturing it. He puzzled over its nature for many years, eventually coming to believe that it "was not a deception" but instead involved "the moments of clearest consciousness we had."[135] He ultimately concluded that Joy is a desire for God.[136] At one point he says that God had been shooting "arrows of Joy" at him "ever since childhood."[137] He attributes one of his crucial insights into the nature of Joy to his reading of Samuel Alexander's 1920 book *Space, Time, and Deity*. In that work, Alexander describes a "distinctive religious appetite, comparable to the appetite for food or drink."[138] Alexander claims that this religious appetite is caused by God and that experiencing it provides insight into God's nature.[139]

Several commentators have argued that Lewis's writing suggests an argument based on Joy. This argument has come to be known as "the argument from desire."[140] The argument has captured the heart of at least one commentator: Peter Kreeft declares that "[n]ext to Anselm's famous 'ontological argument,' I think [the argument from desire] is the single most intriguing argument in the history of human thought."[141]

The following lines from *Mere Christianity* indicate the nature of the argument:

> Creatures are not born with desires unless satisfaction for those desires exists. A baby feels hunger; well, there is such a thing as food. A duckling wants to swim: well, there is such a thing as water. Men feel sexual desire: well, there is such a thing as sex. If I find in myself a desire which no experience in this world can satisfy, the most probable explanation is that I was made for another world.[142]

In light of Lewis's various remarks on Joy and discussions of the argument in the secondary literature, I believe that the essence of the argument may be captured as follows:

Lewis's Argument from Desire

1. All normal human beings have an innate, natural desire (Joy) that is for some thing, x, where x lies beyond the natural world.
2. Every desire that is innate and natural to all normal human beings can be satisfied.
3. So: Joy can be satisfied (from 1 and 2).
4. If Joy can be satisfied, then there is something that lies beyond the natural world.
5. Therefore, there is something that lies beyond the natural world (from 3 and 4).

The most interesting premises here are the first two. In support of the first premise, Lewis remarks that "[m]ost people, if they had really learned to look into their own hearts, would know that they do want...something that cannot be had in this world."[143] Steve Lovell offers the following:

> Given that even the best the material world has to offer leaves many of us deeply unhappy, that even some of the most staunch of atheists admits a desire for 'something more,' that over 90% of the world's population engage in some form of religious practise, and that the longing for transcendence is a recurring theme in both religious and secular literature it would be, at the very least, *reasonable* to posit a natural desire for something beyond this world as an explanation of these facts.[144]

What about the second premise? Why should we think that all our natural, innate desires can be satisfied? Russell appears to reject such a notion outright: "The fact that I feel a *need* for something more than human is no evidence that the need can be satisfied, any more than hunger is evidence that I shall get food."[145] In his 1941 essay "The Weight of Glory," Lewis writes:

> A man's physical hunger does not prove that man will get any bread.... But surely [it] proves that he ... inhabits a world where eatable substances exist. In the same way, though I do not believe ... that my desire for Paradise proves that I shall enjoy it, I think it a pretty good indication that such a thing exists and that some men will. A

many may love a woman and not win her; but it would be very odd if
the phenomenon called "falling in love" occurred in a sexless world.[146]

Lewis's remarks indicate that Russell's hunger example does not do
much to support the rejection of the second premise of the argument
from desire, but Russell nevertheless makes a relevant point: In general, we do not think that the mere fact that something is desired
indicates that the desired thing exists. What reason is there to think
that natural desires *do* point to the existence of the desired object?[147]

Three interesting kinds of arguments for (2) (the claim that all natural, innate desires are capable of being satisfied) exist. The first of
these is an inductive argument based on our experience of natural
desires other than Joy. As Lewis notes, we observe that we naturally desire food, and food exists; we naturally desire sex, and sex
exists. It is not hard to add to this list: We naturally desire sleep, and
sleep exists. So there is lots of inductive evidence that our innate,
natural desires can be satisfied; thus, it is likely that Joy can be satisfied as well.[148] A second line of argument is based on the idea that
"if natural desires did not have correlating objects, there would be
something fundamentally wrong, awry, disjointed, illogical, unfair,
twisted, fraudulent, or out of kilter about reality."[149] If (2) is false,
then the universe is absurd in a certain way; but the universe is not
absurd in this way, so (2) is true. Finally, it might be suggested that
(2) or something that entails it is self-evident and can simply be seen
to be true.[150]

Let us consider these three approaches in reverse order. For my
part, I cannot simply see that (2) is true; after sincere reflection, it
does not strike me as self-evident. Russell apparently thought he
could see it to be false. To my way of thinking, (2) is precisely the
sort of claim that needs to be argued for or against. Readers who find
(2) to be obviously true may as well skip ahead to the concluding
section of this chapter.

What of the absurdity of the universe if (2) is false? Here we must
keep in mind the distinction between *absurdity* (of the relevant sort)
and *inexplicability*. To deny (2) is not to assert that the universe or
some feature of it cannot be *explained*. To deny (2) is rather to assert

that there is something "out of kilter" about the universe in that it is part of human nature to desire something that does not exist. As I have suggested elsewhere, the question of whether the universe fundamentally makes sense is one of the central questions about which theists and atheists tend to disagree, and hence any argument put forth by either party to the debate that simply assumes that the universe does (or does not) make sense in this way is not particularly helpful.[151] That the universe fails to conform to our natural desires is an implication the atheist is unlikely to find surprising or implausible. It is natural to wonder about the *explanation* of a natural desire that cannot be satisfied; I will make a proposal about this later.

Finally, let us consider the inductive case for premise (2). Recall the natural desires to which Lewis initially draws our attention: hunger, sexual desire, and a duckling's desire for water (or to swim). The inductive case goes like this: All *examined* natural desires can be satisfied; therefore, *all* natural desires (examined or unexamined) can be satisfied.[152] Since Joy is a natural desire, it follows that Joy is capable of satisfaction, and hence some sort of supernatural entity that can satisfy it exists.

I see two weaknesses with this inductive approach. One feature of simple inductive arguments of this sort is that they can be countered by other simple inductive arguments for an opposed conclusion. Consider the following example. Imagine a sports team with a long history that has never lost a home game and has never won on a Tuesday. Despite playing many games at home and many games on Tuesdays, the team has never played a home game on a Tuesday. Let us suppose that for the first time the team is scheduled to play at home on a Tuesday. If all we have to go on are the facts I have just mentioned, can we draw any conclusions about whether the team is likely to win the Tuesday home game? I do not think so. The reason we cannot is that we have two conflicting simple inductive arguments that nullify each other. On the one hand, we can reason that because the team has won all past home games, it is likely to win this one. On the other hand, we can reason that because the team has lost all past Tuesday games, it is likely to lose this one. The two arguments cancel each other out, leaving us with no idea whether the team is more likely to win or lose the Tuesday home game.

I believe that a similar situation obtains with respect to the inductive case that Joy can be satisfied. In the example I just described, the problematic game belongs to two relevant classes of games: games played by the team at home, and games played by the team on Tuesdays. Its membership in the first class suggests victory, whereas its membership in the second class suggests defeat. Similarly, Joy belongs to two relevant classes of desires. One of these classes is the class of natural desires, and its membership in this class (let us suppose for the moment) suggests that Joy can be satisfied. But Joy also belongs to a second class of desires, namely, the class of human desires for things that are not part of the known natural universe. And Joy's membership in this class of desires suggests that it is *not* capable of satisfaction. The reason for this is simply that most desires in this second category are for things that do not exist. Throughout human history, people have had desires involving all kinds of entities that do not belong to the known natural universe, and it is clear that the vast majority of these desires involve objects that do not exist. So, we have two opposed inductive arguments that cancel each other out. On the one hand, we can reason that because Joy belongs to the class of natural desires, Joy probably can be satisfied. On the other hand, we can reason that because Joy belongs to the class of human desires for things that are not part of the known natural universe, Joy probably cannot be satisfied. The inductive case that Joy can be satisfied therefore fails, just as the inductive case that the team will win its Tuesday home game fails.

A second (independent) weakness of the inductive approach lies in the fact that, putting aside the issue of whether Joy can be satisfied, it is clear that Joy is quite different from the other natural desires that Lewis mentions. Those other desires share a number of features that Joy lacks. For instance, they are all desires for things that are part of the natural world. Furthermore, they are all such that their satisfaction never brings permanent contentment and fulfillment. In maintaining that Joy is a desire for union with God, Lewis is committed to the view that Joy is not a desire for something that is part of the natural world and that it *is* a desire whose satisfaction brings (or would bring) eternal bliss. It is clear that Lewis conceives of Joy as being unlike other natural desires in some important ways. What, then, is the basis for maintaining that it *is* like them in that it is capable of being satisfied? The inductive argument for the conclusion that Joy can be satisfied seems to be countered by what we might call a "meta-inductive argument": All *examined* inductive arguments from the nature of natural desires to the nature of Joy fail; therefore, *all* such inductive arguments fail. Joy's unique status among natural desires seems to undermine the inductive case for the second premise of the argument from desire.

Robert Holyer comments on this type of criticism as follows:

> [O]ne could question the extent to which Joy is like other natural desires. . . . However, even if the challenger has some success with this line of argument, the most he could do is to diminish the similarity between Joy and other natural desires and hence weaken the argument. The fact that it is still a desire, albeit of a somewhat different sort, would seem to limit the extent to which this sort of challenge could vitiate the argument.[153]

Holyer seems to be suggesting that no matter how different from all other natural desires Joy turns out to be, the fact that it is a natural desire will still constitute *some* reason to believe that Joy can be satisfied. But this seems wrong. If Joy is sufficiently different from all other natural desires, the fact that it is a natural desire will tell us nothing at all about whether it is a desire that can be satisfied. Here is a simple example that illustrates this point: If we know of a particular swan that it is unlike all other swans in many significant ways, the fact that it is a swan may give us no reason to believe that it is white, even if all other swans we have observed are white. The many known differences between this swan and other swans we have observed means that the fact that it is a swan tells us little about its particular characteristics.[154] I conclude that the inductive case that all natural desires can be satisfied is very weak at best, and further that the second premise of our initial formulation of the argument lacks adequate support. I see no good reason to believe that Joy, even if it is part of human nature, is capable of satisfaction.

There is one final way of understanding the argument from desire that merits consideration. We might construe it as based on an inference to the best explanation. As I noted earlier, it is natural to wonder what explains the fact (if it is a fact) that Joy is part of human nature. That God crafted us so that we would experience Joy would certainly account for Joy's existence. So we might understand the argument this way:

Lewis's Argument from Desire (Revised)

1. All normal human beings have an innate, natural desire (Joy) that is for some thing, x, where x lies beyond the natural world.
2. The best explanation of (1) is that a mindlike Higher Power instilled Joy in human nature.
3. Therefore, there is a mindlike Higher Power that instilled Joy in human nature (from 1 and 2).

Is there a plausible explanation for this (alleged) feature of human nature that does not involve a supernatural entity? I believe that we can develop the basic elements of just such an explanation by drawing once again on evolutionary psychology. Interestingly, Lovell considers a suggestion along these very lines:

> We can...understand how a creature acquires its natural traits in evolutionary terms. Evolution will encourage those traits that are an aid to survival and reproduction. If the possession of a particular desire would be an aid to these, then evolution will favour it. In this manner the trait will become prevalent in, and perhaps therefore natural to, the descendants of the creature in which it arose. But many desires would not be at all useful to survival or reproduction unless they are desires for things that can really be obtained.... [I]n an environment that contains lakes or is near to the sea the desire to go swimming might (for some reason) confer an evolutionary advantage. But in an environment void of such expanses of water, the desire might only encourage a fruitless search for places to swim, which would be a waste of time and energy and would therefore be no aid to survival

or reproduction. In this way, we come to see why it is that so many natural desires have correlating objects, but we do so in a way that need not require that they *all* do. Suppose a desire for communion with God . . . does confer an evolutionary edge; why would its doing so require the existence of God . . . ?[155]

This is a promising start, but a crucial element is missing: We need some plausible account of *how* the desire for something beyond the natural world provides those beings that have it with an evolutionary advantage over those that lack it *even if* no such transcendent object exists.

Two important facts about Joy as it is described by Lewis constitute the foundation of such an account. The first important fact is that one of the main effects of Joy is that it prevents a person from deriving lasting contentment from earthly things. This fact is important because deriving lasting contentment from earthly things can be quite disadvantageous, evolutionarily speaking. Dissatisfaction can benefit us in the long run. This idea is evident in Ronald Dworkin's criticism of the use of psychotropic drugs as a "treatment" for ordinary unhappiness (as opposed to genuine psychological disorders). Dworkin labels the happiness produced in this way "Artificial Happiness" and observes that "[p]eople with Artificial Happiness don't feel the unhappiness they need to move forward with their lives."[156] To see the evolutionary drawbacks of lasting contentment, consider a male human who is perfectly content as long as his basic needs (food, shelter, and sex) are satisfied. Once such needs are satisfied, he will have no motivation whatsoever to acquire additional wealth, power, status, or success; indeed, he will have no motivation to do anything at all, other than perhaps ensure that his basic needs continue to be satisfied. Contrast this male with a second male who has the same basic drives but who *never* achieves lasting contentment, regardless of his earthly accomplishments. Everything else being equal, the second male will likely do better than the first in the competition for limited resources and access to the most desirable females. Indeed, a male who would derive lasting contentment from *some* level of earthly success, no matter how high, always stands the risk of being bested by a male who would never derive lasting contentment from any amount of earthly goods. Evolutionarily speaking, a good strategy is never to be entirely satisfied with one's lot in life. Lasting contentment breeds inaction, which in turn breeds reproductive failure – at least when the competition is not entirely content. Robert Wright describes the basic idea here as follows:

> [W]e are designed to feel that the next great goal will bring bliss, and the bliss is designed to evaporate shortly after we get there. Natural selection has a malicious sense of humor; it leads us along with a series of promises and then keeps saying "Just kidding." . . . Remarkably, we go our whole lives without ever really catching on.[157]

The second important fact about Joy is that what Joy is a desire for is not at all obvious. Lewis spent years trying to understand the nature of Joy. This fact is important because if one wants something but doesn't know what, one is likely to conclude that what one wants is more of some earthly good. So as long as the true object of Joy is unclear, Joy functions as a sort of catalyst for one's more fundamental desires. And those fundamental desires, of course, have been instilled by evolution because they tend to produce behaviors that lead to evolutionary success. In light of all this, it is easy to see why the disposition to experience Joy might be selected for by evolution: No matter how many earthly goods we acquire, Joy relentlessly whispers, "It's not enough." Joy prevents us from falling into the genetically disadvantageous trap of lasting contentment; it ensures that our basic fitness-enhancing drives will never cease to operate entirely. It is Lewis himself who suggests perhaps the simplest and clearest illustration of this concept: "Joy is not a substitute for sex; sex is very often a substitute for Joy."[158] And Lewis's very next sentence captures the more general relationship between Joy and the basic drives that I am attempting to describe here: "I sometimes wonder whether all pleasures are not substitutes for Joy."[159] Joy can function in the way I have suggested even if its object does not exist. By causing us to strive for the infinite, it prevents us from being entirely satisfied by the finite, and in this way causes us to survive and reproduce more successfully than we otherwise would.

One objection that might be raised against this account is that it is merely a "just so story." The term "just so story" is taken from Rudyard Kipling's book by that name. The book consists of fanciful accounts of how various animals got to be the way they are – for example, "How the Whale Got His Throat," "How the Leopard Got His Spots," and "The Beginning of the Armadillos." The point of labeling an evolutionary explanation of some trait a "just so story" is to suggest that the explanation is merely a plausible (or plausible-sounding) possibility that is not supported by empirical evidence. With respect to the evolutionary explanation of Joy that I have sketched, the point is well taken, as I have provided no empirical evidence to support my account. However, in the present context, this point is not damaging. The reason is that the theistic explanation of Joy lacks empirical evidence as well.[160] What we have are essentially two competing "just so stories." If this is right, then we have a stalemate. And a stalemate in this context means failure for the argument from desire, which is supposed to provide some positive reason to believe that a transcendent object exists.

It seems, then, that we are left with two possible explanations for the fact that Joy is part of human nature. The first explanation is that the disposition to experience Joy has been selected for by evolution because it enhances the fitness of those beings that have it, even though Joy's object does not exist. The second explanation is that "we cry out for eternity, because God has put such desire into our hearts. Our hearts are restless until they rest in God, because they were designed by God to rest in God alone."[161] The first of these explanations may seem a bit odd or even disturbing in that it involves the claim that it is in our nature to desire something that does not exist. As Lovell observes, "[r]ather than helping the atheist avoid the conclusion that the world is ultimately irrational, this objection simply offers us a way of understanding how it is that the world came to be so absurd."[162] This is exactly right; but I do not see that the mere fact that a view is disturbing or implies that the world is absurd (in the relevant sense) constitutes a reason for thinking that the view in question is false. Indeed, evolutionary psychology predicts many similar oddities. For instance, it predicts that human beings will tend to hold a number of false beliefs, that families will tend not to be perfectly harmonious units but instead will produce various kinds of conflict among their members, and that contemporary humans will be susceptible to various phobias involving things that, for most of us, represent little or no danger, like spiders and small animals.[163] Some thinkers attribute more extreme absurdities to evolution. For example, Arthur Koestler suggests that evolutionary processes are responsible for a lack of coordination between older and newer parts of the human brain and that this lack of coordination is one important cause of, among other things, the remarkably violent history of the human race. Koestler writes: "[W]hen one contemplates the streak of insanity running through human history, it appears highly probable that *homo sapiens* is a biological freak, the result of some remarkable mistake in the evolutionary process."[164] From the point of view of evolutionary psychology, then, the presence in human nature of a desire that cannot be satisfied is not particularly surprising.

The upshot of all of this is that the fact (if it is a fact) that Joy is part of human nature does not constitute much of a reason for thinking that a transcendent entity exists. The initial version of the argument from desire that we considered is unconvincing because none of the ways of supporting its second premise (that all natural desires can be satisfied) succeeds. The revised version of the argument fails because there is a naturalistic explanation for the (alleged) fact that Joy is part of human nature that is at least as plausible as the explanation that involves a transcendent being.

2.5 CONCLUSION

Toward the beginning of this chapter I suggested that none of the three arguments we have considered was intended by Lewis to constitute a decisive proof of the existence of a Higher Power but rather that he intended the three together to amount to a solid cumulative case for the existence of such a Power. Now that we have examined each of Lewis's three arguments in some detail, it is worth considering the overall weight of Lewis's cumulative case. As should be clear by now, my own view is that the cumulative case constituted by the three arguments is not terribly weighty. It seems to me that recent work in evolutionary psychology has done much to weaken Lewis's overall argument.

Nevertheless, Lewis's arguments were ahead of their time in at least two ways. First, they all rest on a substantive conception of human nature. The rise of behaviorism in psychology in the 1920s marked the rejection by many psychologists of the very idea of human nature, a rejection that lasted for around fifty years.[165] It is only relatively recently that the idea of human nature has returned to the psychological mainstream, and, interestingly, this is due in large part to the rise of evolutionary psychology.[166] Evolutionary psychology and Lewis's Christian apologetics therefore rest on a common axiom: That there is such a thing as human nature. They differ, of course, when it comes to explaining how this human nature came to be.

Second, two of Lewis's three arguments – the moral argument and the argument from reason – involve topics that are the subject of much work in contemporary philosophy. Whether and how morality and intentionality can fit into a nontheistic universe are hotly contested issues on the current philosophical scene. Whether they realize it or not, many contemporary naturalists are grappling with challenges posed by Lewis.

Having examined Lewis's arguments for the existence of a Higher Power, we are now ready to turn to his attempt to provide at least a partial case for the conclusion that this Higher Power is in fact the God of Christianity. This attempt is contained in Lewis's book *Miracles*, in which he tries to establish the plausibility of miracles in general and of the Resurrection of Christ in particular. *Miracles* is, in part, a direct response to Hume's famous essay "Of Miracles." Thus, in the next chapter we find ourselves once again in the midst of a clash between those twin titans, Hume and Lewis.

THREE

MIRACLES

3.1 INTRODUCTION

Graham Greene's short story "The Second Death" centers on the deathbed fears of a sinful man. His fears stem from a mysterious event that happened while he was a child. He had been declared dead and was being carried out to be buried "when a doctor stopped them just in time."[1] Reflecting on this childhood incident, the dying man remarks:

> [W]hen I came around that other time, I thought I'd been dead. It wasn't like sleep at all. Or rest in peace. There was someone there all round me, who knew everything. Every girl I'd ever had. Even that young one who hadn't understood.... it must have been a dream, mustn't it? The sort of dream people do get when they are ill. And I saw what was coming to me too. I can't bear being hurt. It wasn't fair. And I wanted to faint and I couldn't, because I was dead.... [S]uppose it was true. Suppose I had been dead. I believed it then, you know, and so did my mother. But you can't trust her. I went straight for a couple of years. I thought it might be a sort of second chance. Then things got fogged and somehow ... [i]t didn't seem really possible. It's not possible.[2]

The narrator of the story is the dying man's companion, who has rushed to his bedside to try to comfort him as he faces death. He assures the dying man that "[m]iracles of that sort don't happen nowadays" and "anyway, they aren't likely to happen to you, are they?"[3] The dying man seizes on his friend's suggestions but ultimately is unable to drive away his fears before dying:

> "There were some others," he said. "But the stories only went round among the poor, and they'll believe anything, won't they? There were lots of diseased and crippled they said he'd cured. And there was a man, who'd been born blind, and he came and just touched his eyelids and sight came to him. Those were all old wives' tales, weren't they?" he asked me, stammering with fear, and then lying suddenly still and bunched up at the side of the bed.[4]

Among the questions raised by the story is this one: Is it ever reasonable to believe that a miracle has occurred? The story suggests that it can be difficult even for those directly involved in miracles to be sure that a miracle has actually taken place.[5] Surely the difficulty is even greater when one is trying to assess the accuracy of a secondhand report of a miracle. Is it ever reasonable to believe that such reports are true?[6] This question is the central topic of the present chapter.

3.2 DEBATING MIRACLES IN THE EIGHTEENTH CENTURY

In eighteenth-century Europe, a debate about miracles raged. More precisely, a debate about the miracles associated with Christianity, particularly the Resurrection of Christ, raged. The debate arose as a consequence of the fact that many Christian philosophers of the time maintained that the occurrence of the Christian miracles, particularly the Resurrection, provide the basis for a proof of the central claims of Christianity. Samuel Clarke bluntly put it this way in 1705: "The Christian Revelation is positively and directly proved, to be actually and immediately sent to us from God, by the many infallible *Signs and Miracles*, which the author of it worked publicly as the Evidence of his Divine Commission."[7] One of the more popular presentations of this sort of argument at the time was Thomas Sherlock's *The Tryal of the Witnesses of the Resurrection of Jesus*, which employed the clever format of a jury trial on the question "Whether the Witnesses of the

Resurrection of Christ are guilty of giving false evidence or no?"[8] Following presentations by "Mr. A," who argues in favor of the guilt of the apostles, and "Mr. B," who defends their innocence, the jury returns a unanimous verdict: "Not guilty."[9]

The earthly stakes in this debate were high, particularly for those who criticized the argument for Christianity based on miracles. Thomas Woolston, a well-known critic of the argument, was convicted of blasphemy for his work *Six Discourses on the Miracles of Our Savior*. Unable to pay the fine for blasphemy, he died in prison in 1733.[10] Another critic, Peter Annett, who wrote a critical response to Sherlock's *Tryal*, was eventually sentenced to be pilloried for the views he put forth in a later work.[11]

Hume's own contribution to this debate is section X, "Of Miracles," of his *Enquiry Concerning Human Understanding*, the first version of which appeared in 1748, thirty-one years prior to the publication of his *Dialogues Concerning Natural Religion*. In "Of Miracles," Hume never explicitly mentions the Resurrection at all, and he refers to Christianity by name only in the last two paragraphs. He casts the topic of his essay as miracles in general rather than any particular alleged miracle. Despite this, the ongoing debate about miracles at the time together with the fact that Hume repeatedly refers to the dead being raised makes it clear that the central miracle with which Hume is concerned is the Resurrection of Christ.

These days, "Of Miracles" is widely considered to be one of the most important texts on miracles ever written, even by those who find it unconvincing. It is standard reading for courses in the philosophy of religion. And it apparently impressed Lewis enough that he wrote a book-length response to it, for, as we shall see, the central argument of Lewis's *Miracles* culminates with a response to Hume's essay. But before examining "Of Miracles" and Lewis's reply, it will be useful to consider another anti-miracle argument suggested by Hume as well as Lewis's response to it. In the course of responding to this argument Lewis introduces an analogy that is central to his response to Hume's argument in "Of Miracles."

3.3 A PRELIMINARY SKIRMISH

Speakers using the expression "Hume's argument against miracles" are typically referring to the argument found in Hume's essay "Of Miracles." But Hume's writing contains another argument worthy of this title. In *The Natural History of Religion*, Hume describes a view often called "Deism":

> Many theists, even the most zealous and refined, have denied a *particular* providence, and have asserted, that the Sovereign mind or first principle of all things, having fixed general laws, by which nature is governed, gives free and uninterrupted course to these laws, and disturbs not, at every turn, the settled order of events by particular volitions.[12]

According to Deism, God sets up the laws that govern the physical universe and then simply lets nature take its course according to these laws. Deists deny that God engages in "particular volitions"; once nature is up and running, God does not intervene in any way. In short, the God of Deism does not work miracles.

Why accept Deism? On the same page Hume suggests that "[c]onvulsions in nature, disorders, prodigies, miracles" are "the most opposite to the plan of a wise superintendent."[13] The idea seems to be that the only reason God could have for performing miracles would be to rectify some previous error or oversight. Miracles are improvised patches or "fix-its." They are crude devices for which an all-knowing God would have no use. This suggests the following argument against miracles:

Hume's Deistic Argument

1. An omnipotent, omniscient, and morally perfect God would never make mistakes.
2. If (1), then such a God would never perform miracles.
3. Therefore, an omnipotent, omniscient, and morally perfect God would never perform miracles.

In *Miracles*, Lewis provides what is, by my lights, a devastating refutation of this argument. Lewis's strategy is to reject the claim that justifies the second premise of the argument, the claim that the only possible function of a miracle is to rectify a divine blunder.

The strongest component of Lewis's response to the argument introduces an analogy that lies at the heart of his response to Hume's argument in "Of Miracles." This is "the analogy between God's relation to the world, on the one hand, and an author's relation to his book on the other."[14] Lewis first observes that "miracles or abnormal events may be bad art, or they may not."[15] They are bad art (and indicate an error or lack of skill on the part of the author) when they are used as ad hoc plot devices: "The ghost story is a legitimate form of art; but you must not bring a ghost into an ordinary novel to get over a difficulty in the plot."[16] On the other hand, they are not bad art (and hence do not indicate an error on the part of the author) if they are "what you are really writing *about*."[17] The application of this point to Hume's Deistic argument is as follows. If the Resurrection, for instance, is really one of the main things that God's "story" is about – if it is one of the main *purposes* of the entire Creation – then its occurrence, even though it involves divine interference with the course of nature, does not indicate a previous error on God's part. And this is exactly Lewis's position:

> Some people probably think of the Resurrection as a desperate last moment expedient to save the Hero from a situation which had got out of the Author's control.... [On the contrary,] Death and Resurrection are what the story is about; and had we but eyes to see it, this has been hinted on every page, met us, in some disguise, at every turn.... If you have hitherto disbelieved in miracles, it is worth pausing a moment to consider whether this is not chiefly because you thought you had discovered what the story was really about? – that atoms, and time and space and economics and politics were the main plot? And is it certain you were right?[18]

Miracles might be crude patches to keep the universe running along as it must so that God can secure some further goal, or they might be among the things for the sake of which everything else exists. Hume's Deistic argument assumes that the former option is the only possibility; therefore, that argument fails. Lewis's response here seems to be me to be entirely convincing. However, as the title of this section suggests, this is but a preliminary skirmish. Hume's main assault on miracles is to be found in "Of Miracles." It is to that work that we now turn.

3.4 HUME'S MAIN ASSAULT

Hume's "Of Miracles" has been the object of an astounding amount of commentary. There has been tremendous debate over what the argument or arguments of the essay are, and whether those arguments are any good. Contemporary philosophical work on the essay has failed to produce anything even remotely resembling a consensus concerning these issues. In his 2000 book *Hume's Abject Failure*, John Earman declares that the argument of "Of Miracles" is "largely derivative" and "almost wholly without merit where it is original."[19] Earman's critique ends with the assertion that Hume's essay is "a confection of rhetoric and *schein Geld*."[20] On the other hand, in his 2003 book *A Defense of Hume on Miracles*, Robert Fogelin defends the view that "Hume's treatment of miracles, when properly understood, exhibits a level of richness, subtlety, coherence, and force not generally appreciated."[21]

It is with considerable trepidation that I enter into such contentious (and crowded!) philosophical waters. In what follows I attempt to formulate what I take to be Hume's central argument in "Of Miracles" as clearly as possible. I will provide textual support for my interpretation where appropriate, and I will sometimes draw on the words of other commentators to explain or emphasize particular points, but material pertaining to scholarly debates about the proper interpretation of Hume's work will be largely relegated to the notes. The task before us is to get as clear as possible on what Hume tries to prove in "Of Miracles" and how he tries to prove it.

Let us begin with the ultimate conclusion of Hume's central argument. The conclusion of the argument is not that miracles are impossible. It is not that miracles never in fact occur. It is not that a perfect God would never perform miracles (as in the Deistic argument). It is not that it is never reasonable for anyone to believe that a miracle has occurred. It is not even that it is never reasonable for anyone to believe that a miracle has occurred solely on the basis of testimony. Hume's conclusion, rather, is that "no human testimony can have such force as to prove a miracle, and make it a just foundation for any system of religion."[22] The second clause of this statement is important. It indicates that Hume's conclusion applies not to all testimony but only to a particular kind of testimony. Specifically, it applies to what we may call *religious testimony*, which we may define as testimony by human beings that is intended to support a particular "system of religion." Hume's claim is that it is never reasonable to believe that a miracle has occurred on the basis of religious testimony alone.

To see how Hume endeavors to establish this conclusion, we will need to get clear on his understanding of some key concepts, particularly the concepts of *proof* and *miracle*. Let us begin with the former concept. Early in "Of Miracles," Hume describes the proper procedure to follow when it comes to forming our beliefs about what he calls "matters of fact."[23] Into this category fall all claims that cannot be known a priori, or independently of experience. Historical claims – including, for instance, Christian claims about the Resurrection of Christ – fall into this category. Hume writes:

> A wise man . . . proportions his belief to the evidence. In such conclusions as are founded on an infallible experience, he expects the event with the last degree of assurance, and regards his past experience as a full *proof* of the future existence of that event. In other cases, he proceeds with more caution: He weighs the opposite experiments. . . . A hundred instances or experiments on one side, and fifty on another, afford a doubtful expectation of any event; though a hundred uniform experiments, with only one that is contradictory, reasonably beget a pretty strong degree of assurance.[24]

In every observed instance, night has been followed by a sunrise. This observed constant conjunction constitutes what Hume in the passage just quoted calls "infallible experience." Therefore, the observed constant conjunction constitutes a proof that the next night will be followed by a sunrise. The important thing to note here is that the claim that experience provides us with a *proof* that the sun will rise tomorrow does not imply that the relevant experiences render the probability that the sun will not rise tomorrow *zero*.[25] Rather, the claim that experience affords us with a proof that the sun will rise tomorrow implies that the probability that the sun will not rise tomorrow is extremely small – so small that, under most circumstances, it is perfectly reasonable to put aside the remote possibility that it will not.[26] Thus, in the light of his past experience, a wise man will be extremely confident in his belief that the sun will rise tomorrow. At the other extreme, suppose I am drawing colored marbles from an urn. I have drawn one hundred marbles, fifty of which are white, and fifty of which are black. Under these circumstances, I should not believe that the next marble I draw will be white, nor should I believe that it will be black; rather, I should suspend judgement (although I can be confident that it will be white *or* black rather than some third color).

In the midst of the passage just quoted, Hume makes the following remark: "All probability . . . supposes an opposition of experiments and observations, where the one side is found to overbalance the other, and to produce a degree of evidence, proportioned to the superiority."[27] On the basis of this claim and the rest of the passage, I attribute to Hume the following principle:

Probability Principle: We should rate the occurrence of event A as more probable than the occurrence of event B if and only if: The evidence provided by our experience supports the occurrence of A to a greater extent than it supports the occurrence of B.

Next, let us consider how Hume conceives of miracles. He offers the following definition: "A miracle is a violation of the laws of nature."[28] This is somewhat tricky; If laws of nature are to be understood as true, exceptionless generalizations (e.g., the dead never rise), then the very concept of a miracle would be self-contradictory (since true generalizations, by definition, are never violated). This understanding of laws of nature would provide Hume with a quick but utterly unconvincing disproof of the very possibility of miracles. Fortunately, the text makes it pretty clear that Hume did not intend to defend this disappointing argument.

A better way of understanding how Hume conceives of laws of nature in this context is proposed by both Earman and Fogelin.[29]

The idea is that when Hume speaks of "laws of nature" here, he is thinking of propositions or statements to the effect that certain regularities hold without exception. Such propositions merit the title "laws of nature" only if there is a lot of experience-based evidence that supports them and none (putting aside any religious testimony) that tells against them; they are, as Hume puts it, supported by "a firm and unalterable experience."[30] A miracle, then, is any event that violates one of these well-supported generalizations. On this understanding of miracles, they are possible, but the available experience-based evidence (again, excluding religious testimony) indicates that they are very unlikely. As Hume puts it, "the proof against a miracle, from the very nature of the fact, is as entire as any argument from experience can possibly be imagined."[31] In light of all of this, we can state the first premise of Hume's argument as follows:

1. For any miracle M, our experience provides us with a (Humean) proof that M did not occur (excluding any religious testimony that supports the occurrence of M).

It should be noted that this premise is consistent with the possibility of there being testimony that would make it reasonable to believe that a miracle has occurred. However, such testimony would have to conform to very high evidential standards in order to outweigh the other evidence against the occurrence of the miracle. Hume remarks that "no testimony is sufficient to establish a miracle, *unless* the testimony be of such a kind, that its falsehood would be more miraculous, than the fact, which it endeavors to establish."[32]

To arrive at the next main premise of Hume's argument, let us consider some of what Hume has to say about testimony. He begins by noting that it is experience that tells us how reliable testimony is: "[O]ur assurance in any argument of this kind is derived from no other principle than our observation of the veracity of human testimony, and of the usual conformity of facts to the reports of witnesses."[33] Thus, testimony constitutes evidence that the reported events actually occurred only to the extent that testimony has been accurate in the past. If all observed human assertions had also been observed to be true, then a single piece of testimony would constitute a proof (in the Humean sense) that the reported events had occurred. At the other extreme, if all observed humans were known to be pathological liars, then testimony would not count as evidence for the occurrence of the reported events at all. As it stands, the reliability of testimony lies somewhere between these two extremes, and some kinds of testimony have been observed to be more reliable than others.

In Part II of "Of Miracles," Hume argues that past experience indicates that religious testimony in support of miracles is a particularly unreliable brand of testimony. This is an important part of Hume's argument, and it indicates a limitation on the scope of his argument. The argument is not intended to show that it is never reasonable to believe that a miracle has occurred on the basis of testimony; rather, it is intended merely to show that it is never reasonable to believe that a miracle has occurred on the basis *of a certain kind of testimony* – namely, *religious testimony*, as defined earlier.[34]

The heart of Hume's position here is straightforward: History is filled with reports of miracles that support one system of religion or another, and most of these reports have subsequently been revealed to be false. "How many stories of this nature, have, in all ages, been detected and exploded in their infancy? How many more have been celebrated for a time, and have afterwards sunk into neglect and oblivion?"[35] In addition, Hume notes that religious testimony about miracles is "observed chiefly to abound among ignorant and barbarous nations" but that "as we advance nearer the enlightened ages" such accounts are viewed with increasing skepticism.[36] Finally, Hume observes that the various systems of religion each have their own reports of miracles that support the system in question. However, since (at least in the case of monotheistic religions) the systems are incompatible with each other, the majority of these alleged miracles must not have happened. All of these considerations are intended to show that we can be confident that most religious testimony in support of miracles is false.

Hume also offers a suggestion about human nature that helps to explain why such accounts are often widely believed, at least for a time. He proposes that this is a consequence of "the strong propensity of mankind to the extraordinary and the marvelous."[37] In short, people simply love wild stories. Hume provides two illustrations of this aspect of human nature. The first is the "greediness" with which "the miraculous accounts of travelers are received," including "descriptions of sea and land monsters, their relations of wonderful adventures, strange men, and uncouth manners."[38] This passion for stories about land and sea monsters continues unabated in our own time, as evidenced by the persistent myths of Bigfoot and Nessie, the Loch Ness monster. We may add to this catalog of wild stories accounts of space monsters in the form of tales of alien abduction. Hume's second illustration of our propensity to believe juicy stories also persists to the present day:

> There is no kind of report, which rises so easily, and spreads so quickly ... as those concerning marriages; insomuch that two young persons of equal condition never see each other twice, but the whole neighborhood immediately join them together.[39]

Moreover, Hume argues, this propensity is least restrained when it comes to religious testimony: "[I]f the spirit of religion join itself to the love of wonder, there is an end of common sense; and human testimony, in these circumstances, loses all pretensions to authority."[40] As Fogelin puts it, "for Hume, it is an empirical fact, amply illustrated by history, that testimony concerning religious miracles is notoriously unreliable."[41] This gives us Hume's second premise:

2. For any religious testimony, T, to the effect that miracle M occurred, our experience contains much evidence that T is false.

From premises (1) and (2) we may infer:

3. So: For any religious testimony, T, to the effect that miracle M occurred, the evidence provided by our experience supports the falsity of T to a greater extent than it supports the occurrence of M.

Recall Hume's Probability Principle:

Probability Principle: We should rate the occurrence of event A as more probable than the occurrence of event B if and only if: The evidence provided by our experience supports the occurrence of A to a greater extent than it supports the occurrence of B.

Hume illustrates the Probability Principle in these lines:

> When anyone tells me, that he saw a dead man restored to life, I immediately consider with myself, whether it be more probable, that this person should either deceive or be deceived, or that the fact, which he relates; should really have happened.[42]

From the Probability Principle and premise (3), we may infer:

4. So: For any religious testimony, T, to the effect that miracle M occurred, we should rate the falsity of T as more likely than the occurrence of M.

And this together with Hume's maxim that "a wise man...proportions his belief to the evidence" implies that a wise man will, when confronted with religious testimony for a miracle, believe that the testimony is false rather than that the miracle occurred.[43] This gives us Hume's conclusion that "no human testimony can have such force as to prove a miracle, and make it a just foundation for any system of religion."[44]

Here, then, is the complete formulation of Hume's central argument in "Of Miracles":

Hume's Argument against Miracles

1. For any miracle, M, our experience provides us with a (Humean) proof that M did not occur (excluding any religious testimony that supports the occurrence of M).
2. For any religious testimony, T, to the effect that miracle M occurred, our experience contains much evidence that T is false.
3. So: For any religious testimony, T, to the effect that miracle M occurred, the evidence provided by our experience supports the falsity of T to a greater extent than it supports the occurrence of M (from 1 and 2).
4. So: For any religious testimony, T, to the effect that miracle M occurred, we should rate the falsity of T as more likely than the occurrence of M (From 3 and the Probability Principle).

5. Therefore, it is never reasonable to believe that miracle M occurred solely on the basis of religious testimony T to the effect that M occurred (from 4 and the maxim that a wise man proportions his belief to the evidence).

It is worth observing that both premises (1) and (2) are required to establish premise (3). Without premise (2), the possibility of religious testimony that renders the occurrence of a miracle more probable than the falsity of the testimony in question is left open. Without premise (1), the possibility that the occurrence of a given miracle is quite plausible independently of any religious testimony in support of it is left open. And if this is a possibility, then it might be reasonable for us to believe some such miracles on the basis of testimony of a sort that is, in general, unreliable. Here is a simple example that illustrates this point. Suppose I have been working on this chapter in a windowless office all night. Larry the Liar, whose testimony is generally unreliable, enters and informs me that the sun has just risen. Under these circumstances, it may be reasonable for me to believe what he says because the reported event is independently plausible.[45] Fogelin aptly describes how premises (1) and (2) work together as follows:

> [P]art 1 fixes the appropriate level of scrutiny for evaluating testimony with respect to miracles; part 2 considers the quality of the testimony that has hitherto been brought forth in support of religious miracles and concludes that it comes nowhere near to meeting the appropriate standards. . . . [T]he wise reasoner is fully justified in rejecting all testimony given in support of a miracle intended to serve as the foundation of a system of religion.[46]

As I suggested earlier, the nature of the eighteenth-century debate about miracles together with Hume's repeated reference to the raising of the dead indicates that, though he never mentions it specifically, the religious miracle that "Of Miracles" is really about is the Resurrection of Christ. Hume's central message is: It is not reasonable to believe that Christ was raised from the dead solely on the basis of religious testimony (e.g., the Christian Bible) alleging that He was.

As we have seen, Hume's conclusion is that "no human testimony *can* have such force as to prove a miracle, and make it a just foundation for any system of religion."[47] The presence of the word "can" here makes it tempting to attribute to Hume the view that there are no *conceivable* circumstances under which religious testimony could make it reasonable to accept that a miracle has occurred. It should be clear by now that this is not Hume's view. In ordinary speech, we often say that certain things can or cannot occur, where such claims are conditional on certain tacit assumptions. The context typically makes it clear what these assumptions are. For instance, suppose I launch into a diatribe outlining the mishmash of errors, distortions, lies, and bad reasoning that typically issues forth from cable news political "analysts." I might conclude my diatribe with the assertion that "no argument offered by a cable news political analyst *can* have such force as to prove its conclusion." What I mean, of course, is that *given the horrific track record of such arguments*, it could never be reasonable to accept the conclusion of such an argument on the basis of the argument itself. Hume's position, similarly, is that *given the horrific track record of religious testimony supporting the occurrence of miracles (together with the evidence against the occurrence of any given miracle provided by experience)*, it could never be reasonable to believe that a miracle has occurred on the basis of such testimony alone. For all Hume argues in "Of Miracles," Christ may have risen from the dead. Hume's position is that, be that as it may, it is not reasonable for *us* to believe that the Resurrection occurred on the basis of testimony alleging that it has. Supporters of religion have cried "Miracle!" too many times.

3.5   LEWIS'S COUNTERATTACK

The opening chapter of *Miracles* contains the following lines:

> Many people think one can decide whether a miracle occurred in the past by examining the evidence 'according to the ordinary rules of historical inquiry'. But the ordinary rules cannot be worked until we have decided whether miracles are possible, and if so, how probable they are. For if they are impossible, then no amount of historical

evidence will convince us. If they are possible but immensely improbable, then only mathematically demonstrative evidence will convince us: and since history never provides that degree of evidence for any event, history can never convince us that a miracle occurred. If, on the other hand, miracles are not intrinsically improbable, then the existing evidence will be sufficient to convince us that quite a number of miracles have occurred. The result of our historical enquiries thus depends on the philosophical views which we have been holding before we even began to look at the evidence. This philosophical question must therefore come first.[48]

Lewis is specifically concerned with Christian miracles, and he is most concerned with the central Christian miracle, the Resurrection. The philosophical questions he sets for himself are these: Are these miracles possible? If so, putting aside the historical evidence for them, how probable is it that they occurred? More specifically, are they sufficiently probable independently of the historical evidence that when the historical evidence is also taken into account, it is reasonable to believe that they really occurred? The central project of *Miracles* is to establish that the correct answer to this last question is yes.

Lewis defines a miracle as "an interference with Nature by a supernatural power."[49] His procedure in *Miracles* is to consider and criticize various reasons one might have for giving the last question just posed a negative answer. The first reason he considers is rooted in Naturalism, according to which nothing outside of nature exists. If Naturalism is true, then miracles are plainly impossible, as there is no supernatural power outside of nature that could interfere with nature. Lewis rejects this reason for doubting the Christian miracles on the grounds that Naturalism is false, and he relies on the argument from reason to refute Naturalism.

He next considers this position: Even if a supernatural power does exist, nature is not the sort of thing with which such a power can interfere. Rejecting this view involves Lewis in a discussion of the nature of the laws of nature, the details of which need not concern us here.[50] His next target is the view that even if a supernatural power does exist and *could* interfere with nature, the supernatural power is not the sort of thing that *would* interfere with nature. One

135

basis for this position is a view Lewis calls "Pantheism," according to which the supernatural power is entirely passive. Lewis rejects this view primarily on the grounds that if Pantheism were true, nature itself would not exist.[51] Another basis for a noninterfering supernatural power is Deism; we considered Lewis's criticism of this view in section 3.3.

Thus, in the first twelve chapters of *Miracles*, Lewis takes it that he has established that there is an active supernatural power that might interfere with nature and that nature is the sort of thing that could be interfered with by such a power. Lewis then turns his attention to Hume's famous argument from "Of Miracles." He begins by making a rather Humean point himself: "Most stories about miraculous events are probably false: if it comes to that, most stories about natural events are false. Lies, exaggerations, misunderstandings and hearsay make up perhaps more than half of all that is said and written in the world."[52] Because of this, Lewis says, "[w]e must . . . find a criterion whereby to judge any particular story of the miraculous."[53] As we will see, the criterion Lewis arrives at stems directly from his main criticism of Hume's argument.

Before developing his main criticism, however, Lewis levels a charge of circularity against Hume. He summarizes the essence of Hume's argument this way: "There is, in fact, 'uniform experience' against Miracle; otherwise, says Hume, it would not be a Miracle. A miracle is therefore the most improbable of all events. It is always more probable that the witnesses were lying or mistaken than that a miracle occurred."[54] Here is the charge of circularity:

> Now of course we must agree with Hume that if there is absolutely 'uniform experience' against miracles, *if in other words they have never happened,* why then they never have. Unfortunately we know the experience against them to be uniform only if we know that all the reports of them are false. And we can know all the reports to be false only if we know already that miracles have never occurred. In fact, we are arguing in a circle.[55]

The crux of Lewis's criticism is that Hume simply takes as a premise the claim that no miracle has ever occurred. It should go without

saying that if Hume really makes such an assumption at the out-
set, it renders his argument utterly unconvincing. Does Hume do
this?

I do not think that he does. The crucial phrase here is "universal
experience." Lewis takes this to refer to all the experiences of every
human being who has ever lived. Interpreted in this way, Hume's
claim is that no human who has ever lived has experienced a miracle.
And, as Lewis points out, it is hard to see how we could know this
unless we already knew that no miracle has ever occurred. However,
I do not think this is the correct way to understand Hume's argument.
Notice how I stated the first premise of Hume's argument:

1. For any miracle, M, our experience provides us with a (Humean)
    proof that M did not occur (excluding any religious testimony
    that supports the occurrence of M).

In particular, note the reference to *our* experience. This indicates that
the relevant experience is not that of every human who has ever lived
but rather the experiences of *Hume's audience*. And Hume's audience
is, of course, limited to people who were born long after the time
of Christ. Hume's argument is directed toward people who have not
observed any miracles themselves. It is the experience of *these* people
that Hume claims provides *them* with a (Humean) proof that any
given miracle did not occur (putting aside religious testimony to the
contrary). Therefore, Hume is not simply assuming that no miracle
has ever occurred; rather, he is making the plausible assumption that
most readers of his essay have not directly observed any miracles
themselves. So Lewis's first objection misses its mark.[56]

However, Lewis immediately offers a far more interesting objection:

> The whole idea of Probability (as Hume understands it) depends on
> the principle of the Uniformity of Nature. Unless Nature always goes
> on in the same way, the fact that a thing had happened ten million
> times would not make it a whit more probable that it would happen
> again. . . . Probabilities of the kind that Hume is concerned with hold
> inside the framework of an assumed Uniformity of Nature.[57]

Lewis's remarks here seem to be directed toward comments like the following:

> A wise man...proportions his belief to the evidence....He weighs the opposite experiments....A hundred instances or experiments on one side, and fifty on another, afford a doubtful expectation of any event; though a hundred uniform experiments, with only one that is contradictory, reasonably beget a pretty strong degree of assurance.[58]

On the basis of comments like this I have attributed the following principle to Hume:

Probability Principle: We should rate the occurrence of event A as more probable than the occurrence of event B if and only if: The evidence provided by our experience supports the occurrence of A to a greater extent than it supports the occurrence of B.

Lewis's point is that the Probability Principle itself relies on what he calls the "principle of the Uniformity of Nature" according to which "Nature always goes on in the same way."[59] Earlier, I suggested that, according to Hume, in light of his past experience a wise man will be extremely confident in his belief that the sun will rise tomorrow. But this confidence is based on the assumption that the natural universe will continue to behave in the future as it has behaved in the past. And this claim relies in turn on the assumption that no supernatural power will interfere with nature and make it behave differently than it has in the past. The observed is a reliable guide to the unobserved only if the unobserved resembles the observed, and we can be sure the unobserved resembles the observed only if we can be sure no miracles occur. Thus, Lewis's objection may be cast this way: The Probability Principle is true only if the principle of the Uniformity of Nature is true. And the latter principle is true only if miracles never occur. Therefore, Hume's argument against miracles relies on the assumption that miracles never occur after all (though not in the way Lewis suggests in his first objection).

Here, again, is Hume's argument:

Hume's Argument against Miracles

1. For any miracle, M, our experience provides us with a (Humean) proof that M did not occur (excluding any religious testimony that supports the occurrence of M).
2. For any religious testimony, T, to the effect that miracle M occurred, our experience contains much evidence that T is false.
3. So: For any religious testimony, T, to the effect that miracle M occurred, the evidence provided by our experience supports the falsity of T to a greater extent than it supports the occurrence of M (from 1 and 2).
4. So: For any religious testimony, T, to the effect that miracle M occurred, we should rate the falsity of T as more likely than the occurrence of M (from 3 and the Probability Principle).
5. Therefore, it is never reasonable to believe that miracle M occurred solely on the basis of religious testimony T to the effect that M occurred (from 4 and the maxim that a wise man proportions his belief to the evidence).

I believe that Lewis would reject premise (4), as this is the premise that relies on the Probability Principle. Lewis would point out that the Probability Principle is true only if miracles never occur. Thus, Hume ultimately begs the question posed against the Christian by simply assuming that miracles never occur. If Hume could provide a good argument for the uniformity of nature, he could save the argument in "Of Miracles." Of course, if he could do that, the argument in "Of Miracles" would be entirely superfluous.

This objection is an interesting one; however, it may be a double-edged sword. Steve Lovell suggests that anyone who hopes to establish the occurrence of a miracle on the basis of testimony must also assume that nature is uniform, at least to a significant degree.[60] As Hume points out, the case for miracles based on testimony relies on "our observation of the veracity of human testimony, and of the usual conformity of facts to the reports of witnesses."[61] If nature is not sufficiently uniform, however, then observations about the veracity of human testimony tell us nothing about miracles. If nature is not sufficiently uniform, past experience tells us nothing about the unobserved; instead, anything goes.

Both parties to the debate can avoid this double-edged sword by noting that reasoning based on past experience can be quite reliable even if nature is not *perfectly* uniform; all that is required is that nature is *almost* uniform.[62] Perhaps anticipating this point, Lewis provides a justification for the belief that nature is *almost* perfectly uniform. The justification for this belief, he suggests, is rooted in our "sense of the fitness of things":

> 'In science,' said the late Sir Arthur Eddington, 'we sometimes have convictions which we cherish but cannot justify; we are influenced by some innate sense of the fitness of things'. This may sound a perilously subjective and aesthetic criterion; but can one doubt that it is a principal source of our belief in Uniformity? A universe in which unprecedented and unpredictable events were at every moment flung into Nature would not merely be inconvenient to us: it would be profoundly repugnant. We will not accept such a universe on any terms whatever. It is utterly detestable to us. It shocks 'our sense of the fitness of things'.[63]

It simply *seems right* that the universe is (at least almost) uniform. But can we have confidence that this feeling of rightness is a reliable guide to the way the universe actually is? Lewis appeals to his Argument from Reason to answer this question:

> If all that exists is Nature . . . if our own deepest convictions are merely the by-products of an irrational process, then clearly there is not the slightest ground for supposing that our sense of fitness and our consequent faith in uniformity tell us anything about a reality external to ourselves. . . . If Naturalism is true we have no reason to trust our conviction that Nature is uniform. It can be trusted only if a quite different Metaphysic is true. If the deepest thing in reality, the Fact which is the source of all other facthood, is a thing in some degree like ourselves – if it is a Rational Spirit and we derive our rationality from It – then indeed our conviction can be trusted.[64]

So we can rely on our innate sense of the fitness of things so long as there is a Higher Power that "is more like a mind than it is like anything else we know."[65] Thus, according to Lewis, we can use knowledge of the observed to acquire knowledge of the unobserved only if Naturalism is false.

The final element of Lewis's response to Hume's argument is a criterion by which to judge the probability of any given miracle (independently of the historical evidence for the miracle). Lewis says that we must rely on our innate sense of fitness to evaluate the probability of a given miracle.[66] The probability that a given miracle has occurred (independently of any historical evidence for it) is directly proportional to its level of fitness. If its level of fitness is sufficiently high, the miracle may be so probable that the available historical evidence for it renders reasonable the belief that it really happened. In relying on "fitness," Lewis claims not to be doing anything new: "Even those who think all stories of miracles absurd think some very much more absurd than others: even those who believe them all (if anyone does) think that some require a specially robust faith. The criterion which both parties are using is that of fitness."[67]

Thus, Lewis rejects the Probability Principle and, along with it, the fourth premise of Hume's argument. The Probability Principle directs us to consider *only* past experience when assessing the probability that a miracle has occurred. Lewis maintains that we must instead take into account the miracle's level of fitness. This may lead us to assign a much higher probability to the miracle's occurrence than we would assign it if we went on past experience alone.[68] It is our innate sense of fitness, then, that not only allows us to know that nature is (nearly) uniform, but also helps us identify those rare occasions on which nature is interfered with by a Higher Power. As Lewis cleverly puts it, "[t]heology offers you a working arrangement, which leaves the scientist free to continue his experiments and the Christian to continue his prayers."[69]

This discussion has taken several twists and turns, so allow me to summarize what I take to be Lewis's most interesting objection to Hume's argument. The objection runs as follows: Hume's argument against miracles requires at least the assumption that nature is *almost* perfectly uniform. But we are justified in believing this assumption only if we can trust our sense of fitness, and we can do this only if there is a supernatural Higher Power that is the source of our rationality. If there is such a Power, then (contra Hume) past experience is not the only relevant factor when it comes to determining the probability of a given miracle. We should instead rely on our sense of fitness to make this assessment. Thus: If we are justified in believing that nature is almost perfectly uniform, then Hume's Probability Principle is false. But if we are not justified in believing that nature is almost uniform, then we are also not justified in accepting the Probability Principle. Therefore, either the Probability Principle is false (if we are justified in accepting the near-uniformity of nature), or we are not justified in accepting the principle (if we are not justified in accepting the near-uniformity of nature). Either way, we cannot reasonably rely on the Probability Principle, and hence the support for the fourth premise of Hume's argument is undercut. The following argument captures the main steps of Lewis's reasoning:

Lewis's Objection to Hume's Argument against Miracles

1. Either we are justified in believing that nature is almost uniform, or we are not.
2. If we are justified in believing that nature is almost uniform, then the Probability Principle is false.
3. If we are not justified in believing that nature is almost uniform, then we are not justified in believing the Probability Principle.
4. So: Either the Probability Principle is false, or we are not justified in believing it.
5. If (4), then we should not accept Hume's fourth premise.
6. Therefore, we should not accept Hume's fourth premise.

Lewis is not content with merely refuting Hume's argument; he also wants to show that the Christian miracles have high levels of fitness – sufficiently high that, when the historical evidence is also taken into account, it is reasonable to believe that they occurred. In the next section we examine Lewis's attempt to establish the fitness

142

of what he labels "the Grand Miracle" – the Incarnation ("that God became Man"), of which the Resurrection is a key component.[70]

3.6 THE FITNESS OF THE INCARNATION

The chapter in which Lewis attempts to establish the fitness of the Incarnation is by far the longest chapter of *Miracles*. He begins by appealing to the analogy introduced in his response to Hume's Deistic argument – God as Author and His Creation as His Novel:

> Let us suppose we possess parts of a novel. . . . Someone now brings us a newly discovered piece of manuscript and says, 'This is the missing part of the work. This is the chapter on which the whole plot of the novel really turned. . . .' Our business would be to see whether the new passage, if admitted to the central place which the discoverer claimed for it, did actually illuminate all the parts we had already seen and 'pull them together'. . . . Something like this we must do with the doctrine of the Incarnation. Here, instead of . . . a novel, we have the whole mass of our knowledge. The credibility will depend on the extent to which the doctrine, if accepted, can illuminate and integrate that whole mass.[71]

The passage gives us some sense of how Lewis understands fitness in this context. The Incarnation is fit to the extent that it coheres with, unites, and explains other things we know.

To make his case, Lewis identifies several (in his view) known features of the universe and outlines their connection to the Incarnation. These features are: (i) the "composite existence" of human beings,[72] (ii) descent and re-ascent, (iii) "Selectiveness," (iv) "Vicariousness," (v) that humans find dirty jokes funny, and (vi) that humans find the dead uncanny. Let us briefly consider each of these in turn.

In speaking of the "composite existence" of human beings Lewis is referring to his view that human beings have a supernatural component as well as a natural component. The natural component is the physical body; the supernatural component is the part that is capable of having knowledge. That humans are composite in this way is entailed by Lewis's argument from reason. The connection between our composite existence and the Incarnation is fairly straightforward. The Incarnation involves a special kind of union between the supernatural and the natural, but something like this union takes place in the case of every ordinary human being. As Lewis puts it, our own composite existence is "a faint image of the Divine Incarnation itself – the same theme in a very minor key."[73]

Lewis sees descent and re-ascent at the heart of the Incarnation. According to that doctrine, God descends "from the heights of absolute being" down to earth, "down to the very roots and seabed of the Nature He has created."[74] The point of the descent is to bring humanity (and, in fact, all of nature) back up with Him, to make humanity and nature into something far better than they were before. Lewis claims that this same pattern can be found throughout nature, that it is "written all over the world."[75] The Incarnation offers a tidy explanation for the universality of this pattern: "The pattern is there in Nature because it was first there in God."[76] As examples of this pattern, he mentions vegetable and animal reproduction (e.g., the seed falls to the ground and then grows upward) and "our moral and emotional life" (our initial spontaneous desires must be controlled or killed, and from there we can ascend to virtue).[77]

"Selectiveness" manifests itself in the Incarnation by God's selection, out of all of humanity, of a tiny group of people to be directly involved in the Incarnation itself. A particular woman is selected to be the mother of God the Son; a small group of men are chosen to be His disciples.[78] Again, Lewis says, we find the same pattern in nature. Out of the vastness of space, only a tiny portion contains matter. Of the zillions of stars, only a relatively small number have planets. Of the planets in our solar system, just one supports life. Of the many species of life on our planet, just one can reason. Of the many humans, only a few "attain excellence of beauty, strength, or intelligence."[79]

In speaking of "Vicariousness" in the Incarnation, Lewis is referring to Christ suffering for the sins of humanity; Christ, in a sense, takes the place of humanity. Lewis claims that this is also "a characteristic of Nature."[80] Vicariousness exhibits itself in Nature primarily in the form of interdependency: "Everything is indebted to everything else, sacrificed to everything else, dependent on everything else."[81] I am reminded here of the concept of a food chain about which I learned in middle school; each creature in the chain depends for its sustenance on creatures below it in the chain. Lewis specifically mentions the interdependency between bees and flowers, parasite and host, and mother and unborn child.[82]

To this point we have examined four themes that, according to Lewis, can be found both in the Incarnation and in nature. Thus, Lewis's case for the fitness of the Incarnation so far is rooted in *common themes*. The relationship between the two remaining features of the universe Lewis considers and the Incarnation is somewhat different; here the idea seems to be that the Christian view of the universe, of which the Incarnation is a central element, *explains* the features in question.

Let us start with dirty jokes. Lewis's case for a connection between Christianity and dirty jokes is, to my way of thinking, one of his more ingenious contributions to the history of ideas. The key to this connection is the Fall of Man (which, while distinct from the Incarnation, prepares the way for it). According to Lewis's account of the Fall, one of its consequences was a loss of control by humans over their desires: "And desires began to come up into the mind of man, not as his reason chose, but just as the biochemical and environmental facts happened to cause them."[83] Among these is, of course, sexual desire, which seems to be among the least controllable of our various desires. Our inability to control sexual desire leads to various incongruities, many of which are downright hilarious. Any male who has gone through puberty is familiar with the phenomenon of the uncontrollable (and often unprovoked) erection. Such events often occur at the most inopportune times, as when, say, one is asked to come up to the front of the class to complete a math problem on the chalkboard. It is the incongruity, the juxtaposition of sophisticated, noble intellect and uncontrollable, base desire that leads to humor. Imagine a math whiz asked to approach the board and solve a calculus problem that is entirely within his intellectual capacity rendered unable to do so by his stubborn, erect member, and you should get a sense of what Lewis has in mind here. Through the Fall of Man, the dirty joke is born; because of the Fall, we (correctly) find ourselves to be ridiculous.

Another consequence of the Fall is that it makes death possible. In death the two components of the composite human being (supernatural and natural) separate, leaving behind a lifeless corpse. The Fall corrupted nature, and the existence of corpses is both an aspect and a reminder of this corruption. This, according to Lewis, is why we find corpses to be unnerving, unnatural, uncanny.

This completes Lewis's case for the fitness of the Incarnation. It also completes the central argument of *Miracles*. It is important to keep in mind that Lewis does not see his central argument as by itself making it reasonable to believe that the Incarnation occurred. Instead, Lewis seeks to complete the preliminary philosophical project of establishing that our sense of fitness shows us that the probability that the Incarnation occurred is sufficiently high that *when the historical evidence is also taken into account*, it is reasonable to conclude that the Incarnation really happened.[84]

In arriving at this conclusion, Lewis has, if his argument is successful, refuted Naturalism, Pantheism, Deism, and Hume's influential argument that it is never reasonable to believe that a miracle has occurred on the basis of religious testimony alone. Success in all these tasks would render *Miracles* a remarkably significant work of philosophy. Whether Lewis has succeeded in all of them is the topic of the next section.

3.7 LEWIS'S MITIGATED VICTORY AND THE TRILEMMA

The most significant weakness I see in Lewis's argument is his claim that we are justified in believing that nature is (almost) uniform only if there is a supernatural Higher Power that is the source of our rationality. The weakness of the claim lies in the fact that either it is a mere assertion or it depends on the argument from reason, which, as I argued in the previous chapter, is not decisive. With this claim unsupported, Lewis's case against the Probability Principle falls apart. It is clear enough that we all know that nature is at least nearly uniform; *how* we know this is an interesting philosophical question, but Lewis has not established that this knowledge requires a Higher Power outside of nature.

Despite this weakness, Lewis has identified a significant shortcoming in Hume's main argument against miracles. To see this, it will be helpful to consider some areas of agreement between Hume and Lewis and look at precisely where they part ways. I believe that both writers would maintain that, in light of the general unreliability of religious testimony concerning miracles, our initial, default attitude toward such testimony, prior to any serious investigation, should be one of skepticism. That Hume holds such a view should be uncontroversial; I attribute it to Lewis as well, primarily on the basis of remarks like this one: "Most stories about miraculous events are probably false: if it comes to that, most stories about natural events are false. Lies, exaggerations, misunderstandings and hearsay make up perhaps more than half of all that is said and written in the world."[85]

We find ourselves confronted with a mind-boggling array of testimony concerning miraculous events. Hume and Lewis agree that we know that at best a tiny fraction of these accounts are true. How on earth are we supposed to find the needle of truth in this haystack of falsity? Hume's answer is that we cannot. Even if some of these accounts are true, because all we have to go on is experience, we could never reasonably conclude of a particular account that it is true. Lewis's answer is that we can find the truth by relying on our sense of fitness. Some of these alleged miracles simply make more sense than others; some of them make enough sense that the historical evidence together with their fitness makes it reasonable for us to conclude that they really happened. The Resurrection of Christ is a good candidate for such a miracle.[86] As Lewis puts it, "[w]hatever men may *say*, no one really thinks that the Christian doctrine of the Resurrection is exactly on the same level with some pious tittle-tattle about how Mother Egaree Louise miraculously found her second best thimble by the aid of St Anthony."[87]

Who is right? The answer is that it depends. If we had a good philosophical argument for the existence of a Higher Power outside of nature, and it could be shown that it was plausible that this Higher

Power could and would intervene in nature in a particular way, then it seems possible that these considerations could make it reasonable to believe that such intervention had actually occurred, if the right sort of historical evidence were also available.[88] If this is right, then Hume's case against miracles implicitly depends on the assumption that we have no such argument. In a nutshell, Lewis has not shown that the Probability Principle is false, but Hume is not warranted in taking it to be obviously true.

An interesting question here is whether Hume himself thought that his argument against miracles implicitly depends on the claim that there is no good argument for the existence of a Higher Power. Terence Penelhum suggests that he did not: "The fact that [Hume] presents [the argument against miracles] before he enters any discussion of natural theology indicates that he considers [the argument against miracles] to be decisive even if some form of natural theology has been agreed to be successful."[89] Evidence that Penelhum is right about this can be found toward the end of Hume's essay itself:

> Though the Being to whom the miracle is ascribed, be . . . Almighty, [the alleged miracle] does not, upon that account, become a whit more probable; since it is impossible for us to know the attributes or actions of such a Being, otherwise than from the experience which we have of his productions, in the usual course of nature. This still reduces us to past observation, and obliges us to compare the instances of the violation of truth in the testimony of men, with those of the violation of the laws of nature by miracles, in order to judge which of them is more likely and probable.[90]

Hume claims that even if we somehow knew that an omnipotent supernatural power existed, the argument against miracles would succeed because we would still have to rely on past experience *alone* to assess the likelihood that a given piece of religious testimony in support of a miracle was true. On this particular point Hume seems to be mistaken, as Lewis has shown.[91]

In any case, an important conclusion from all of this is that neither Hume's argument in "Of Miracles" nor Lewis's case for the fitness of the Incarnation sketched in the previous section can stand on its own. Lewis's case for fitness must rest on a sufficiently convincing argument for the existence of a Higher Power, whereas Hume's argument against miracles depends on the claim that there is no such argument. Without such an argument we are left with experience as our only guide, and I think Hume's argument establishes at least this much: *If experience is our only guide,* then it is not reasonable to infer that the Christian account of Christ's Resurrection is correct on the basis of the testimony in its favor.

This result has implications for Lewis's famous "Trilemma." One version of the Trilemma appears in *Mere Christianity*:

> A man who was merely a man and said the sort of things Jesus said would not be a great moral teacher. He would either be a lunatic ... or else he would be the Devil of Hell. ... Now it seems to me obvious that He was neither a lunatic nor a fiend: and consequently, however strange or terrifying or unlikely it may seem, I have to accept the view that He was and is God.[92]

The opening line of the passage indicates that the Trilemma is a reaction to the view that Jesus was not divine but was a great moral teacher, a view held by, among others, Thomas Jefferson, the author of the Declaration of Independence and founder of the U.S. Republican Party.[93] The Trilemma goes like this: Christ was (a) insane, (b) evil, or (c) God. But Christ was neither (a) nor (b); therefore, He was (c).

There are two important things to see about the Trilemma. The first is that it rests on a comparison of the plausibility of various possible explanations of the available historical evidence about Christ. Lewis's position is that (c) is the most plausible of the three possible explanations of the historical evidence and hence should be accepted. The second (and related) point to see here is that (a), (b), and (c) do not exhaust all of the logically possible explanations. In fact, it is far from clear that they exhaust all the plausible explanations; it has been argued, for example, that another plausible explanation is that Christ mistakenly but sanely believed himself to be divine.[94] Here is another explanation that is at least logically possible: At some point during his life, Christ was replaced by a robot duplicate created by extremely technologically advanced aliens. In fact, the aliens made two identical robots. After the Crucifixion and while the first robot was lying inert in the tomb, the aliens teleported in, replaced the inert robot with a functional one, and teleported out. Later, the functional robot emerged from the tomb, walked around on earth for some period of time, encountered various acquaintances of Christ who believed the robot to be Christ, and later floated into the sky, whereupon, after vanishing from sight, it was either retrieved by the aliens or self-destructed.

These observations about the Trilemma suggest two strategies for resisting it. First, one might accept that (a), (b), and (c) are the only options on the table, but argue that (c) is not the most plausible option. An example of this strategy is the atheist's trilemma: Christ was mad, bad, or God; he wasn't God or the devil, so he must have been mad. Psychiatrists have in fact proffered proposals along these lines. For instance, one psychiatrist has recently and tentatively suggested that Jesus might have "had a latent homosexual fixation as the result of a negative Oedipus complex."[95] Second, one might deny that we are faced with a Trilemma at all; perhaps we should say that Christ was mad, bad, God, mistaken but sane, or an alien robot(s).

The second strategy makes it clear that the Trilemma works only if lots of logically possible alternatives can be excluded. Let us consider three logically possible options, two of which it seems reasonable to put on the table at least initially, the third of which can be excluded from the start. Lewis takes the possibilities of Christ being insane or a liar seriously enough to include them in the Trilemma; what gets them onto the table? The answer seems to be: experience. Our common experience contains plenty of liars and lunatics, particularly in the context of religion. All of us, believer and nonbeliever alike, surely recognize that there is an abundance of religious nuts and shysters out there. Next, consider the alien robot option. Even after it occurs to us, we (rightly, I think) are reluctant to take it seriously. Why is this? Again, a big part of the answer seems to be experience. Our common experience contains nothing like the alien robot scenario, and so we are inclined to think, reasonably, that *the universe just doesn't work that way*. Because of this, the alien robot option cannot get onto the table of plausible explanations unless there is some independent evidence in its favor.

A challenge for supporters of Lewis's Trilemma is that the Christian explanation of the historical evidence about the life and death of Christ (the God option) is much more like the alien robot option than it is like the liar or lunatic option in that our experience tells against it. If your experience is anything like mine, it includes a fascinating panoply of liars and lunatics, but no gods or aliens. Thus, the God option can get onto the table of plausible explanations only if there is some independent evidence in its favor.

I believe that Lewis recognized this point. Lewis's presentation of the Trilemma in *Mere Christianity* follows his moral argument and his criticism of Dualism. He briefly mentions the Trilemma in *Miracles*, but only very late in his overall argument.[96] A rudimentary version of the argument appears in the introductory chapter of *The Problem of Pain*, where it is presented as a Dilemma (mad and bad are collapsed into a single possibility).[97] It appears there as a fourth "strand" of Christianity; earlier strands involve the recognition of a great being or spirit that is a source of awe and of morality. We see, therefore, that while the Trilemma makes an appearance in each of Lewis's three main books of Christian apologetics, it never appears at the start of his effort to establish the rationality of Christian belief. Why not simply introduce the Trilemma right off the bat? The answer, I think, is that Lewis saw that without the right sort of philosophical foundation, the Trilemma is roughly as convincing as this argument: Christ was a lunatic, a liar, or an alien robot; since he was not a lunatic or a liar, he must have been an alien robot.

Where does all of this leave us? Hume was right in thinking that experience presents a *formidable* obstacle to any historical case for the Resurrection of Christ, but wrong in thinking that experience presents an *insurmountable* obstacle to such a case. Lewis correctly saw that the historical case could succeed despite Hume's argument – but only if an adequate philosophical foundation for such a case could be established. His shortcoming, in my view, is that he was unable to provide such a foundation.

3.8 CONCLUSION

I have argued that Lewis's proposed solution to the problem of pain is incomplete, that his cumulative case for the existence of a Higher Power is, overall, not terribly weighty, and that (consequently) his effort to establish an adequate philosophical foundation for a historical case for the Resurrection of Christ fails. However, the arguments we have considered leave us with puzzles for atheist and Christian alike. The most challenging puzzle for the atheist that has emerged in the preceding discussion is accounting for the emergence of intentionality, whereas the most challenging puzzle for the Christian that has emerged is accounting for the presence of non-victim-improving natural child suffering in the world.

In the fourth and final chapter we turn to the relationship between faith and reason, the argument from design, and the nature of true religion. In examining these topics we will find some surprising areas of agreement among our three thinkers. For all their differences, they share some important common ground. And if C. S. Lewis, David Hume, and Bertrand Russell all accept a certain proposition, we ought to take that proposition quite seriously indeed.

FOUR

FAITH, DESIGN, AND TRUE RELIGION

4.1 INTRODUCTION

The discussion to this point has focused primarily on areas of disagreement among Lewis, Hume, and Russell. The present chapter is
devoted to an examination of some areas of agreement among the
three thinkers. In particular, we will focus on the nature of faith, the
status of arguments from design, and the nature of true religion. We
will see that the things about which the three agree are fundamental
and sometimes surprising.

4.2 FAITH

4.2.1 Lewis and Russell on Faith

Faith is often contrasted with reason. The popular expression "taking
a leap of faith" expresses this idea; the leap alluded to is a leap beyond
what can be established by reason and evidence.[1] The contemporary
humanist and Russell scholar A. C. Grayling succinctly summarizes
this popular view:

> Faith is a negation of reason. Reason is the faculty of proportioning
> judgment to evidence, after first weighing the evidence. Faith is belief
> even in the face of contrary evidence. Soren Kierkegaard defined faith
> as the leap taken despite everything, despite the very absurdity of what
> one is asked to believe.[2]

A famous remark by Tertullian, an early Christian thinker, illustrates this conception of faith in action: "The Son of God died; it must needs be believed because it is absurd. He was buried and rose again; it is certain because it is impossible."[3] On this view, believing something "on faith" is an irrational activity. Russell saw faith as irrational in this way: "I think faith is a vice, because faith means believing a proposition when there is no good reason for believing it. That may be taken as a definition of faith."[4] Seeing faith as a vice, Russell sought the opposed virtue, which he referred to by a variety of names, including "veracity," "truthfulness," and "intellectual integrity." He characterizes this virtue as "the habit of deciding vexed questions in accordance with the evidence, or of leaving them undecided where the evidence is inconclusive."[5] Russell shows particular scorn for those who argue that certain propositions ought to be believed not because they are true or supported by the preponderance of the evidence but for some other reason, for instance, that widespread acceptance of such propositions will have good consequences:

> As soon as it is held that any belief, no matter what, is important for some other reason than that it is true, a whole host of evils is ready to spring up. Discouragement of inquiry . . . is the first of these, but others are pretty sure to follow. . . . Sooner or later unorthodoxy will come to be considered a crime to be dealt with by the stake, the purge, or the concentration camp. I can respect the men who argue that religion is true and therefore ought to be believed, but I can only feel profound moral reprobation for those who say that religion ought to be believed because it is useful, and that to ask whether it is true is a waste of time.[6]

Elsewhere Russell offers further reasons why veracity should be inculcated and faith discouraged. He maintains that knowledge is one of two essential ingredients in a good human life (the other being love), and surely veracity is more likely to lead to knowledge than faith.[7] One of Russell's most extended discussions of veracity appears in his 1944 essay "The Value of Free Thought." There, he characterizes the free thinker (who possesses the virtue of veracity) as someone who is free from the force of tradition and "the tyranny of his own passions" when it comes to belief formation.[8] Russell writes:

"He will not bow to the authority of others, and he will not bow to his own desires, but he will submit to the evidence."[9] A citizenry of free thinkers will avoid being subject to a tyrannical government, says Russell, and individual free thinkers will avoid a certain kind of intellectual cowardice – namely, that of believing certain claims despite a lack of evidence because one is too afraid to face the prospect that such claims are false.[10] Thus, a free thinker is not someone who simply believes whatever he happens to feel like believing, free to change his beliefs on a whim. He is free in that he is free from all influences save one: the evidence.

Lewis is in complete agreement with Russell when it comes to the importance of regulating one's beliefs in accordance with the evidence:

> Obviously . . . a sane man accepts or rejects any statement, not because he wants to or does not want to, but because the evidence seems to him good or bad. If he were mistaken about the goodness or badness of the evidence that would not mean he was a bad man, but only that he was not very clever. And if he thought the evidence bad but tried to force himself to believe in spite of it, that would be merely stupid. . . . I am not asking anyone to accept Christianity if his best reasoning tells him that the weight of the evidence is against it.[11]

Lewis also shares Russell's disdain for advocating the acceptance of propositions not because they are true but for some other reason, going so far as to make the method one of the tools of the devil Screwtape in *The Screwtape Letters*: "The great thing is to make him value an opinion for some quality other than truth, thus introducing an element of dishonesty and make-believe."[12] Elsewhere Lewis warns against "foolish preachers" who are "always telling you how much Christianity will help you and how good it is for society," whereas "if Christianity is untrue, then no honest man will want to believe it," and "if it is true, every honest man will want to believe it, even if it gives him no help at all."[13]

Given Lewis's agreement with Russell on these points, Lewis must either accept Russell's view that faith is a vice or reject the view that faith requires believing what is unsupported by the evidence. Lewis takes the second option, claiming that "faith is based on reason."[14] He defines faith as "the art of holding on to things your reason has once accepted, in spite of your changing moods."[15] He offers the following example to illustrate how a mood can overpower reason and alter a person's beliefs:

> [M]y reason is perfectly convinced by good evidence that anaesthetics do not smother me and that properly trained surgeons do not start operating until I am unconscious. But that does not alter the fact that when they have me down on the table and clap their horrible mask over my face, a mere childish panic begins inside me. I start thinking I am going to choke, and I am afraid that they will start cutting me up before I am properly under. In other words, I lose my faith in anaesthetics.[16]

A crucial feature of the example is that the beliefs about suffocating and being cut while still conscious are not based on any new evidence that has come to light; the new beliefs are produced by emotions that are not rooted in evidence. Faith is the virtue that prevents this sort of thing; on Lewis's account, "[t]he battle is between faith and reason on one side and emotion and imagination on the other."[17]

Russell and Lewis both recognized an important fact about human beings: We are not purely rational belief-forming machines. We are susceptible to a variety of emotions, and these emotions influence everything from our actions to our health to our beliefs. Lewis puts the point this way:

> [T]hough Reason is divine, human reasoners are not. When once passion takes a part in the game, the human reason, unassisted by Grace, has about as much chance of retaining its hold on truths already gained as a snowflake has of retaining its consistency in the mouth of a blast furnace.[18]

Russell and Lewis lamented this feature of human nature. Lewis lamented it because it makes possible a whole slew of attacks on Christian belief that cannot be effectively countered merely by the use of reason. In Lewis's view, the evidence favors Christianity. But because human beings cannot be counted on to believe in accordance with the evidence, merely showcasing the evidence is not, by itself, sufficient for conversion, or for the preservation of belief in the already converted. Lewis remarks: "[I]f you examined a hundred people who had lost their faith in Christianity, I wonder how many of them would turn out to have been reasoned out of it by honest argument? Do not most people simply drift away?"[19] This view is also evident in *The Screwtape Letters*, where Screwtape routinely encourages his nephew Wormwood to focus his efforts on exploiting the emotions of the "patient" he is trying to draw away from Christianity. The third sentence of Screwtape's first letter to Wormwood is this sarcastic remark: "It sounds as if you supposed that *argument* was the way to keep him out of the Enemy's [God's] clutches."[20] And the letter ends like this: "Do remember that you are there to fuddle him. From the way some of you young fiends talk, anyone would suppose it was our job to *teach!*"[21]

Russell thought that the evidence did not point toward Christianity. He lamented the influence of emotions on belief formation because he thought that such emotions, primarily fear, were the main causes of belief in harmful superstitions, including Christianity:

> Religion is based...primarily and mainly upon fear. It is partly the terror of the unknown and partly...the wish to feel that you have a kind of elder brother who will stand by you in all your troubles and disputes. Fear is the basis of the whole thing – fear of the mysterious, fear of defeat, fear of death.[22]

Russell and Lewis agreed that one ought to follow the evidence when it comes to forming one's beliefs, though they disagreed about where the evidence leads when it comes to Christianity. And both saw human emotion as among the primary obstacles to forming one's beliefs properly. This is why the capacity to resist such emotions is so important. Note the striking similarity between the following pair of passages. The first is from *Mere Christianity*:

> [M]oods will change, whatever view your reason takes.... That is why Faith is such a necessary virtue: unless you teach your moods 'where they get off', you can never be either a sound Christian or even a sound atheist, but just a creature dithering to and fro, with its beliefs really dependent on the weather and the state of its digestion.[23]

The second is from Russell's 1930 essay "The Sense of Sin":

> Men must not allow themselves to be swayed by their moods, believing
> one thing at one moment and another at another.... Do not be content
> with an alternation between moments of rationality and moments of
> irrationality. Look into the irrationality closely with a determination
> not to respect it, and not to let it dominate you.... Do not allow your-
> self to remain a vacillating creature, swayed half by reason and half
> by infantile folly.[24]

4.2.2 Christian Obstinacy

John Beversluis would reject the interpretation of Lewis's views on
following the evidence that I have just given. He writes: "[I]t would
seem that Lewis's concept of rational religion requires that we proportion our beliefs to the state of the evidence at any given time. In
fact, however, this was not his view."[25] Beversluis bases this claim
primarily on Lewis's 1955 essay "On Obstinacy in Belief," alleging
that Lewis there endorses a significant qualification to the view he
puts forth in *Mere Christianity*. However, I think that a careful reading
of the later essay reveals that it is perfectly consistent with Lewis's
earlier view.

In "On Obstinacy in Belief," Lewis distinguishes "the way in which
a Christian first assents to certain propositions" from "the way in
which he afterwards adheres to them."[26] He never explicitly identifies the propositions he has in mind, but the ensuing discussion
suggests that the proposition that the Christian God exists is among
them. Here is a passage that seems to be at odds with the view I
ascribed to Lewis in the previous section:

> But we have now to consider something quite different; their [Chris-
> tians'] adherence to their belief after it has once been formed. It is here
> that the charge of irrationality and resistance to evidence becomes
> really important. For it must be admitted at once that Christians do
> praise such an adherence as if it were meritorious; and even, in a
> sense, more meritorious the stronger the apparent evidence against
> their faith becomes.[27]

It certainly *looks* as if Lewis is suggesting that his general rule that one should believe in accordance with the evidence admits of one exception: Once one becomes a Christian, one should no longer believe in accordance with the evidence when it comes to Christianity itself. Rather, one should continue to believe Christianity *regardless of the evidence against it*. If this interpretation is correct, Lewis has made a radical break with his view in *Mere Christianity* that "a sane man accepts or rejects any statement, not because he wants to or does not want to, but because the evidence seems to him good or bad."[28] In the later essay, is Lewis suggesting that Christians ought to indulge in a kind of insanity?

I have already made it clear that I think an interpretation of the later essay that does not force us to this conclusion is available. The time has come for me to provide this interpretation. It will turn out, I think, that what Lewis calls "Christian obstinacy" is perfectly in line with the general rule that one should believe in accordance with the evidence at all times.[29] To see this, we must examine two examples Lewis discusses in "On Obstinacy in Belief."

One of the examples is described in these lines:

> It is one thing to ask *in vacuo* whether So-and-So will join us tonight, and another to discuss this when So-and-So's honour is pledged to come and some great matter depends on his coming. In the first case it would be merely reasonable, as the clock ticked on, to expect him less and less. In the second, a continued expectation far into the night would be due to our friend's character if we had found him reliable before. Which of us would not feel slightly ashamed if, one moment after we had given him up, he arrived with a full explanation of his delay? We should feel that we ought to have known him better.[30]

In this example, the increasing lateness of the hour constitutes growing evidence against the proposition that So-and-So will arrive. Yet, Lewis suggests, we should adhere to our belief that he will arrive. Why? One way of understanding the passage is that Lewis is suggesting that we ought to persist in believing that So-and-So will arrive despite the fact that, on balance, the evidence tells against it. But a careful reading of the passage reveals that this is not what Lewis has in mind. Notice the last line. The case Lewis describes is one in which we know something about So-and-So's character. Lewis's idea is that by abandoning our belief that So-and-So will arrive because of the lateness of the hour, we would be failing to give sufficient weight to another piece of evidence at our disposal, namely, the nature of So-and-So's character. The lateness of the hour is merely a part of the evidence, not all of it. Adherence to the belief that So-and-So will arrive is required by the rule that one should believe in accordance with the *total* available evidence. Our acquaintance with So-and-So provides us with evidence that we would not otherwise have, and this evidence makes all the difference. The relevance of this example to Christian obstinacy is that Lewis thinks that Christians know something about God's character:

> For it seems to us…that we have something like a knowledge-by-acquaintance of the Person we believe in, however imperfect and intermittent it may be. We trust not because "a God" exists, but because *this* God exists. Or if we ourselves dare not claim to "know" Him, Christendom does, and we trust at least some of its representatives in the same way: because of the sort of people they are.[31]

The idea is that Christians ought to adhere to belief in the God of Christianity in the face of certain kinds of evidence against that belief because they have access to additional evidence such that, on balance, adhering to Christian belief is required by the rule that one should believe in accordance with the evidence. This adherence is meritorious not because it involves believing contrary to the available evidence, but rather because it is based on a not-easily-achieved insight into the nature of God's character.

So far not much has been said about what *kind* of evidence against the Christian God's existence Lewis has in mind. A second example discussed by Lewis sheds light on this issue:

> There are times when we can do all that a fellow creature needs if only he will trust us. In getting a dog out of a trap, in extracting a thorn from a child's finger, in teaching a boy to swim or rescuing one who can't, in getting a frightened beginner over a nasty place on a mountain, the one fatal obstacle may be their distrust. We are asking

them to trust us in the teeth of their senses, their imagination, and their intelligence. We ask them to believe that what is painful will relieve their pain and that what looks dangerous is their only safety. We ask them to accept apparent impossibilities: that moving the paw farther back into the trap is the way to get it out – that hurting the finger very much more will stop the finger hurting [etc.].[32]

It is no accident that these examples all involve pain, danger, and/or fear. I think that these are precisely the kinds of cases Lewis has in mind when he speaks of encountering apparent evidence against Christianity. In short, Lewis is thinking here primarily of suffering as apparent evidence against the existence of the Christian God. Lewis connects the examples in the passage I just quoted with Christian obstinacy as follows:

Now to accept the Christian proposition is *ipso facto* to believe that we are to God, always, as that dog or child or bather or mountain climber was to us, only very much more so. . . . If human life is in fact ordered by a beneficent being whose knowledge of our real needs and of the way in which they can be satisfied infinitely exceeds our own, we must expect *a priori* that His operations will often appear to us far from beneficent and far from wise, and that it will be our highest prudence to give Him our confidence in spite of this.[33]

Christianity, properly understood, implies that there will be suffering in the world for which there is no apparent explanation. Christianity includes the proposition that there is an enormous gap between the cognitive abilities and knowledge of human beings and those of God. The truth in the saying that "God works in mysterious ways" is that God sometimes works in ways that are mysterious *to us* – just as, for instance, our efforts to move the dog's paw further into the trap may be quite mysterious (or downright alarming!) to the dog. As Daniel Howard-Snyder puts it, "[w]hen God is in the dock . . . we cannot presume to know quite well the sorts of reasons that *he* would be privy to."[34]

If Christianity implies that there will be suffering for which there is no apparent explanation, it follows that the presence of suffering with no apparent explanation is not really genuine evidence against Christianity at all.[35] If we think of Christianity as a theory, then we can put the point this way: Christianity *predicts* that the world will contain suffering for which there is no obvious explanation. So the presence of such suffering hardly constitutes evidence against the theory. In his discussion of Christian obstinacy Lewis very often (but not always) speaks of obstinacy in the face of *apparent* evidence against Christianity. For example, when first describing Christian obstinacy he says that it is "more meritorious the stronger the *apparent* evidence against their faith becomes."[36] I think it is no accident that Lewis often includes this qualification. His view is that suffering with no obvious explanation may *seem* to be evidence against Christianity, but a fuller understanding reveals that it is not *genuine* evidence against Christianity.

It is worth revisiting the discussion of the problem of pain from Chapter 1 in light of this point. At the end of Chapter 1, I suggested that in *The Problem of Pain* Lewis fails to provide a plausible explanation for the existence of *non-victim-improving natural child suffering*, which is suffering experienced by a child that is not the result of human free action and does not contribute at all to the genuine happiness of the child who experiences the suffering. I suggested that the presence in our world of such suffering constitutes evidence against the existence of the God of traditional Christianity. But such suffering is suffering for which there is no apparent justification. Does it follow from Lewis's position on Christian obstinacy that such suffering is not evidence against Christianity after all?

I think not, and the following simple example should illustrate why. Imagine a scientific theory that predicts both that (i) there are spherical objects and that (ii) there are no blue objects. Suppose we encounter a blue sphere and offer this as evidence against the theory. It is no good for a defender of the theory to point out that the theory predicts the existence of spheres and that because the putative evidence against the theory is a sphere it does not constitute genuine evidence against the theory at all. This defense of the theory fails because the object in question is also blue, and it is its blueness that makes it evidence against the theory.

Consider an instance of suffering that both (i) has no apparent explanation and (ii) is non-victim-improving natural child

162

suffering. If someone were to suggest that such an instance of suffering is evidence against Christianity in virtue of being suffering that has no apparent explanation, then the Lewisian point that Christianity predicts suffering with this feature is both relevant and effective.[37] But I am suggesting that such suffering constitutes evidence against Christianity in virtue of being a case of non-victim-improving natural child suffering. The Lewisian point does not apply to this claim; arguing that such suffering does not constitute genuine evidence against Christianity because it is suffering that has no apparent explanation is no more sensible than arguing that the blue sphere does not constitute evidence against the scientific theory just discussed because it is a sphere. So I am inclined to stick to my initial contention that the fact (if it is a fact) that our world contains non-victim-improving natural child suffering is evidence against Christianity. The gap between the cognitive abilities of human beings and God posited by Christianity may prevent the presence of non-victim-improving natural child suffering from being *decisive* evidence against Christianity, but it does not prevent it from being *evidence* against Christianity.

In any case, Christian obstinacy is perfectly consistent with the rule that one should believe in accordance with all the available evidence. Lewis offers two distinct arguments that support this position. First, the Christian will take the nature of God's character into account when assessing the relevant evidence for and against Christianity. This evidence will often be sufficient to tip the scales in favor of Christianity despite the presence of evidence against it. Second, the Christian will realize that certain features of the world (e.g., that there is suffering that has no obvious explanation) that may on their face appear to be evidence against Christianity are not in fact evidence of this sort after all. To those who lack the insight of the Christian, it may appear as if the Christian is continuing to believe despite overwhelming evidence against Christianity, but this is mere appearance. The Christian's obstinacy is meritorious because it involves a more accurate assessment of the evidence at hand. If this is correct, then, contra Beversluis, Lewis's later essay on obstinacy is not at odds with his commitment to the principle that we ought always to believe in accordance with the evidence. Christian obstinacy is an extension of Lewis's account of faith based on reason.

I therefore stand by my contention that Lewis and Russell believe that we should always strive to follow the evidence but disagree about where the evidence leads. When one thinks that the available evidence supports a given position but finds that many people incline toward a different position, it is tempting to attribute the others' beliefs to irrationality. This is a temptation to which Russell often succumbs when it comes to religious belief, and some of Lewis's remarks in *Mere Christianity* and *The Screwtape Letters* give the impression that Lewis succumbs to the same temptation when it comes to nonbelief. However, in "On Obstinacy in Belief," Lewis offers an assessment of the situation that strikes me as (almost) absolutely correct:

> Men wish on both sides. . . . [T]here is fear-fulfillment as well as wish-fulfillment, and hypochondriac temperaments will always tend to think true what they most wish to be false. Thus instead of the one predicament on which our opponents sometimes concentrate there are in fact four. A man may be a Christian because he wants Christianity to be true. He may be an atheist because he wants atheism to be true. He may be an atheist because he wants Christianity to be true. He may be a Christian because he wants atheism to be true. Surely these possibilities cancel one another out? . . . I do not think they overthrow the view that there is evidence both for and against the Christian proposition which fully rational minds, working honestly, can assess differently.[38]

4.2.3   Hume and Evidentialism

The inquisitive reader is perhaps by this time wondering about Hume's views on faith and reason. Hume seems to think of faith along Russellian lines, as something that is rightly contrasted with reason rather than subsumed under it.[39] Hume's position on arguments for (or against) propositions based on the consequences of accepting such propositions is somewhat different from the straightforward disdain shared by Lewis and Russell. On the one hand, Hume sees that the consequences of accepting a certain proposition tell us nothing about its truth, observing that "it is not certain that an opinion is false, because it is of dangerous consequence."[40] Elsewhere he observes that "the love of truth...never is, nor can be, carried to too high a degree."[41] And, of course, we have already seen his claim in "Of Miracles" that "[a] wise man...proportions his belief to the evidence."[42] In light of remarks like this, David O'Connor classifies Hume as an "evidentialist," one who accepts the principle that "*any* belief is rational only in direct proportion to the balance of evidence in its favor."[43] On the other hand, we also find in Hume the following remark:

> [T]hough the philosophical truth of any proposition by no means depends on its tendency to promote the interests of society; yet a man has but a bad grace, who delivers a theory, however true, which, he must confess, leads to a practice dangerous and pernicious. . . . Truths which are *pernicious* to society, if any such there be, will yield to errors which are salutary and *advantageous*.[44]

This passage suggests that perhaps the passion for the truth can be carried too far if it leads one to promote truths that are pernicious to society. It is important to note, however, that the bad grace manifests itself in the *deliverance* of the pernicious theory, not in the *acceptance* of it. So it may be that Hume thinks that we should always follow the evidence when it comes to the beliefs we hold but not necessarily when it comes to the beliefs we share with others.

It turns out, however, that Hume is not a straightforward evidentialist. To get clear on Hume's views on reason, evidence, and belief, we must briefly consider his larger philosophical project. Hume was arguably as much a psychologist as a philosopher. He was concerned with understanding the nature and limits of the various capacities of the human mind. As he put it, he hoped to "discover, at least in some degree, the secret springs and principles, by which the human mind is actuated in its operations."[45] He was particularly interested in laying out once and for all the limits of human reason, in delineating the subjects about which human reason could be expected to yield knowledge and those that lie beyond its reach. One of the main benefits of this project, in Hume's eyes, is that it would put an end to "abstruse philosophy and metaphysical jargon," thereby freeing humanity of the burden of trying to understand subtle and often obscure philosophical works.[46] Hume acknowledged that this project itself would require some subtle and difficult philosophy but argued that "[w]e must submit to this fatigue, in order to live at ease ever after."[47] As H. O. Mounce puts it, Hume's view is that "to cure the disorder in philosophy, we must . . . first consider what it is in the world that we are fitted to understand."[48]

As Hume carries out his investigation into the limits of reason, he discovers some serious gaps in what reason can do. One of the most famous of these gaps involves the problem of induction. To borrow one of Hume's examples: In the past, all the bread I have eaten has nourished me. Recognizing this, I infer that all bread – even bread I have not eaten or even encountered – nourishes.[49] With respect to this sort of transition, Hume writes: "I shall allow, if you please, that the one proposition may justly be inferred from the other: I know, in fact, that it always is inferred. But if you insist that the inference is made by a chain of reasoning, I desire you to produce that reasoning."[50]

Hume proceeds to argue that there is in fact no adequate chain of reasoning that would license the sort of inference under discussion. He points out that "all inferences from experience suppose, as their foundation, that the future will resemble the past," but there is no good philosophical argument that establishes this supposition.[51]

Let us put aside the question of whether Hume is right about this. What is important for our purpose is the further conclusion Hume draws from the alleged failure of reason to justify induction. One might expect Hume to deny that inductive reasoning can lead to knowledge. But this is not the conclusion Hume draws. In fact, there is already a pretty clear hint that Hume will not draw such a conclusion in the passage I just quoted. In that passage, Hume concedes that "the one proposition may justly be inferred from the other."[52] Yet the inference is not accomplished via any chain of reasoning. Therefore, it must be accomplished in some other way.

The section immediately following the one in which Hume discusses the problem of induction is titled "Skeptical Solution of These Doubts." In it, Hume draws precisely the conclusion I just described:

> [I]n all reasonings from experience, there is a step taken by the mind which is not supported by any argument or process of the understanding.... If the mind be not engaged by argument to make this step, it must be induced by some other principle of equal weight and authority.[53]

Hume identifies the "other" principle or faculty as "Custom or Habit," which he describes as "the great guide of human life."[54] He explains custom's importance in these lines:

> Without the influence of custom, we should be entirely ignorant of every matter of fact beyond what is immediately present to the memory and senses. We should never know how to adjust means to ends, or to employ our natural powers in the production of any effect. There would be an end at once of all action, as well as of the chief part of speculation.[55]

This passage makes it clear that custom can produce knowledge.[56] Custom seems to be an innate instinct or disposition that produces certain beliefs under certain circumstances. Returning to the bread example, when I reflect on all the bread I have eaten, custom causes me to form the belief that the future will resemble the past, and hence I arrive at the conclusion that the bread I eat in the future will nourish me just as the bread I have already eaten did. Or perhaps custom simply causes me to form the belief that all bread nourishes (once I have eaten a lot of nourishing bread).[57]

Beliefs produced by custom may have warrant and hence can be instances of knowledge even though they are not arrived at via any sound philosophical argument.[58] Hume believes in what contemporary philosophers call *properly basic beliefs*.[59] These are beliefs that have warrant that is not derived from any other belief. (Nonbasic beliefs, naturally, are those whose warrant, if any, is derived from other beliefs.) Custom is an important source of properly basic beliefs; indeed, according to Hume, without custom we would lack the knowledge requisite for action of any sort.[60]

Thus, Hume does not maintain that *all* beliefs are warranted only to the extent that they are supported by the total balance of the available evidence. Some beliefs are properly basic. We are justified in accepting such beliefs even if we have no evidence that supports them.[61] This is because no evidence is necessary to support such beliefs; typically (but not always) properly basic beliefs are simply obviously true. Hume seems to include the proposition that the future will resemble the past in this category.[62] So Hume holds what we may call *qualified evidentialism*. This is the view that there are some properly basic beliefs that we are justified in believing even if we have no evidence that supports them, but that we should always believe in accordance with the evidence when it comes to nonbasic beliefs.

It turns out that Russell and Lewis hold precisely this view as well. Russell writes:

[S]ince proofs need premise, it is impossible to prove anything unless some things are accepted without proof. We must therefore ask ourselves: What sort of thing is it reasonable to believe without proof? I should reply: The facts of sense experience and the principles of mathematics and logic – including the inductive logic employed in science. These are things which we can hardly bring ourselves to doubt.[63]

And Lewis has this to say:

I believe that the primary moral principles on which all others depend are rationally perceived. We 'just see' that there is no reason why my neighbor's happiness should be sacrificed to my own, as we 'just see' that things which are equal to the same thing are equal to one another. If we cannot prove either axiom, that is not because they are irrational but because they are self-evident and all proofs depend on them. Their intrinsic reasonableness shines by its own light.[64]

Hume, Lewis, and Russell, therefore, are qualified evidentialists. Each maintains that there are properly basic beliefs that need no evidence (though they do not always agree on what these beliefs are). But they believe that when it comes to beliefs that are not basic, we should always believe in accordance with the evidence available to us at the time.

In the next section we return to a topic that we touched on briefly in Chapter 2: arguments from design. We will once again discover some surprising areas of agreement between our three thinkers on this topic. We will also gain some insight into the views of our three thinkers on the nature of true religion and how it differs from its false imitators. This distinction between true and false (or corrupted) religion, a distinction examined by all three philosophers, will be the focus of the final section of this chapter.

4.3 DESIGN

4.3.1 Hume on Design

In *Dialogues Concerning Natural Religion*, Cleanthes offers the following version of the argument from design:

> Look round the world: Contemplate the whole and every part of it: You will find it to be nothing but one great machine, subdivided into an infinite number of lesser machines, which again admit of subdivisions to a degree beyond what human senses and faculties can trace and explain. All these various machines, and even their most minute parts, are adjusted to each other with an accuracy which ravishes into admiration all men who have ever contemplated them. The curious adapting of means to ends, throughout all nature, resembles exactly, though it much exceeds, the productions of human contrivance; of human design, thought, wisdom, and intelligence. Since therefore the effects resemble each other, we are led to infer, by all the rules of analogy, that the causes also resemble, and that the Author of Nature is somewhat similar to the mind of man, though possessed of much larger faculties, proportioned to the grandeur of the work which he has executed. By this argument *a posteriori*, and this argument alone, do we at once prove the existence of a Deity and his similarity to human mind and intelligence.[65]

The argument relies on two main principles. The first of these is that "[f]rom similar effects we infer similar causes."[66] More precisely:

Cause-and-Effect Principle: The degree to which the *causes* of x and y are similar to each other is directly proportional to the degree to which *x and y* are similar to each other.

The second principle is this one:

Superiority Principle: If being A is the designer of x, and being B is the designer of y, then A is superior to B to the same degree that x is superior to y.[67]

Cleanthes's argument can be formulated this way:

Cleanthes's Argument from Design

1. The universe is (i) very similar to machines that are the result of human intelligence and (ii) far superior to such machines.
2. If (1), then the cause of the universe is (i) very similar to human intelligence and (ii) far superior to human intelligence.
3. Therefore, the cause of the universe is very similar to human intelligence but far superior.

Suppose x = the universe, and y = some man-made machine. The first premise tells us that x and y are quite similar. Applying the Cause-and-Effect Principle, we can infer that the cause of the universe is similar to human intelligence (as this is the cause of the man-made machine). So, A = the intelligence that designed the universe, and B = human intelligence. The first premise also tells us that the universe is far superior to any man-made machine. Applying the Superiority Principle, we can infer that the intelligence that produced the universe is far superior to human intelligence.

This argument appears in Part II of the *Dialogues*. In the remainder of that part, as well as in the subsequent six parts, the argument is subjected to a bewildering variety of objections, the majority of which are suggested by Philo. We will not examine all of these objections. The project at hand is the tricky one that I mentioned but brushed aside in Chapter 1: to determine *Hume's* position on the argument from design. We will begin by considering Philo's first criticism of Cleanthes's argument as well as Cleanthes's response to that criticism in Part III.

Philo's immediate reaction to Cleanthes's argument is to question its first premise. He rejects the claim that that there is much resemblance between the universe and man-made machines at all: "The dissimilitude is so striking that the utmost you can here pretend to is a guess, a conjecture, a presumption concerning a similar cause."[68] Philo goes on to offer an argument against the similarity of the universe to a man-made machine, the details of which do not concern us here. What is important is that Cleanthes clearly takes Philo's main objection to be directed against the similarity claim. This is evident from Cleanthes's opening speech in Part III of the *Dialogues*, where he remarks: "[I]t is by no means necessary that theists should prove the similarity of the works of nature to those of art, because this similarity is self-evident and undeniable."[69] Cleanthes follows up this remark by describing two imaginary cases in which it is supposed to be obvious that intelligent design is at work, arguing that design is similarly obvious in the case of the actual universe. Again, the details of these cases do not concern us here. What does concern us is an important and much-discussed argument that immediately follows Cleanthes's presentation of the two examples. This is the so-called irregular argument, which appears in these lines, spoken by Cleanthes to Philo: "Consider, anatomize the eye; survey its structure and contrivance, and tell me, from your own feeling, if the idea of a contriver does not immediately flow in upon you with a force like that of sensation. The most obvious conclusion, surely, is in favor of design."[70]

The exact nature and function of this irregular argument in the *Dialogues* is a matter of some debate. Some commentators suppose that it is a new kind of argument from design, distinct from Cleanthes's earlier Part II argument.[71] Others suggest that it is not an argument at all but simply a feeling that ultimately adds nothing to the debate.[72] I favor a third possibility: that this irregular argument is not an entirely new and distinct design argument but rather is intended to support Cleanthes's Part II argument. I believe that the irregular argument is designed to get Philo to recognize that the natural universe (or at least some of its parts) is *obviously* similar to a man-made machine. The context in which Cleanthes presents the irregular argument supports this interpretation; Cleanthes has spent all of Part III up to this point trying to establish the obviousness of this resemblance. It would be odd for him suddenly in midstream to offer an entirely new kind of design argument.

If this interpretation is right, then what exactly *is* the irregular argument? How are Cleanthes's remarks supposed to get Philo to recognize the obviousness of the similarity between the human eye and man-made machines? To answer this question, we must return once again to Hume's example involving nourishing bread and his views on custom.

Suppose that I enter a restaurant, starved for nourishment. Shortly after I am seated a waiter brings me a bowl of bread. The bread is of a variety I have not previously encountered. Almost immediately I form the belief that this bread will nourish me; indeed, the belief flows in upon me with a force like that of sensation. What exactly has happened here?

Here is a Humean account of what has gone on in this example. My observation of the bread triggers the operation of a host of innate cognitive faculties. These cognitive faculties operate largely outside of my conscious awareness.[73] The bread on the table, while of a variety I have not previously encountered, *resembles* bread that I have encountered in a variety of ways. The resemblance is, in fact, obvious. This resemblance is registered by my cognitive faculties, though I do not necessarily form the conscious belief that the new bread resembles bread I have previously encountered. Registering the resemblance, my cognitive faculties cause me to form the belief that this new bread will nourish me, thus clearing the way for the bread-eating frenzy that inevitably follows. Custom, that "great guide of human life," has led me to an important piece of knowledge. The knowledge that the bread will nourish me is rooted in its resemblance to bread I have previously encountered, but I did not engage in a chain of reasoning that began with premises about bread I have previously encountered and ended with the conclusion that this new bread would also nourish me. Indeed, as I am a careful reasoner, I am aware that there is no such adequate chain of reasoning, so, were it not for custom, I would find myself sitting helplessly at the table, wondering whether this new bread would nourish me after all.[74]

Here is the crucial feature of the example: The fact that the belief that the bread will nourish me rushes in on me with such force should tell me (if I think about it) that I recognize, at least implicitly the strong similarity between this new bread and bread I have previously encountered. Given the way my cognitive faculties work (when functioning properly), the belief in question would not have rushed in with such force if there were not a strong resemblance between bread familiar to me and the new bread. This is because my faculties would not have produced the belief in question had they not registered the resemblance in question (again, assuming that they are functioning properly).

At this point, a question arises: There are plenty of *other* conclusions I might reasonably have drawn on the basis of the resemblance. Why, for instance, did not the belief that this bread contains flour rush in on me? The Humean answer, I think, is that which of the many beliefs that *might* have been formed on the basis of the resemblance actually *is* formed depends on my interests at the time. In the example, I was very hungry, so naturally I wondered whether the bread would nourish me rather than what its ingredients were or how it was made.

With all of this in mind, let us return to Cleanthes and Philo. When Cleanthes asks Philo to reflect on the eye and "survey its structure," he assumes that such surveillance will trigger Philo's automatic cognitive faculties to produce in Philo "the idea of a contriver."[75] The point of this is to get Philo to recognize that, despite his fancy philosophical arguments against the similarity of the universe to man-made machines, the workings of his own cognitive faculties suggests that he himself implicitly recognizes the similarity. Of course, there is the possibility that the idea of a contriver is a result not of Philo's properly functioning cognitive faculties but rather of some sort of error or bias. Still, the presence of the idea of a contriver constitutes at least a prima facie case for significant similarity between the universe and man-made machines. In this way, Philo's excessive skepticism is challenged by custom. The irregular argument, then, is not an argument in the traditional sense. It is not a series of propositions standing in certain logical relations to each other intended to support a conclusion. Instead, it is a thought experiment posed by Cleanthes intended to bring Philo to the realization that he implicitly accepts the very similarity he has previously denied.

After presenting this irregular argument, Cleanthes says:

> It sometimes happens, I own, that the religious arguments have not their due influence on an ignorant savage and barbarian; not because they are obscure and difficult, but because he never asks himself any question with regard to them. Whence arises the curious structure of an animal? From the copulation of its parents? And these whence? From *their* parents? A few removes set the objects at such a distance to him that they are lost in darkness and confusion; nor is he actuated by any curiosity to trace them farther.[76]

Our innate cognitive faculties are quietly and continuously clicking away, registering the countless similarities and differences between the various objects we encounter. The similarities and differences these faculties register provide the materials for countless bits of knowledge, the vast majority of which we never acquire. Which bits of knowledge we do acquire at any given time is determined largely by our concerns at that time. The ignorant savage fails to form the belief that the eye is a product of intelligent design for much the same reason that I fail to form the belief that the bread before me contains flour.[77] I am not interested in the ingredients of the bread; the savage is not interested in the origin of the eye. Philo, however, is different. For one thing, he is in the midst of a discussion of the ultimate origin of the universe. For another, he has, according to Cleanthes, a "sifting, inquisitive disposition."[78] Thus, Cleanthes is confident that Philo's cognitive faculties can be counted on to produce the idea of a designer, thereby forcing Philo to acknowledge the similarity between the eye and man-made machines. And, since Philo's only objection to Cleanthes's argument at this point is directed against the similarity claim, once Philo acknowledges the similarity he will have nothing left to say against Cleanthes's original argument. He should be rendered speechless – at least temporarily.

And this is exactly what happens. When Cleanthes stops speaking, Pamphilus (who, you will recall, recounts to Hermippus the entire discussion involving Cleanthes, Philo, and Demea) observes that Philo is "a little embarrassed and confounded."[79] This is a significant development; as William Sessions points out, "[t]his is one of those rare moments of (reported) action in the *Dialogues*, and we are obliged to take it most seriously."[80] My theory about the cause of Philo's silence is that Philo has in fact carried out the thought experiment Cleanthes asked him to carry out. Philo has reflected on the eye, and the idea of a designer has rushed in on him with some force. Cleanthes has been successful in forcing Philo to recognize the similarity between "the works of nature" and "those of art."[81] Hume has Philo fall into embarrassed silence at this moment to signal that Cleanthes has scored a victory. This is good evidence, I think, that Hume himself is at least somewhat sympathetic to Cleanthes's similarity claim.

This is just one piece of the puzzle that is the *Dialogues*. To determine Hume's ultimate verdict regarding Cleanthes's design argument we must examine some other sections of the *Dialogues*, particularly the final part, Part XII. Some background information will be useful before we consider Part XII itself.

Throughout Parts II–VIII, Philo presents a bewildering array of possible alternative explanations for the natural universe other than Cleanthes's favored intelligent designer hypothesis. Among these are the hypotheses (i) that the world is an animal body and God is its soul (rather than its designer), (ii) that the world is a kind of vegetable and hence was produced by "vegetation" (growth?) rather than by intelligent design, and (iii) that the universe contains a finite number of atoms moving at random and the present configuration arose by chance.[82] At the end of Part VIII, Philo offers the following verdict on the various "religious systems" that have been considered:

> All religious systems . . . are subject to great and insuperable difficulties. Each disputant triumphs in his turn, while he carries on an offensive war, and exposes the absurdities, barbarities, and pernicious tenets of his antagonist. But all of them, on the whole, prepare a complete triumph for the skeptic, who tells them that no system ought ever

to be embraced with regard to such subjects... A total suspense of judgment is here our only reasonable recourse.[83]

Throughout much of the *Dialogues*, Cleanthes argues for *anthropomorphism*, the view that the universe is the product of a divine Mind that is both significantly similar to, and comprehensible by, the human mind. Demea argues for *mysticism*, the view that the universe is the product of an infinite and perfect divine Mind that is utterly beyond the grasp of human reason. And Philo, for his part, pushes a kind of *skepticism*, according to which human reason is incapable of acquiring any determinate knowledge about the cause (or causes) of the universe.

At the end of Part XI, Demea is scandalized by Philo's suggestion that in light of the mixture of good and evil in the universe, the most probable hypothesis is that the cause of the universe is morally indifferent (and hence not perfectly good, as Demea and traditional Christianity would have it). He storms out, leaving Cleanthes and Philo to finish the discussion. Philo's first speech in Part XII contains the following startling apparent reversal of his earlier endorsement of skepticism:

> Cleanthes, with whom I live in unreserved intimacy; you are sensible that, notwithstanding the freedom of my conversation and my love of singular arguments, no one has a deeper sense of religion impressed on his mind, or pays more profound adoration to the Divine Being, as he discovers himself to reason in the inexplicable contrivance and artifice of nature. A purpose, an intention, a design strikes everywhere the most careless, the most stupid thinker; and no man can be so hardened in absurd systems as at all times to reject it.[84]

This unexpected apparent revelation that Philo in fact accepts Cleanthes's basic position is followed not too long after by a speech in which Philo essentially restates and endorses Cleanthes's original design argument from Part II.[85]

What are we to make of Philo's apparent display of his true anthropomorphic colors? This reversal is one of the central stumbling blocks to discerning Hume's views in the *Dialogues*. In his introduction to the *Dialogues*, J. C. A. Gaskin reports the comment of a colleague who had just read the work for the first time: "What does the dashed fellow actually *believe* in the end?"[86] Many commentators agree that Demea's departure immediately prior to Philo's apparent reversal is significant but disagree about just what it signifies. David O'Connor suggests that Philo's speech at the start of Part XII is "less about the truth and falsity of the design hypothesis than about re-establishing an amiable and social atmosphere," remarking that the two "seem to be acting in a way that is fairly common among friends... when a conversation has become too sharp."[87] In O'Connor's view, the friendship that exists between Philo and Cleanthes gives us reason to doubt the sincerity of Philo's abrupt adoption of Cleanthes's views.

William Sessions takes a somewhat different view:

> [S]o long as Demea is present... we cannot credit his arguments as conveying Philo's true views, either in their (mostly negative) conclusions or in their (generally skeptical) bent. Thus, in particular, the details of Philo's controversial starting of cavils and objections in Parts 2–11 against Cleanthes' design argument must be taken with a grain of salt; they do not necessarily represent Philo's own true views.... Philo can speak his true mind only when, in Part 12, he is in non-combative conversation alone with his old friend Cleanthes.[88]

Well, such is the way of philosophy. This much is clear: Demea's departure and the friendship between Cleanthes and Philo does not, by itself, tell us whether Philo's reversal is sincere. We must look for other clues as to Philo's actual view.

O'Connor and Sessions agree that Philo's reversal, sincere or not, is followed by a series of qualifications that greatly waters down his initial apparent complete acceptance of Cleanthes's anthropomorphism. Much of this "hollowing out" of Cleanthes's anthropomorphism occurs in a long speech by Philo in which he argues that the debate between theists and atheists is a purely verbal dispute.[89] Philo claims that theists and atheists agree that the cause of the universe resembles the human mind to some degree but disagree about *how strong* this resemblance is.[90] He claims that honest theists and atheists will make certain concessions to the other side. The theist, for her part, ought to admit that "there is a great and immeasurable, because incomprehensible, difference between the *human* and the *divine* mind."[91] The atheist, for her part, ought to recognize that there is "a certain degree of analogy among all the operations of nature ... whether the rotting of a turnip, the generation of an animal, and the structure of human thought."[92] Since all known natural processes resemble each other to *some* extent, the atheist should make the further concession that it is probable that "the principle which first arranged and still maintains order in this universe bears ... some remote inconceivable analogy to the other operations of nature and, among the rest, to the economy of human mind and thought."[93]

The concessions Philo describes would yield a position that is closer to Philo's original skepticism than it is to Cleanthes's anthropomorphism. The compromise position includes the claims (i) that the difference between the divine mind and the human mind is *incomprehensible* and (ii) that the similarity between the human mind and the divine mind, while existent, is *inconceivable*. Philo also insists that the moral attributes of the divine mind are quite unlike the virtues of benevolence and justice, as those virtues are understood by human beings:

> I must also acknowledge, Cleanthes, that, as the works of Nature have a much greater analogy to the effects of *our* art and contrivance than to those of *our* benevolence and justice; we have reason to infer that the natural attributes of the Deity have a greater resemblance to those of men than his moral have to human virtues.[94]

Philo is here alluding to his earlier presentation of the problem of pain in Parts X and XI. During that discussion, Philo was quite confident that the presence of suffering in the universe blocks any inference from the universe to a just and benevolent Designer: "Here, Cleanthes, I find myself at ease in my argument. Here I triumph."[95] Philo's later remarks during the "hollowing out" of his concession to Cleanthes indicate that he stands by his earlier claim to victory. The hollowing out culminates near the end of Part XII (and of the *Dialogues*) with Philo suggesting that "the whole of natural theology ... resolves itself into one simple ... proposition, *That the cause or causes of order in the universe probably bear some remote analogy to human intelligence,*" and that this proposition is "not capable of extension, variation, or more particular explication."[96]

Further evidence that the compromise position is closer to Philo's skepticism than it is to Cleanthes's anthropomorphism can be seen by reflecting on this question: Suppose that skepticism about natural religion (as expressed by Philo's remarks at the end of Part VIII) were true; what *practical* implications would natural religion have for how we should live? The answer is clear: essentially none, other than perhaps that we should not try to use human reason to understand God. According to Philo, the compromise position has exactly the same lack of practical relevance. He suggests that it "affords no inference that affects human life, or can be the source of any action or forbearance."[97]

In light of all this, I think that the following argument captures Philo's final position:

Philo's Hollowed-Out Argument from Design

1. The universe is (i) somewhat similar to machines that are the result of human intelligence and (ii) contains a lot of suffering.
2. If (1), then the cause of the universe is (i) somewhat similar to human intelligence but (ii) not benevolent or just in the same sense that just or benevolent human beings are.
3. Therefore, the cause of the universe is somewhat similar to human intelligence but not benevolent or just in the same sense that just or benevolent human beings are.[98]

The conclusion of this argument is vague. This is intentional; Philo remarks that the conclusion suggested by natural theology is "somewhat ambiguous."[99]

The purpose of this discussion has been to determine the nature of Hume's own views on the argument from design. I believe that Hume's own views do not perfectly match the views of any one character in the *Dialogues*. I mentioned in Chapter 1 that Hume worked on the *Dialogues* off and on for roughly thirty years. I think the *Dialogues* is Hume's attempt to work out the implications of three ideas.

The first of these is that it is important to delineate the limits of human reason. As we saw earlier in this chapter, finding the limits of human reason was one of Hume's central goals. In that same discussion I noted that Hume was concerned to put a stop to bad philosophy, much of which he thought was produced by thinkers who attempt to push human reason beyond its limits. Hume was particularly skeptical of the idea that human reason can be used to determine much of interest about the existence and nature of God. In the *Dialogues*, Philo presses skepticism about natural religion to extremes. The character of Philo gives Hume an opportunity to develop the best arguments for skepticism about natural religion that he can.

However, Hume was, I think, also deeply cognizant of the fact that the universe certainly *seems* to be a product of intelligent design. Hume felt the naturalness of this view quite strongly. In the first paragraph of *The Natural History of Religion*, he remarks that "[t]he whole frame of nature bespeaks an intelligent author."[100] He makes similar claims no less than nine additional times through that same work.[101] And we saw earlier that Hume even has the skeptical Philo temporarily rendered speechless in the face of the apparent obviousness of design. The character of Cleanthes gives Hume an opportunity to develop the best design argument that he can and to evaluate it.

Finally, Hume felt the force of the problem of evil, particularly evil in the form of suffering. In *Natural History*, Hume tells us that "with good reasoners," unexpected evils "are the chief difficulties in admitting a supreme intelligence."[102] We saw in Chapter 1 that two of the twelve sections of the *Dialogues* are devoted to the problem of evil, and I noted in the present section that Philo views suffering in the world as the basis of his strongest criticism of Cleanthes's design argument. The character of Philo (and to a lesser extent Demea) provides Hume with the opportunity to examine the implications that suffering has for natural religion.

The influence of these three ideas (skepticism, design, and suffering) is evident in the compromise position described by Philo in the final section of the *Dialogues*. Skepticism manifests itself in the vagueness and the minimalist nature of that position. Design manifests itself in the fact that the compromise includes the notion that the cause of the universe is something like the human mind. And the problem of evil manifests itself in the fact that, according to the compromise position, the moral attributes of the cause of the universe are the least comprehensible to us of all its attributes. There may in fact be a God with a much richer and more determinate nature than the vague cause of the universe depicted by the compromise position, but the nature of such a God lies beyond the reach of human reason. As Susan Neiman puts it, "it is reason, not God, that was the primary target of Hume's work."[103]

Ultimately, therefore, I believe that the best guess about Hume's own views on the design argument is that they are captured by Philo's compromise position. This position represents the culmination of Hume's efforts to work out the implications of skepticism, design, and evil. Indeed, there is reason to believe that Hume grappled with these issues intermittently throughout his entire adult life. In a letter written on March 10, 1751, Hume reports that he has just recently destroyed a manuscript on natural religion that he wrote before he was twenty years old. He describes the destroyed manuscript this way:

> It begun with an anxious Search after Arguments, to confirm the common Opinion; Doubts stole in, dissipated, return'd, were again dissipated, return'd again; and it was a perpetual struggle of a restless Imagination against Inclination, perhaps against Reason.[104]

This same "perpetual struggle" continues in the *Dialogues*, and Philo's final compromise position at the end of the work represents the closest Hume ever got to a clear, decisive resolution of the struggle.[105]

4.3.2   Lewis on Design

We considered Lewis's view on the argument from design early in Chapter 2, so we need only remind ourselves of that view here. Lewis's position on the design argument is captured by Philo's assessment of it in Part XI of Hume's *Dialogues* that "however consistent the world may be, allowing certain suppositions and conjectures with the idea of such a Deity, it can never afford us an inference concerning his existence."[106] In *Mere Christianity*, Lewis says that if we had to base our knowledge about God's nature exclusively on what we know of the observable physical universe, "we should have to conclude that the He was a great artist (for the universe is a very beautiful place), but also that He is quite merciless and no friend to man (for the universe is a very dangerous and terrifying place.)"[107]

Consider the following proposition:

Hume's Conditional: If all our knowledge of God must be based entirely on the observable physical universe, then we cannot know that God is omnipotent, omniscient, and perfectly good.

Lewis and Hume both accept this conditional. Hume also affirms the antecedent of the conditional and hence holds that we cannot know that God is omnipotent, omniscient, and perfectly good. Lewis, by contrast, rejects the antecedent. His case for a good God rests not on the observable physical universe but rather on human nature. For Hume, the argument from design lies at the very heart of natural religion. For Lewis, it is a red herring.

4.3.3   Russell on Design

Russell also endorses Hume's conditional. Furthermore, in at least some places, he seems to support the conditional by much the same reasoning that Philo and Lewis do: "[I]f you are going to judge of the Creator by the creation you would have to suppose that God also is partly good and partly bad, that He likes poetry, music, art, and He also likes war and slaughter."[108] Russell was fond of suggesting that a perfect God could (and would) have done much better than the universe we find ourselves in:

> When you come to look into this argument from design, it is a most astonishing thing that people can believe that this world, with all the things that are in it, with all its defects, should be the best that omnipotence and omniscience have been able to produce in millions of years. I really cannot believe it.[109]

At different points in his life, Russell held different views on whether the evil we find in the universe is consistent with the existence of an omnipotent, omniscient, and perfectly good God. In 1939, he wrote that the existence of this sort of God "can be actually disproved," and the basis of the proof seems to be the existence of evil.[110] In 1944, he allowed that the creation of a universe containing some evil by an omnipotent, omniscient, perfectly good God "is logically possible."[111] However, he never wavered in his endorsement of the thesis that arguments from design cannot by themselves establish the existence of the traditional God of Christianity. Like Hume and Lewis, Russell saw evil in the universe as one of the major stumbling blocks for such arguments.

Many have pointed to Darwin's theory of evolution as putting a dagger through the heart of the argument from design, and in some places Russell endorses this view. For instance, in "Why I Am Not a Christian," he writes:

> [S]ince the time of Darwin we understand much better why living creatures are adapted to their environment. It is not that their environment was made to be suitable to them but that they grew to be suitable to it, and that is the basis of adaptation. There is no evidence of design about it.[112]

To the extent that evolutionary theory is plausible, it does make trouble for certain versions of the design argument. However, there are other versions that the theory does not touch. For instance, Cleanthes's design argument from Part II of Hume's *Dialogues* is untouched by evolutionary theory. This is because that argument is based on the similarity between the entire universe and man-made machines. Evolutionary theory does not (and is not intended to) explain all the order in the universe; it is only intended to explain how all currently existing species might have arisen from a single simple organism, and perhaps why all currently existing species are so well suited to the environments in which they live. But there are other features of the universe about which the theory simply has nothing to say. For example, contemporary fine-tuning arguments take as their starting point the observation that the values of the constants in the fundamental laws of physics all fall into the tiny range required for life to arise, even though there appears to be a huge range of possible values these constants might have had.[113] Evolutionary theory does not provide an explanation for these "anthropic coincidences."

Later, Russell championed a different kind of objection. This one focuses on omnipotence:

> Design implies the necessity of using means, which does not exist for omnipotence. When we desire a house, we have to go through the labor of building it, but Aladdin's genie could cause a palace to exist by magic. The long process of evolution might be necessary to a divine Artificer who found matter already in existence, and had to struggle to bring order out of chaos. But to the God of Genesis and of orthodox theology no such laborious process was needed.[114]

It is likely that Russell got this objection from John Stuart Mill, who, as it happens, was Russell's godfather. In Part II of his essay "Theism," Mill writes:

> It is not too much to say that every indication of Design in the Kosmos is so much evidence against the Omnipotence of the Designer. For what is meant by Design? Contrivance: the adaptation of means to an end. But the necessity for contrivance – the need of employing means – is a consequence of the limitation of power. . . . A man does not use machinery to move his arms. If he did, it could only be when paralysis had deprived him of the power of moving them by volition. . . . The evidences, therefore, of Natural Theology distinctly imply that the author of the Kosmos worked under limitations.[115]

This is a clever attempt to turn the argument from design on its head. The idea is that the very features of the universe that suggest the existence of an intelligent designer also suggest that the designer is not omnipotent. The presence in nature of means to ends indicates intelligent design, but the use of means to achieve ends simultaneously indicates a lack of power in the designer. An omnipotent designer would simply bring about his ends directly, without using any means at all, as in Mill's example of moving one's arms and Russell's example of building a house. The implication is that a design produced by an omnipotent designer would be devoid of any indication that it had been designed at all.

The argument relies on the following principle:

Mill's Principle: The use of means to achieve an end always indicates a lack of power in the being who uses the means.

This principle is false for at least two reasons. First, there is the simple point that an end is a goal, and it is possible to have as one's goal the attainment of a particular end *by a particular means*. For instance, it is perfectly conceivable to have as one's goal moving one's arm *using complicated gadgetry*. One may have this as one's goal even if one is capable of moving one's arm in the usual more direct fashion. An inability to move one's arm directly is *one* possible reason one might use complicated machinery to effect the move, but it is not the *only* possible reason. Applying this point to Russell's earlier remarks, we can say that while it may not have been necessary for the God of traditional Christianity to use evolution to create human beings, it is possible that God's goal was not merely that there be human beings but that human beings come into existence via evolution.

A second reason the principle is false is that some ends are impossible to bring about directly. Recall Lewis's view (discussed in Chapter 1) that omnipotence does not include the ability to do absolutely anything. Some things are simply impossible (in Lewis's terminology, they are "intrinsically impossible").[116] If there are ends such that bringing them about directly is intrinsically impossible, then the fact that a given being uses a means to achieve them does not imply a lack of power in that being. Lewis provides a plausible example of such an end. In Chapter 1 we also considered Lewis's idea that one of God's main goals for humanity is that human beings come to love Him *freely*. Because of the nature of free will, this is not a goal that can be directly brought about by God. It can be attained only by somewhat indirect means (recall Screwtape's remark that "[God] cannot ravish. He can only woo").[117] Thus, Mill's principle is false, and Russell's Mill-inspired argument fails.

We also find in Russell yet another way of arguing for Hume's conditional. This argument must be carefully distinguished from the approach taken by Philo in Part XII of the *Dialogues* and by Lewis in *Mere Christianity*. They argue that if all our knowledge of God must be based entirely on the observable physical universe, then we must conclude that God is not perfectly good. Hume's conditional follows immediately from this claim. Another strategy, however, is to argue that there are many hypotheses about the nature of the Designer

185

that explain the observable physical universe equally well. If all we have to go on is the observable physical universe, there is no reason to favor any one of these hypotheses over the others. This also leads to Hume's conditional. Russell presents the argument this way:

> There would seem . . . to be no evidence that the course of events has been planned either by an omnipotent or by a non-omnipotent Deity; there is also no evidence that it has not been planned. Nor, if there be a Deity, is there any evidence as to his moral attributes. He may be doing His best under difficulties; He may be doing His worst, but be unable to prevent the accidental emergence of a little bit of good now and then. Or, again, His purposes may be purely aesthetic; He may not care whether His creatures are happy or unhappy, but only whether they provide a pleasing spectacle. All these hypotheses are equally probable, in the sense that there is not a shred of evidence for or against any of them. . . . Of possible hypotheses there is no end, but in the absence of evidence we have no right to incline toward those that we happen to find agreeable.[118]

With a little imagination, it is not hard to add hypotheses to those Russell lists. Russell's 1903 essay "A Free Man's Worship" opens with an imagined Creator who creates our universe simply for the drama and spectacle of it all.[119] Hume gets into the act as well, letting his imagination run wild by way of Philo's speculations:

> This world, for aught [one] knows . . . was only the first rude essay of some dependent, inferior deity who afterwards abandoned it, ashamed of his lame performance: It is the work only of some dependent, inferior deity, and is the object of derision to his superiors: It is the production of old age and dotage in some superannuated deity; and ever since his death has run on at adventures, from the first impulse and active force which it received from him. . . .[120]

Science fiction abounds with further hypotheses. In Kurt Vonnegut's *The Sirens of Titan* (spoiler coming!), earth and all life on it exist entirely for the sake of manufacturing a replacement part for a stranded interstellar traveler's spaceship.[121] In the fourth book of Douglas Adams's *Hitchhiker's Guide to the Galaxy* series (another spoiler coming!), God's Final Message to His Creation is revealed to be: "We apologize for the inconvenience."[122]

Lewis, Hume, and Russell all identified a fundamental weakness common to all design arguments: The furthest such arguments can take us is to the existence of some intelligent designer or other. If the universe is indeed an artifact of some sort, it is an artifact about which we know relatively little. We cannot be sure which parts are the important parts in the eyes of the designer and which, if any, are merely the means to some end, or accidental by-products. We are certainly in no position to judge the ultimate purpose or purposes of the artifact. Given our current state of knowledge, ascertaining the purpose of the universe is about as likely as inferring a clock from knowledge of one of its springs. Given this, it is hard to see how we could arrive at any determinate conclusions concerning the nature of the designer if all we have to go on is the physical universe.

Contemporary debate about intelligent design tends to focus on evolutionary theory. But the demise of evolutionary theory would, at best, eliminate one part of one alternative to the traditional Christian version of the design hypothesis. Countless alternatives would remain untouched. The fact that few in the West defend (or even consider) such alternatives is irrelevant to this point. Perhaps contemporary critics of intelligent design would do well to emphasize its ultimately disappointing results: It leads directly to Philo's compromise position, a position that "affords no inference that affects human life, or can be the source of any action or forbearance."[123] Recall Paul the Apostle's claim that God's nature can be "understood and seen through the things he has made."[124] The dream that this remark is often understood as representing, the dream of inferring the existence of an all-powerful, all-knowing, perfectly good God from the existence of the observable physical universe alone, is dead. The murderer of that dream was not Darwin but Hume.[125]

4.4 TRUE RELIGION

4.4.1 Hume: True Religion and Sick Men's Dreams

William Sessions suggests that the *Dialogues* contains a distinction between theology and piety, where piety is "practical religion, how one lives as well as thinks and feels."[126] Recall Philo's suggestion that the results of natural religion amount to the following proposition: "That the cause or causes of order in the universe probably bear some remote analogy to human intelligence."[127] Shortly after reaching this conclusion, Philo reflects on its practical implications. Using Sessions's distinction, we can say that Philo offers the following account of piety to go with his theology:

> [W]hat can the most inquisitive, contemplative, and religious man do more than give a plain, philosophical assent to the proposition [just given], as often as it occurs, and believe that the arguments on which it is established exceed the objections which lie against it? Some astonishment, indeed, will naturally arise from the greatness of the object; some melancholy from its obscurity: Some contempt of human reason that it can give no solution more satisfactory with regard to so extraordinary and magnificent a question.[128]

All that unaided reason can tell us about the cause of the universe (which we call "God") is that it probably is something like a human mind. The proper emotional response to this result is to feel a mixture of astonishment (at God's mysterious greatness), melancholy (at the disappointingly meager fruits of human reason in this area), and contempt (for human reason for not doing better with respect to such an important issue). This sums up Hume's views on *true religion* – the beliefs and attitudes that properly executed natural religion yields. Humean true religion has almost no implications for how we ought to act in everyday life. It includes no claims about an afterlife; in the *Enquiry Concerning Human Understanding*, Hume argues that natural religion fails to establish the existence of an afterlife.[129] He writes: "No new fact can ever be inferred from the religious hypothesis; no event foreseen or foretold; no reward or punishment expected or dreaded, beyond what is already known by practice and observation."[130]

In light of all this, the following remark by Philo is puzzling: "A person, seasoned with a just sense of the imperfections of natural reason, will fly to revealed truth with the greatest avidity.... To be a philosophical skeptic is, in a man of letters, the first and most essential step towards being a sound, believing Christian."[131] Read literally, the passage suggests that recognition of the disappointing results of natural religion will eventually lead the reflective thinker to Christianity in the following way: Noticing the many defects of human reason in general and its inability to produce much of anything of interest in the particular area of religion, a reflective thinker will turn to revealed religion for knowledge of God. The substantial gaps in our knowledge of God left by human reason are to be filled in by the word of God as contained in the Christian Bible. Thus, recognition of the failings of the human mind is the first step in conversion to Christianity.

There is good reason, however, not to take Philo's remarks at face value. These remarks at the very end of the *Dialogues* are connected with Part I, the topic of which is the proper method of educating the young. There, Demea outlines a curriculum aimed at instilling firm and unshakeable religious belief in its students. The study of religion is to be saved for last; all other subjects are to be examined first. Throughout the study of the other subjects, the imperfection and deficiency of human reason is repeatedly emphasized. In a university run on Demea's principles, each course would end with the professor remarking, "And so we see from our study of (calculus, or geology, or chemistry, or sociology, etc.) how prone to error human reason is." The goal is to instill in the students doubt about their ability to think through much of anything on their own, particularly when it comes to the existence and nature of God. Once this self-doubt is in place, they are ready to be exposed to something in which they can have confidence – the word of God:

> Having thus tamed their minds to a proper submission and self-diffidence, I have no longer any scruple of opening to them the greatest mysteries of religion, nor apprehend any danger from that assuming arrogance of philosophy, which may lead them to reject the most established doctrines and opinions.[132]

The same distrust of human reason that makes the students receptive to revealed religion in the first place insulates their religious beliefs from philosophical refutation; after all, philosophical arguments against God's existence or goodness are products of human reason, and the students have learned all too well how unreliable that particular faculty is.

Toward the end of Part I, Philo offers a devastating criticism of Demea's approach. Philo points out that religious believers in different ages use different apologetic strategies, sometimes extolling the virtues of human reason, sometimes emphasizing its shortcomings. He explains the contemporary (i.e., eighteenth-century) strategy as follows:

> [A]t present, when the influence of education is much diminished and men, from a more open commerce of the world, have learned to compare the popular principles of different nations and ages, our sagacious divines have changed their whole system of philosophy and talk the language of *Stoics*, *Platonists*, and *Peripatetics*, not that of *Pyrrhonians* and *Academics*. *If we distrust human reason we have now no other principle to lead us into religion.*[133]

The last line of the passage strikes at the heart of Demea's system of education. Globalization has made it clear that there are multiple incompatible alleged words of God: How are we to know which of these, if any, is genuine? Philo's point in the final sentence is that we must rely on reason to evaluate the various texts and determine which, if any, constitutes genuine divine revelation. If we cannot rely on human reason at all, then we will have no good way of deciding which alleged revealed religion to believe. Therefore, in the context of globalization, Demea's method of education contains the seeds of its own failure.

A consequence of this is that if becoming a philosophical skeptic is the first step toward becoming a Christian, the skepticism in question must not be too extreme, or no step past the first one can be taken. Any additional steps toward Christianity must be based on an evaluation of the various religious texts by human reason.[134] And Hume's essay "Of Miracles," discussed in the previous chapter, contains Hume's views on the results of that project: "[N]o human testimony can have such force as to prove a miracle, and make it a just foundation for any system of religion."[135]

At the start of Part X of the *Dialogues*, Demea suggests that the best way to instill religious belief in people is to get them to recognize their own misery and imbecility. In response to this proposal, Philo remarks, "I am indeed persuaded . . . that the best and indeed the only method of bringing everyone to a due sense of religion is by just representations of the misery and wickedness of man."[136] What Philo says here is, strictly speaking, something he believes; nevertheless, the statement is misleading. Philo thinks that recognition of human misery should lead to doubt about God's goodness, but he knows that Demea will misunderstand Philo's remark so as to think that Philo agrees with him. I believe that Philo's remark at the very end of the *Dialogues* that becoming a philosophical skeptic is "the first and most essential step towards being a sound, believing Christian" is much like his earlier remark in Part X.[137] It is, strictly speaking, something Philo (and perhaps Hume as well) believes. However, Hume at any rate also believes that no further steps toward Christianity can be taken by human reason. The only way to get from Philo's compromise position to Christianity is by way of an irrational leap of faith.[138] It may be a psychological fact about human beings that skepticism causes them to turn to revealed religion, but the move from skepticism to revealed religion is not a reasonable one. Philo's remark may in fact be intended as a kind of *warning* against precisely this irrational move.[139] Hume may also be warning the reader not to expect Philo's compromise position to become widely believed simply because it happens to be the most reasonable position. Like Lewis and Russell, Hume is well aware of the fact that humans are not simply rational truth seekers.

When we consider all of Hume's writings on religion, we see that his overall view is that human reason can take us no further than Philo's compromise position. Acceptance of this compromise position, together with the astonishment, melancholy, and contempt described earlier, constitutes true religion. True religion has no implications for ordinary life. There is no need to separate the church of true religion from the state, because true religion has no political implications whatsoever. Hume of course recognizes that his true religion has few adherents, and he is careful to distinguish it from popular religion, "religion as it has commonly been found in the world."[140] In Part XII of the *Dialogues*, Philo criticizes popular religion, noting its "pernicious consequences on public affairs," which include "civil wars, persecutions, subversions of government, oppression, [and] slavery."[141] He suggests that it is the prevalence of popular religion that makes the separation of church and state such a good idea: "Is there any maxim in politics more certain and infallible than that both the number and authority of priests should be confined within very narrow limits, and that the civil magistrate ought, for ever, to keep his *fasces* and *axes* from such dangerous hands?"[142]

Hume's other writings make it clear that his own views on this issue are close to those of Philo. In *The Natural History of Religion*, he writes: "Survey most nations and most ages. Examine the religious principles, which have, in fact, prevailed in the world. You will scarcely be persuaded, that they are any thing but sick men's dreams" or "playsome whimsies of monkeys in human shape."[143] In his essay "Of Superstition and Enthusiasm," Hume distinguishes two "corruptions of true religion."[144] The two corruptions are, naturally, superstition, which is rooted in terror, and enthusiasm, which is rooted in elation. Each has its own advantages and disadvantages, but Hume's view concerning their value in comparison to true religion is made by clear by the fact that he presents them as evidence for the claim that "the corruption of the best things produces the worst."[145]

We have seen that Hume thinks that reason does not lead to Christianity; but does he count it too as a corruption of true religion, nothing but a sick man's dream? He has no qualms about including Catholicism in this category: "[T]here is no tenet in all paganism, which would give so fair a scope to ridicule as this of the *real presence*."[146] Of course, the doctrine of transubstantiation is one that is explicitly rejected by reformed Christianity, so this remark leaves us without a verdict concerning the status of that kind of Christianity. We know that Hume had good reason to suppress any overt criticism of reformed Christianity, but there are two passages in the *Natural*

History that suggest that he considers all versions of Christianity to be corruptions of true religion. The first passage is this one:

> Were there a religion ... which [sometimes painted the Deity in the most sublime colours, as the creator of heaven and earth; sometimes degraded him nearly to the level with human creatures in his powers and faculties;] while at the same time it ascribed to him suitable infirmities, passions, and partialities, of the moral kind: That religion, after it was extinct, would also be cited as an instance of those contradictions, which arise from the gross, vulgar, natural conceptions of mankind. ... Nothing indeed would prove more strongly the divine origin of any religion, than to find (and happily this is the case with Christianity) that it is free from a contradiction, so incident to human nature.[147]

Despite the disingenuous disclaimer in parentheses here, it is clear that in the passage in brackets Hume is alluding in a not-so-subtle way to the Christian doctrine of the Incarnation. This is made even clearer by the fact that in an earlier proof of the *Natural History* the text apparently read as follows:

> Were there a religion. ... which [sometimes degraded him so far to a level with human creatures as to represent him wrestling with a man, walking in the cool of the evening, showing his back parts, and descending from Heaven to inform himself of what passes on earth] ...[148]

A second tell-tale passage occurs at the end of a section in which Hume observes that when it comes to religious controversies the most absurd opinion typically prevails. He writes: "To oppose the torrent of scholastic religion by such feeble maxims as these, that *it is impossible for the same thing to be and not to be*, that *the whole is greater than a part*, that *two and three make five*; is pretending to stop the ocean with a bullrush."[149] Note the third of Hume's "feeble maxims." Hume selects a mathematical truth as an example of an obvious truth with which certain popular religions conflict. But what popular religion conflicts with the claim that $2 + 3 = 5$? It is likely that Hume is again not-so-subtly alluding to Christianity; in this case, it is the doctrine of the Trinity that seems to be Hume's target. With its three Persons of the Trinity but just one God, this doctrine may be thought to run afoul of the obvious mathematical truth that $1 + 1 + 1 = 3$ (rather than 1).[150]

We can conclude, therefore, that Hume does consider reformed Christianity to be a kind of popular religion, to be counted among "sick men's dreams" or "playsome whimsies of monkeys in human shape."[151] It is one of many widely accepted doctrines which lie beyond the boundaries of rationality but which humans are nevertheless drawn to believe. Hume's view of Christianity is much the same as that of the teenage Lewis: It is "a kind of endemic nonsense into which humanity tend[s] to blunder."[152]

4.4.2   Lewis and Russell: True Religion as the Conquest of Selfishness

Russell's best-known writings on religion give the impression that he saw religion in all its forms as an evil with almost no redeeming value. Recall the opening lines of his essay "Has Religion Made Useful Contributions to Civilization?": "My own view on religion is that of Lucretius. I regard it as a disease born of fear and as a source of untold misery to the human race."[153] Russell admits only two contributions to civilization made by religion: the fixing of the calendar and the chronicling of eclipses.[154] The essay concludes with these lines:

> Religion prevents our children from having a rational education; religion prevents us from removing the fundamental causes of war; religion prevents us from teaching the ethic of scientific co-operation in place of the old fierce doctrines of sin and punishment. It is possible that mankind is on the threshold of a golden age; but, if so, it will be necessary first to slay the dragon that guards the door, and this dragon is religion.[155]

It may come as a surprise, then, to discover that in some of his earlier writing, Russell maintained that there are elements of religion that are worth preserving. Russell's 1912 essay "The Essence of Religion" is a careful attempt to isolate those elements of religion that are beneficial and can survive the "decay of traditional religious beliefs."[156] Russell argues that what is both good about and essential to religion

194

are not the traditional "dogmas" (belief in God, immortality, the divinity of Christ, etc.) but rather a certain outlook on the universe and corresponding emotional attitude:

> The dogmas have been valued, not so much on their own account, as because they were believed to facilitate a certain attitude towards the world, an habitual direction of our thoughts, a life in the whole, free from the finiteness of self and providing an escape from the tyranny of desire and daily cares. Such a life on the whole is possible without dogma, and ought not to perish through the indifference of those to whom the beliefs of former ages are no longer credible.[157]

Russell distinguishes the finite self and the infinite self. The finite self "sees the world in concentric circles around the *here* and *now*, and itself as the God of that wished-for heaven."[158] The infinite self, on the other hand, "shines impartially" and "aims simply at the good, without regarding the good as mine or yours."[159] These two selves are naturally in conflict, and the essence of religion is the conquest of the finite self by the infinite self. This conquest "requires a moment of absolute self-surrender," a moment "which to the finite self appears like death."[160] Upon the "death" of the finite self, "a new life begins, with a larger vision, a new happiness, and wider hopes."[161]

Then, the author of the infamously scathing "Why I Am Not a Christian" has this to say: "There are in Christianity three elements which it is desirable to preserve if possible: worship, acquiescence, and love."[162] Worship is a combination of "contemplation with joy, reverence, and sense of mystery."[163] There are two types of worship worthy of preservation: worship of ideal goodness and worship of what actually exists. These together yield a desire to mold what actually exists into the ideal good – that is, to make the world as good as possible. Acquiescence is acceptance of "evil which it is not within our power to cure."[164] This frees us from fruitless anger; "the realization of necessity is the liberation from indignation."[165] Finally, there is love. According to Christ, the two greatest commandments are to "love the Lord your God with all your heart, and with all your soul, and with all your mind," and to "love your neighbor as yourself."[166] The first sort of love depends on dogma. Accordingly,

Russell suggests that "[i]n a religion which is not theistic, love of God is replaced by worship of the ideal good."[167] But love for one's fellow human beings can and should be preserved despite the loss of dogma. This love is "given to all indifferently" and "does not demand that its object shall be delightful, beautiful, or good."[168] It "breaks down the walls of self that prevent its union with the world," and "[w]here it is strong, duties become easy, and all service is filled with joy."[169]

What we have here is what might be described as a Russellian account of true religion, religion that is worth preserving. This true religion is grounded in the conquest of the finite self by the infinite self. Such conquest yields a desire to make the world as good as possible, a calm acceptance of the evils that one cannot eliminate, and universal love for one's fellow human beings. These three elements of religion are "intimately interconnected; each helps to produce the others, and all three together form a unity in which it is impossible to say which comes first."[170] And "[a]ll three can exist without dogma."[171]

On May 20, 1946, Lewis gave a talk to the Oxford Socratic Club called "Religion without Dogma?" He said: "[T]he essence of religion . . . is the thirst for an end higher than natural ends; the finite self's desire for, and acquiescence in, and self-rejection in favour of, an object wholly good and wholly good for it."[172]

This account of the essence of religion is strikingly similar to Russell's. Even the language the two use is similar. Compare Lewis's remark to this one by Russell: "The essence of religion . . . lies in the subordination of the finite part of our life to the infinite part."[173] Moreover, a careful examination of Lewis's understanding of Christianity reveals that Lewis sees the struggle against the finite self as lying at the heart of Christianity.

One illustration of this is Lewis's interesting take on the Fall of Man. In the Genesis account of the Fall, the Fall is motivated by a desire on the part of humans to be like God with respect to *knowledge*. The serpent tempts the humans by telling them that if they eat the fruit from the forbidden tree, they will "be like God, knowing good and evil."[174] Lewis puts forth a different proposal. In his version of the Fall, the humans want to be like God with respect to *power* rather than knowledge. They want a kind of self-sufficiency and independence: "[T]hey desired to be on their own, to take care for their own future.... They wanted some corner in the universe of which they could say to God, 'This is our business, not yours.'"[175] (Compare this to Russell's account of the finite self as the self that "sees the world in concentric circles around the *here* and *now*, and itself as the God of that wished-for heaven.")[176] Lewis identifies the first human sin as an act of selfishness – it is a "turning from God to self."[177] This act fundamentally alters human nature: "[A] new species, never made by God, had sinned itself into existence."[178] As a result, "[w]e are not merely imperfect creatures who must be improved: we are ... rebels who must lay down our arms."[179] Russell describes the conquest of the finite self by the infinite self as a kind of death for the finite self, remarking that this conquest "requires a moment of absolute self-surrender," a moment "which to the finite self appears like death."[180] Lewis similarly suggests that "to surrender a self-will inflamed and swollen with years of usurpation is a kind of death."[181] Moreover, it is a death that must be endured not just once but over and over: "Hence the necessity to die daily; however often we think we have broken the rebellious self we shall still find it alive."[182]

Screwtape describes the result of this self-conquest as follows:

> The Enemy [God] wants ... man ... to be so free from any bias in his own favour that he can rejoice in his own talents as frankly and gratefully as in his neighbour's talents – or in a sunrise, an elephant, or a waterfall.... He wants to kill their animal self-love as soon as possible; but it is His long-term policy ... to restore to them a new kind of self-love – a charity and gratitude for all selves, including their own.[183]

This is the impartial love for all human beings commanded by Christ and praised by Russell. Despite their disagreement about the status of Christian dogma, it turns out that Russell and Lewis hold similar views on the essence of religion. Lewis sees acceptance of Christian dogma as they key to preserving this essence, whereas Russell seeks to abandon the dogma but preserve the essence.

A number of recent writers have endorsed a turn to mysticism as a way of preserving the benefits of monotheistic religions like Christianity while avoiding the sometimes violent conflicts that arise over disagreements about dogma.[184] The essence of this move is the one proposed by Russell: Abandon the divisive dogma while preserving the positive emotional benefits, most notably the conquest of selfishness. Lewis, by contrast, supports the conquest of selfishness through acceptance of Christianity. Yet Lewis was aware of the needless violence, intolerance, and persecution that often accompany religious belief, including Christian belief. In a letter written in 1961, he refers to "the ghastly record of Christian persecution" which "had begun in Our Lord's time."[185] And in *The Four Loves*, he speaks of "Christendom's specific contribution to the sum of human cruelty and treachery," observing that "[w]e have shouted the name of Christ and enacted the service of Moloch."[186] Lewis thought that the way to solve the problem of religious violence is not to abandon Christian dogma altogether but rather to understand it correctly and to recognize the proper roles of government and organized religion. Lewis's views on this and related matters are the focus of the next section, which is also the final section of the book.

4.4.3 Lewis on Disputes about Dogma and the Separation of Church and State

In the Preface to *Mere Christianity*, Lewis likens mere Christianity to "a hall out of which doors open into several rooms."[187] The rooms represent the various denominations of Christianity. The Preface ends with the following paragraph:

> When you have reached your own room, be kind to those who have chosen different doors and to those who are still in the hall. If they are wrong they need your prayers all the more; and if they are your enemies, then you are under orders to pray for them. That is one of the rules common to the whole house.[188]

This captures Lewis's straightforward view on interdenominational Christian violence: Such violence is at odds with mere Christianity, which is common to all denominations. Prayer and kindness are to take the place of violence. In "Answers to Questions on Christianity," Lewis goes even further, remarking that "[d]ivisions between Christians are a sin and a scandal, and Christians ought at all times to be making contributions toward re-union."[189]

What about Christian violence against non-Christians? In a 1952 letter, Lewis offers much the same prescription regarding how Christians ought to treat those who reside outside the mansion of Christianity altogether:

> I think that every prayer which is sincerely made even to a false god or to a very imperfectly conceived true God, is accepted by the true God and that Christ saves many who do not think they know Him.... But of course anxiety about unbelievers is most usefully employed when it leads us, not to speculation but to earnest prayer for them and the attempt to be in our own lives such good advertisements for Christianity as will make it attractive.[190]

A common source of religious violence and persecution is the attempt by the state to impose a particular religion on its citizens. Lewis opposes any attempt by the state to impose Christianity. This is not to say that Lewis is opposed to the existence of a Christian society; indeed, in *Mere Christianity* he offers some suggestions about what such a society might be like.[191] But he believes that the proper way to bring about such a society is from the bottom up rather than from the top down. The way to achieve such a society is to convince all the citizens of the truth of Christianity and have them implement Christian principles on their own rather than for a Christian government to impose Christian principles on a non-Christian citizenry. For instance, Lewis rejects the idea that the clergy should "put out a political programme," describing this idea as "silly."[192] He says that the clergy are simply not qualified for politics; in asking them to put forth a political program, we would be "asking them to do a...job for which they have not been trained."[193] While Lewis defends a traditional conception of Christian marriage in which the husband is

199

the "head" and divorce is permitted only in very rare circumstances or not at all, he also says this:[194]

> A great many people seem to think that if you are a Christian yourself you should try to make divorce difficult for every one. I do not think that. At least I know I should be very angry if the Mohammedans tried to prevent the rest of us from drinking wine. My own view is that the Churches should frankly recognize that the majority of the British people are not Christians and, therefore, cannot be expected to live Christian lives.[195]

He goes on to suggest that there ought to be two kinds of marriage, one kind governed by the state, the other governed by the church.[196]

In "On the Transmission of Christianity," Lewis argues against the notion that the British government ought to attempt to instill Christianity in the young by way of education. Much of Lewis's argument is aimed at showing that such a program would be futile and hence leaves it unclear whether he would support such a program if he thought it could succeed. But he also says this: "Where the tide flows towards increasing State control, Christianity, with its claims in one way personal and in the other way ecumenical and both ways antithetical to omnicompetent government, must always in fact . . . be treated as an enemy."[197] This suggests that Lewis sees Christianity itself as placing definite limits on the legitimate power of the state, and the context of the remark suggests that he sees government-run Christian education as lying beyond these limits (though he does go on to support the establishment of private Christian schools).[198]

In a 1958 letter, Lewis expresses his views on the legitimate limits of government rather more forcefully. The topic is whether homosexual acts should be made illegal:

> [N]o *sin*, simply as such, should be made a *crime*. Who the deuce are our rulers to enforce their opinions about sin on us? – a lot of professional politicians, often venal time-servers, whose opinion on a moral problem in one's life we should attach very little value to. . . . We hear too much of the State. Government is at its best a necessary evil. Let's keep it in its place.[199]

And in "Answers to Questions on Christianity," he says, "I detest every kind of religions compulsion."[200]

Finally, let us consider Lewis's essay "Meditation on the Third Commandment." The third commandment says: "You shall not make wrongful use of the name of the Lord your God."[201] The topic of the essay is whether there ought to be a Christian political party. Lewis opposes the idea. The main danger he sees with a Christian party is that it will inevitably represent at most one part of Christianity. The problem with this is that it "will be not simply a *part* of Christendom, but *a part claiming to be the whole*."[202] And this, in turn, may have very bad consequences:

> If ever Christian men can be brought to think treachery and murder the lawful means of establishing the *regime* they desire, and faked trials, religious persecution and organized hooliganism the lawful means of maintaining it, it will, surely, be by just such a process as this.[203]

Lewis's essay has the title it does because he believes that a Christian party would violate the third commandment. His understanding of that commandment is made clear in these lines: "On those who add 'Thus said the Lord' to their merely human utterances descends the utter doom of a conscience which seems clearer and clearer the more it is loaded with sin. All this comes from pretending that God has spoken when He has not spoken."[204]

If the development of a Christian party is a violation of the third commandment, how, then, can Christians exert political influence? Lewis's answer to this question is: "He who converts his neighbor has performed the most practical Christian-political act of all."[205]

Despite their many disagreements we have seen that there are significant and sometimes surprising areas of agreement among Lewis, Hume, and Russell. All three reject the view that we can reason from the nature of the observable physical universe to the existence of a perfect God. All three recognize organized religion's potential for explosive violence and are aware of Christianity's sins in this regard. Hume and Russell see Christianity as rooted in irrational emotions rather than reason, a sick man's dream from which Western civilization ought to awaken, and see the rejection of its ridiculous doctrines as the way to avoid the violence it sometimes engenders. Lewis sees Christianity as rooted in reason; he thinks that we can come to know God by first knowing ourselves. He sees the key to avoiding Christian violence as understanding Christianity correctly and preventing its misuse politically.

One of the most important areas of agreement among our three thinkers concerns how humans ought to go about forming their beliefs. All three thinkers share a common prescription: *Follow the evidence!*[206] And all three see that among the many obstacles to following this prescription is governmental interference. If people are to be able to exercise the virtue that Lewis calls "faith" and Russell calls "veracity," they must live under a political system that permits its citizens to believe in accordance with the evidence. Lewis identifies democracy as such a system: "[A]s long as we remain a democracy, it is men who give the State its powers. And over these men, until all freedom is extinguished, the free winds of opinion blow."[207] But political interference is not the only obstacle to following the evidence. Culture can also be an obstacle. If one lives in a culture in which careful attention to evidence and intellectual honesty are devalued, this can make it difficult to exercise the virtue of faith. Unfortunately, government alone can only put in place a structure that allows for intellectual honesty; it cannot make its citizens value such honesty. Concern for honesty must come from within.

Within the writings of Lewis, Hume, and Russell, you will find arguments made, reasons offered in support of the positions put forth, and objections acknowledged. You will find a burning passion for the truth and respect – indeed reverence – for evidence. This shared passion and reverence not only unites these three intellectual giants; it makes them exemplars we would all do well to emulate.

NOTES

Introduction

1. Plato, *Phaedo*, trans. G. M. A. Grube (Indianapolis: Hackett, 1977), 12, 64a.
2. Michel de Montaigne, "That to Philosophize Is to Learn to Die," in Michel de Montaigne, *Essays* (Chicago: The Great Books Foundation, 1966), 2.
3. David Hume, "My Own Life," in E. C. Mossner (ed.), *The Forgotten Hume* (New York: Columbia University Press, 1943), 9.
4. Ibid.
5. Ibid., 183.
6. Walter Hooper (ed.), *Letters of C. S. Lewis*, revised edition (Orlando, FL: Harcourt, 1993), 509.
7. Ibid., 45.
8. Remarkably, Aldous Huxley also died on this day.
9. Bertrand Russell, *Autobiography* (London: Routledge, 2000), 726.
10. Ibid., 727. Although Russell wrote these words when he was eighty years old, he lived for an additional eighteen years.
11. Ibid., 728.
12. Bertrand Russell, "How to Grow Old," in *Portraits from Memory* (New York: Simon & Schuster, 1965), 52–3.
13. James F. Sennett and Douglas Groothius (eds.), *In Defense of Natural Theology: A Post-Humean Assessment* (Downers Grove, IL: InterVarsity Press, 2005), 9. For a prominent recent example of Hume's influence, see Richard Dawkins, *The God Delusion* (New York: Houghton Mifflin, 2006). The central atheistic argument of the book, the "Ultimate 747 Gambit," owes much to Part IV of Hume's *Dialogues Concerning Natural Religion*.
14. Peter van Inwagen, "Quam Dilecta," in *God and the Philosophers: The Reconciliation of Faith and Reason*, ed. Thomas V. Morris (Oxford: Oxford University Press, 1994), 33.
15. Ibid.

16. Walter Hooper (ed.), *The Collected Letters of C. S. Lewis, Volume II: Books, Broadcasts, and the War 1931–1949* (New York: HarperCollins, 2004), 20–1.

1. The Love of God and the Suffering of Humanity

1. Kenneth L. Woodward, "Countless Souls Cry Out to God," *Newsweek*, January 10, 2005, 37.
2. Voltaire, *Candide*, trans. L. Bair (New York: Bantam Books, 1959), 29. Among the more interesting of the assorted horrors is the severing of one buttock of various characters.
3. G. W. Leibniz, *Theodicy*, trans. E. M. Huggard (LaSalle, IL: Open Court, 1985), 128.
4. Russell also discussed the problem of evil, though it is probably not really accurate to say that he "grappled" with it; his view (at least sometimes) seemed to be that the evil in our world decisively establishes the nonexistence of the traditional God of monotheism. See, for example, Russell's 1939 essay "The Existence and Nature of God," in *Russell on Religion*, ed. L. Greenspan and S. Andersson (New York: Routledge, 1999), 94. Also see Chapter 4, section 4.3.3.
5. J. C. A. Gaskin, *Hume's Philosophy of Religion*, second edition (Atlantic Highlands, NJ: Humanities Press International, 1988), 5.
6. David O'Connor, *Hume on Religion* (New York: Routledge, 2001), 5.
7. See, for example, A. J. Ayer, *Hume: A Very Short Introduction* (Oxford: Oxford University Press, 2000), 32.
8. David Hume, *Dialogues Concerning Natural Religion*, second edition (Indianapolis: Hackett, 1998), 58.
9. Ibid.
10. Ibid., 59.
11. Ibid., 69.
12. Ibid., 63.
13. Ibid., 75.
14. See Chapter 2, section 2.2.3.
15. Ibid. Shortly after Philo reaches this conclusion, Demea recognizes Philo's true colors; not long after that, Demea leaves the conversation altogether.
16. Hume, *Dialogues*, 7.
17. For an apt characterization of Philo's "two-track" strategy, see O'Connor, *Hume on Religion*, 189–90. That Philo's position has these two "tracks" to it sheds light on how both defenders and critics of the problem of evil have found support in the words of Philo. For a criticism of the problem of evil that draws on the first, skeptical track, see Stephen J. Wykstra, "The Humean Obstacle to Evidential Arguments from Suffering: On Avoiding the Evils of 'Appearance'," *International Journal for Philosophy of Religion* 16 (1984), 73–93. For a defense of the problem of evil that

draws on the second, atheistic track, see Paul Draper, "Pain and Pleasure: An Evidential Problem for Theists," *NOUS* 23 (1989), 331–50.

18. Hume, *Dialogues*, 66.
19. I say "more or less" because, strictly speaking, an additional principle is required, namely, something like this: If God wants p to be the case, and God could bring it about that p, then God brings it about that p.
20. Hume, *Dialogues*, 69.
21. Ibid., 69–73.
22. See, for example, *The Problem of Evil: Selected Readings*, ed. Michael L. Peterson (Notre Dame, IN: University of Notre Dame Press, 1992), 3.
23. C. S. Lewis, *Surprised by Joy: The Shape of My Early Life* (New York: Harcourt, 1955), 63. This autobiographical work describes in some detail Lewis's departure from and later return to Christianity.
24. Walter Hooper (ed.), *Letters of C. S. Lewis*, revised edition (Orlando, FL: Harcourt, 1993), 52.
25. Walter Hooper (ed.), *The Collected Letters of C. S. Lewis, Volume II: Books, Broadcasts, and the War 1931–1949* (New York: HarperCollins, 2004), 702–3.
26. Ibid., 145.
27. Lewis, *Surprised by Joy*, 237.
28. Hooper (ed.), *Letters*, 288. The first letter to Greeves was written on October 12, 1916, the second on October 18, 1931.
29. Ibid., 212.
30. C. S. Lewis, *All My Road Before Me: The Diary of C. S. Lewis, 1922–1927* (New York: Harvest Books, 2002), 332.
31. Hume, *Dialogues*, 74.
32. Ibid., 75.
33. C. S. Lewis, *The Problem of Pain* (New York: HarperCollins, 2001), 1.
34. Ibid., 1–3.
35. Ibid., 16.
36. Matthew 19:26.
37. Thomas Aquinas, *Summa Theologica* (New York: Benziger Brothers Inc., 1947), 139, I, q. 25, a. 4.
38. Lewis, *Problem of Pain*, 18. Lewis's language here is close to that of the seventeenth-century Cambridge Platonist Ralph Cudworth, who declared "that which implies a contradiction is a nonentity and therefore cannot be the object of divine power." Ralph Cudworth, *A Treatise Concerning Eternal and Immutable Morality*, ed. S. Hutton (Cambridge: Cambridge University Press, 1996), 25.
39. Lewis, *Problem of Pain*, 18.
40. Ultimately, this definition may not be adequate either, but its shortcomings are not relevant to our discussion. For an examination of the concept of omnipotence that highlights some of the shortcomings of Lewis's analysis of omnipotence, see Erik Wielenberg, "Omnipotence Again," *Faith and Philosophy* 17:1 (January 2000), 26–47.

41. Lewis, *Problem of Pain*, 20.
42. Ibid., 21.
43. Ibid., 22.
44. Ibid., 23–4.
45. Hume, *Dialogues*, 70.
46. Ibid.
47. Lewis, *Problem of Pain*, 24–5. Lewis does emphasize that God can and does interfere with nature on some occasions (to maintain otherwise would be to deny the occurrence of miracles); what he means to reject is the notion that God could interfere in such a way as to prevent all suffering. This passage makes it clear that Lewis is assuming a libertarian account of free will according to which S performs act A freely only if S could have performed an action other than A.
48. The free will defense goes back at least to Augustine; see his *On Free Choice of the Will*, trans. T. Williams (Indianapolis: Hackett, 1993). The best-known contemporary development of the free will defense is probably Alvin Plantinga's. Plantinga's defense has been published multiple times; for one presentation, see Alvin Plantinga, "The Free Will Defense," Chapter 2 of *The Analytic Theist: An Alvin Plantinga Reader*, ed. J. F. Sennett (Grand Rapids, MI: Eerdmans, 1998), 22–49.
49. For a discussion of the precise nature of Lewis's goals in *The Problem of Pain*, see the final section of this chapter.
50. Lewis, *Problem of Pain*, 31–2.
51. Ibid., 32.
52. Ibid., 38.
53. Ibid., 34–5.
54. Ibid., 41.
55. Ibid., 46.
56. Ibid., 46–7.
57. C. S. Lewis, *The Screwtape Letters* (New York: Touchstone, 1996), 4, letter VIII.
58. As I noted above, this is just one component of divine goodness.
59. Lewis also says that "the free will of rational creatures" is itself good; Lewis, *Problem of Pain*, 63.
60. Ibid., 85.
61. Ibid., 87.
62. Ibid., 86.
63. Ibid., 90.
64. Ibid., 91.
65. Ibid., 93.
66. Ibid., 70.
67. Peter van Inwagen, "The Magnitude, Duration, and Distribution of Evil: A Theodicy," in *God, Knowledge, and Mystery: Essays in Philosophical Theology* (Ithaca NY: Cornell University Press, 1995), 110.
68. Lewis, *Problem of Pain*, 96.

69. Ibid., 94–5. Lewis himself may have fallen into this category; for an autobiographical account of his suffering, see C. S. Lewis, *A Grief Observed* (New York: HarperCollins, 2001).
70. Matthew 19:23–4.
71. Lewis, *Screwtape Letters*, 101, letter XXVIII.
72. Lewis, *Problem of Pain*, 116. These remarks about the absence of security may have their origin in the loss of security Lewis felt upon the death of his mother when he was a child; see *Surprised by Joy*, 21.
73. Lewis, *Problem of Pain*, 97–8.
74. This is not to say that there is no action that I performed freely: It may be the case that the drinking and video game playing were done freely. What was not done freely was drinking and playing video games *because these things were commanded by God*.
75. Genesis 22:12.
76. Lewis, *Problem of Pain*, 100–1.
77. Well, almost; Lewis also discusses animal suffering, but our discussion is limited to human suffering.
78. Interestingly, the second premise is the premise in which Philo seems to have the least confidence.
79. Lewis signals his awareness of the difficulty in the last sentence of the passage that I quoted at the beginning of the present section.
80. Leo Tolstoy, *The Death of Ivan Ilyich*, trans. L. Solotaroff (New York: Bantam Books, 1981), 49.
81. Note Screwtape's advice to Wormwood: "Murder is no better than cards if cards can do the trick. Indeed, the safest road to Hell is the gradual one – the gentle slope, soft underfoot, without sudden turnings, without milestones, without signposts." Lewis, *Screwtape Letters*, 54, letter XII.
82. Tolstoy, *Death of Ivan Ilyich*, 50–1.
83. Ibid., 55–6.
84. Lewis, *Problem of Pain*, 91.
85. Tolstoy, *Death of Ivan Ilyich*, 83.
86. Ibid., 126–7.
87. Ibid., 119.
88. Ibid., 132.
89. Ibid., 133.
90. Note the parallels between Ivan's death and Christ's death: After suffering for an extended period of time (three days – surely no coincidence), Ivan dies for the sake of others.
91. Ibid.
92. The two roles of pain that are illustrated by the case of Ivan Ilyich are also illustrated by certain episodes in Lewis's *Chronicles of Narnia*. For a discussion of these ideas, see Erik Wielenberg, "Aslan the Terrible: Painful Encounters with Absolute Goodness," in *The Chronicles of Narnia and Philosophy*, ed. Greg Bassham and Jerry Walls (Chicago: Open Court, 2005), 221–30.

93. Tolstoy, *Ivan Ilyich*, 118.
94. Lewis, *Problem of Pain*, 33.
95. Hume, *Dialogues*, 69.
96. Ibid., 70.
97. Ibid., 69–73.
98. As one of my students, Loren Faulkner, pointed out.
99. Lewis, *Screwtape Letters*, 41, letter VIII.
100. John Beversluis, *C. S. Lewis and the Search for Rational Religion* (Grand Rapids, MI: Eerdmans, 1985), 113.
101. Lewis himself considers this possibility in *A Grief Observed*, 29–30.
102. Lewis, *Screwtape Letters*, 41, letter VIII.
103. In this respect, God's use of pain is akin to Socrates' use of perplexity. Socrates allegedly brought his interlocutors into a state of perplexity so that they would recognize their own ignorance with respect to some question and would be motivated to search for the correct answer to the question. But the state of being perplexed does not impose a particular answer on the interlocutor; rather, it (ideally) initiates a process of reflection in which the interlocutor is an agent, a process that is not limited to one possible outcome.
104. Beversluis, *Search for Rational Religion*, 117.
105. For a good defense of Lewis's solution to the problem of pain against some of the other objections suggested by this passage, see James Petrik, "In Defense of C. S. Lewis's Analysis of God's Goodness," *International Journal for Philosophy of Religion* 36 (1994), 45–56.
106. Lewis, *Problem of Pain*, 32.
107. Indeed, the claim that God does not love all humans seems to strike at the heart of Christianity itself.
108. Ibid., 110.
109. Matthew 22:39.
110. Lewis seems to consider this sort of objection himself (see *Problem of Pain*, 110–12), but, frankly, I think he could have done better job of responding to it.
111. Ibid., 110.
112. Lewis, *Grief*, 43.
113. This is just one necessary condition on the permissibility of inflicting suffering on another.
114. C. S. Lewis, *Mere Christianity* (New York: HarperCollins, 2001), 89.
115. Ibid., 91.
116. Ibid.
117. Petrik, "Defense of C. S. Lewis's Analysis," 51–2. Lewis also likens God to a surgeon (as well as to a dentist) in *A Grief Observed*, 43.
118. Lewis, *Problem of Pain*, 126.
119. Ibid., 93. In fact, Lewis was troubled by the existence of suffering that did not seem to function as it should. In a 1954 letter, he wrote: "I meet selfish egoists in whom suffering seems to produce only resentment,

hate, blasphemy, and more egoism. They are the real problem." Hooper, *Letters*, p. 441.

120. C. S. Lewis, *Till We Have Faces* (New York: Harcourt, 1984), 294, emphasis added.

121. See, for example: Peter Goldie, *On Personality* (New York: Routledge, 2004), Chapter 3; Immanuel Kant, *The Metaphysics of Morals*, trans. M. Gregor (Cambridge: Cambridge University Press, 1996), 155; R. E. Nisbett, and T. D. Wilson, "Telling More than We Can Know: Verbal Reports on Mental Processes," *Psychological Review* 84 (1977), 231–59; and R. Nisbett and L. Ross, *Human Inference: Strategies and Shortcomings of Social Judgment* (Englewood Cliffs, NJ: Prentice-Hall, 1980), particularly 195–227. A recent accessible book that summarizes much of the relevant evidence from psychology is Cordelia Fine, *A Mind of Its Own: How Your Brain Distorts and Deceives* (New York: Norton, 2006).

122. As far as I know, Lewis never explicitly developed the line of thought sketched here, although its basic components are present in his writing. In an essay written many years after the publication of *The Problem of Pain* and *Mere Christianity*, Lewis does develop the idea that Christianity predicts that God's activities will often *seem to us* to be evil (see Chapter 4, section 4.2.2). The response to the problem of not enough pain I have given here seems, in this respect, to anticipate Lewis's later essay.

123. But see letter XXVIII of *The Screwtape Letters* for some of Lewis's thoughts on death.

124. Notice that I didn't say the amount of pain required for the promotion of *that individual's* genuine happiness; Lewis' view does not require that a given individual's suffering promote that individual's genuine happiness. I will discuss this point in more detail later.

125. As Lewis himself would, I think, acknowledge: "It is so [very] difficult to believe that the travail of all creation which God Himself descended to share, at its most intense, may be necessary in the process of turning finite creatures (with free wills) into – well, Gods." Hooper (ed.), *Letters*, 440.

126. Fyodor Dostoevsky, *The Brothers Karamazov*, trans. A. H. MacAndrew (New York: Bantam Books, 1981), 291.

127. Information about metachromatic leukodystrophy was found at ⟨http://www.ninds.nih.gov/disorders/metachromatic_leukodystrophy/metachromatic_leukodystrophy.htm⟩ (accessed January 4, 2007).

128. Petrik, "Defense of C. S. Lewis's Analysis," 53.

129. Augustine, *Free Choice*, 116.

130. Lewis, *Problem of Pain*, 94–5.

131. Dostoevsky, *Brothers Karamazov*, 296.

132. In fact, Ivan's position seems to be that the suffering of children is so evil that *nothing* could possibly justify it; see, for instance, ibid., 295.

133. At this point, the Christian may point to the suffering and death of Christ as evidence that the answer to this question is "yes"; didn't God sacrifice His own son for the sake of humanity? However, this case is complicated by the fact that the Child God sacrificed was really Himself. Moreover, according to the Second Eucharistic Prayer, at any rate, it was a death He freely accepted. These factors make the suffering and death of Christ quite different from the suffering and death of a nondivine, unwilling child.

134. Augustine, *Free Choice*, 116–17.

135. See William Lane Craig and Walter Sinnott-Armstrong, *God? A Debate between a Christian and an Atheist* (Oxford: Oxford University Press, 2004), 92; and Marilyn McCord Adams, "Horrendous Evils and the Goodness of God," in Marilyn McCord Adams and Robert Merrihew Adams (eds.), *The Problem of Evil* (Oxford: Oxford University Press, 1990), 214.

136. For an interesting proposal about how Lewis's position might be modified and extended to handle the kind of problem under discussion here, see Thomas Talbott, "C. S. Lewis and the Problem of Evil," *Christian Scholar's Review* 17 (September 1987), 36–51.

137. Lewis, *Grief Observed*, 43.

138. Alvin Plantinga's free will defense is widely (though not universally) regarded as a successful defense. This near-consensus has motivated many contemporary atheists to move from defending logical versions of the problem of evil to evidential versions. For an interesting critical discussion of Plantinga's free will defense, see Quentin Smith, *Ethical and Religious Thought in Analytic Philosophy of Language* (New Haven, CT: Yale University Press, 1998), 148–57.

139. Lewis, *Problem of Pain*, 27.

140. Ibid., 86, emphasis added.

141. Ibid., 119–47.

142. Hume, *Dialogues*, 69.

143. Lewis, *Problem of Pain*, 19.

144. For a proposal along these lines, see Talbott, "Lewis and the Problem of Evil," 47–51.

145. The possibility of a justification of evil that is known by God but not by us has come to occupy a central role in contemporary philosophical discussions of the problem of evil; this idea receives further attention in the present work in sections 2.3 and 4.2.2 .

146. I should point out that this claim is distinct from the charge of incompleteness I have leveled against *The Problem of Pain*; from the fact that Lewis has not or even cannot account for such suffering it hardly follows that such suffering cannot be accounted for within a Christian framework. This claim is also highly controversial, and I do not pretend to have established it here; proper discussion of it would require a book-length project unto itself.

2. Beyond Nature

1. C. S. Lewis, *Mere Christianity* (New York: HarperCollins, 2001), 138.
2. Ibid., 25.
3. Romans 1:18–20. Not all have understood this passage as endorsing arguments from design. For one alternative interpretation of the passage, see Caleb Miller, "Faith and Reason," in Michael J. Murray (ed.), *Reason for the Hope Within* (Grand Rapids, MI: Eerdmans, 1999), 135–64, particularly 146–9.
4. Lewis, *Mere Christianity*, 24.
5. C. S. Lewis, *The Problem of Pain* (New York: HarperCollins, 2001), 3–4. For similar remarks, see *Mere Christianity*, 29; and C. S. Lewis, *The Four Loves* (New York: Harcourt, Brace, 1960), 21.
6. David Hume, *Dialogues Concerning Natural Religion*, second edition (Indianapolis: Hackett, 1998), 69. For more on this point of agreement between Lewis and Hume, see Chapter 4, section 4.3.2.
7. Walter Hooper (ed.), *The Collected Letters of C. S. Lewis, Volume II: Books, Broadcasts, and the War 1931–1949* (New York: HarperCollins, 2004), 747.
8. Robert Holyer, "C. S. Lewis – The Rationalist?," *Christian Scholar's Review* 18:2 (1988), 148–67.
9. Lewis, *Mere Christianity*, xvii.
10. Ibid., 5.
11. Ibid.
12. Elsewhere, Lewis says that we learn some moral facts "from parents and teachers, and friends and books" (ibid., 12). If we interpret Lewis's claim that moral facts are known "by nature" in the way I have suggested, there is no inconsistency here. A given proposition p might be such that (i) it *could* be known a priori and (ii) is in fact known (by a given person) on the basis of teaching. Many mathematical truths have these two features.
13. C. S. Lewis, *Miracles: A Preliminary Study* (New York: HarperCollins, 2001), 54. See also C. S. Lewis, "The Poison of Subjectivism," in *Christian Reflections* (Grand Rapids, MI: Eerdmans, 1995), 79.
14. Lewis, *Mere Christianity*, 25.
15. Ibid., 24–5.
16. John Beversluis, *C. S. Lewis and the Search for Rational Religion* (Grand Rapids, MI: Eerdmans), 50–1.
17. The logical form of the argument is: (i) If P, then Q; (ii) Q; (iii) therefore, P. This is an invalid argument form, meaning that the truth of the premises does not guarantee the truth of the conclusion.
18. Lewis, *Mere Christianity*, 25.
19. Ibid., 30.
20. Ibid., 29.
21. Ibid.

22. Bertrand Russell, "Has Religion Made Useful Contributions to Civilization?," in A. Seckel (ed.), *Bertrand Russell on God and Religion* (Amherst, NY: Prometheus, 1986), 169.

23. Bertrand Russell, "Why I Am Not a Christian," in Seckel (ed.), *Russell on Religion*, 83. The classic discussion of the relationship between God and morality, by which Russell's objection is obviously inspired, is the Platonic dialogue *Euthyphro*; see, in particular, Plato, *Five Dialogues*, second edition, trans. G. M. A. Grube (Indianapolis: Hackett, 2002), 12, 10a.

24. Lewis, "Poison of Subjectivism," 79.

25. Ibid.

26. Ibid.

27. Ibid., 80.

28. Ibid.

29. Steve Lovell, "Philosophical Themes from C. S. Lewis" (Ph.D. dissertation, University of Sheffield, 2003), Chapter 2, 23.

30. The contemporary literature on divine command theory includes some efforts to develop the notion that God = the Good. Of particular note in this regard are William Alston, "What Euthyphro Should Have Said," in William Lane Craig (ed.), *Philosophy of Religion: A Reader and Guide* (New Brunswick, NJ: Rutgers University Press, 2002), 283–98; and Robert Adams, *Finite and Infinite Goods* (Oxford: Oxford University Press, 1999). The approach suggested by these two works is quite subtle and complex, making use of a number of recent developments in contemporary analytic philosophy, and there is no way of knowing what Lewis would have thought of it. For these reasons, discussion of this contemporary approach is outside the scope of this work; however, I do discuss Adams's view in Erik Wielenberg, *Value and Virtue in a Godless Universe* (Cambridge: Cambridge University Press, 2005), 53–67.

31. Lovell develops a theory he calls "Divine Nature Theory" (DNT) that he maintains secures many of the conclusions Lewis was trying to establish (see Lovell, *Philosophical Themes*, Chapter 2, 26–34). The theory is interesting in its own right, but I think it is incompatible with Lewis's position in "The Poison of Subjectivism" because DNT implies that the moral law is created by God, a view Lewis denies in "Poison."

32. Lewis, *Mere Christianity*, 31, emphasis added.

33. Ibid., 36.

34. Ibid., 30.

35. Lovell explores a proposal along these lines; see Lovell, *Philosophical Themes*, Chapter 2, 25. For an extensive development of this basic idea by a contemporary philosopher, see Thomas Hurka, *Virtue, Vice, and Value* (Oxford: Oxford University Press, 2001).

36. Another option is that God's goodness consists in a combination of all of these factors – that God is good in virtue of being a loving moral law that desires genuine human happiness (and that all of this is necessary

for God to be good). Even if this proposal is coherent, the argument that I will make in section 2.2.4, if successful, tells against it.

37. Apparently the English word "dualism" was first used to refer to Zoroastrianism; see Charles Taliaferro, *Evidence and Faith: Philosophy and Religion since the Seventeenth Century* (Cambridge: Cambridge University Press, 2005), 30.

38. Lewis, *Mere Christianity*, 42.

39. For an account of the crusade against the Cathars, see Jonathan Sumption, *The Albigensian Crusade* (London: Faber and Faber, 1978).

40. Lewis, *Mere Christianity*, 42.

41. Hooper (ed.), *Letters II*, 532.

42. Lewis, *Mere Christianity*, 43.

43. Ibid., 43–4.

44. As one of my students, Courtney Hague, pointed out.

45. Augustine, *Confessions*, revised edition, trans. F. J Sheed (Indianapolis: Hackett, 1993), 26–7.

46. C. S. Lewis, *All My Road before Me: The Diary of C. S. Lewis, 1922–1927* (New York: Harvest Books, 2002), 191.

47. I owe the line of reasoning contained in this paragraph to an anonymous reader.

48. A slightly different version of the argument is based on the principle that all *rational* actions aim at goals regarded as good or worthwhile. But this principle establishes at most that the evil Power of Dualism does not act *rationally*, and I do not see why such a result is problematic for the Dualist; if the Dualist is comfortable with positing a thoroughly depraved and evil Power in opposition to God, it's hard to see why the Dualist should be reluctant to attribute irrationality to such a Power as well.

49. Romans 7:18–19.

50. Charles Freeman, *The Closing of the Western Mind: The Rise of Faith and the Fall of Reason* (New York: Vintage Books, 2005), 122.

51. Immanuel Kant, *Lectures on Ethics*, trans. L. Infield (Indianapolis: Hackett, 1930), 76.

52. Lewis, *Mere Christianity*, 45.

53. Ibid., emphasis added.

54. Recall my suggestion that Lewis offers a cumulative-case argument, of which his moral argument is merely one component. Might other aspects of this cumulative case break the stand-off described here? My short answer is no: The other phenomena Lewis appeals to in making his case for a Higher Power (our ability to reason and a desire that no earthly object can satisfy) do not, as far as I can see, tell against the existence of an evil Higher Power in addition to a good Power.

55. Lewis, *Mere Christianity*, 25, 29.

56. Lewis, *Problem of Pain*, 91.

57. Bertrand Russell, "The Existence and Nature of God," in L. Greenspan and S. Andersson (eds.), *Russell on Religion* (New York: Routledge, 1999), 99. Similar remarks may be found in Bertrand Russell, "Science and Religion," ibid., 137; and Bertrand Russell, "The Sense of Sin," ibid., 186.

58. Bertrand Russell and F. C. Copleston, "A Debate on the Existence of God," ibid., 141.

59. Ibid.

60. Bertrand Russell, "Science and Religion," ibid., 137.

61. Bertrand Russell and F. C. Copleston, "A Debate," ibid., 141.

62. Bertrand Russell, "Existence and Nature," ibid., 99.

63. Bertrand Russell, *Autobiography* (New York: Routledge, 1998), 126.

64. C. S. Lewis, *The Abolition of Man* (New York: HarperCollins, 2001), 83–101; also see ⟨www.religioustolerance.org/reciproc.htm⟩ (accessed January 11, 2007).

65. See Robert D. Hare, *Without Conscience: The Disturbing World of the Psychopaths among Us* (New York: The Guilford Press, 1999), 40–6; and Martha Stout, *The Sociopath Next Door* (New York: Broadway Books, 2005), 36–51. Stout refers to psychopaths as "ice people."

66. Hare, *Without Conscience*, 75–6.

67. Lewis, *Mere Christianity*, 5.

68. Hare, *Without Conscience*, 53.

69. Ibid., 129.

70. Lewis, *Mere Christianity*, 31.

71. Stout, *Sociopath Next Door*, 136.

72. David Hume, *Enquiries Concerning Human Understanding and Concerning the Principles of Morals*, third edition (Oxford: Oxford University Press, 1990), 271.

73. Ibid., 272.

74. Ibid., 273.

75. Ibid., 276.

76. Ibid.

77. Hume at one point actually suggests that these emotional dispositions are a product of the "Supreme Will"; ibid., 294. As we will see, Hume's considered views on religion make it unclear how seriously this remark should be taken. Nevertheless, Hume did make it.

78. Interestingly, Darwin identified the very same pair of emotional dispositions identified by Hume and, like Hume, suggested that they are part of human nature. See Robert Wright, *The Moral Animal: Evolutionary Psychology and Everyday Life* (New York: Random House, 1994), 184.

79. This understanding of evolutionary explanations focuses on *classical fitness* and ignores complications that arise from the concept of *inclusive fitness*; for useful discussions of inclusive fitness, see Wright, *Moral Animal*, 155–79; and David M. Buss, *Evolutionary Psychology: The New Science of the Mind*, second edition (Boston: Pearson Education, Inc., 2004),

13–15. I also ignore here the controversial notion of group selection; for a discussion of group selection in connection with morality, see Michael Shermer, *The Science of Good and Evil* (New York: Henry Holt & Co., 2004), 50–6.

80. Buss, *Evolutionary Psychology*, 48. Buss goes on to discuss one specific fertility clue – a relatively low waist-to-hip ratio.

81. Wright, *Moral Animal*, 196–7; also see Buss, *Evolutionary Psychology*, 254–7.

82. This brief sketch is just that; a number of subtleties and complexities arise in connection with reciprocal altruism and TIT FOR TAT. For an accessible discussion of some of these, see Chapter 9 of Wright's *The Moral Animal* and Chapter 9 of Buss's *Evolutionary Psychology*.

83. Wright, *Moral Animal*, 206.

84. François duc de la Rochefoucauld, *Maxims*, trans. L. Kronenberger (New York: Random House, 1959), 66, 180.

85. Of course, if this sort of explanation is plausible, it may lead one to wonder why psychopathy has not been eliminated through evolution. For a discussion of evolutionary explanations for psychopathy, see Hare, *Without Conscience*, 166–8.

86. To be clear: I do not mean to suggest that the evolutionary explanation I have sketched is nontheistic in the sense that it is incompatible with the existence of God; rather, the idea is that the explanation does not require the existence of God.

87. Lewis, "Poison of Subjectivism," 80.

88. Lovell, *Philosophical Themes*, Chapter 2, 21. Alston briefly mentions this possibility in "What Euthyphro Should Have Said," 291. A longer discussion of this view can be found in William Wainwright, *Religion and Morality* (Burlington, VT: Ashgate, 2005), 62–7. I briefly discuss Wainwright's remarks in Erik Wielenberg, "Response to Maria Antonaccio," *Conversations in Religion and Theology* 4:2 (November 2006), 219–24.

89. I develop just such a theory in Wielenberg, *Value and Virtue*.

90. For some useful discussions of this topic, see Colin McGinn, *Ethics, Evil, and Fiction* (Oxford: Oxford University Press, 1997), 7–60; and Russ Shafer-Landau, *Moral Realism: A Defence* (Oxford: Oxford University Press, 2005), 231–302. A number of recent writers (including McGinn) have suggested that the way we acquire moral knowledge is similar to the way we learn language and that, as in the case of language acquisition, we possess innate cognitive capacities dedicated to morality. This idea is explicated and defended at great length in Marc Hauser, *Moral Minds: How Nature Designed Our Universal Sense of Right and Wrong* (New York: HarperCollins, 2006).

91. Lewis, *Miracles*, 54.

92. For a recent extended defense of this sort of approach, see Michael Heumer, *Ethical Intuitionism* (New York: Palgrave Macmillan, 2005).

93. See Chapter 4, section 4.2.3. The line of reasoning hinted at here assumes the falsity of coherentism. For a useful discussion of this and related issues, see Richard Feldman, *Epistemology* (Upper Saddle River, NJ: Prentice-Hall, 2003), Chapter 4, 39–80.

94. Wright worries about this; see *Moral Animal*, 324–6.

95. Peter Singer, *How Are We to Live? Ethics in an Age of Self-Interest* (Amherst, NY: Prometheus Books, 1995), 226–7.

96. Singer also suggests this idea; see *How Are We to Live?*, 227.

97. For a brief sketch of a similar account, see Steven Pinker, "Evolution and Ethics," in J. Brockman (ed.), *Intelligent Thought* (New York: Vintage Books, 2006), 142–52.

98. Hume, *Dialogues*, 57.

99. Lewis, *Miracles*, 18.

100. Ibid., 43.

101. Anscombe's criticisms together with an account of the ensuing discussion and Lewis's response on that occasion are contained in G. E. M. Anscombe, "A Reply to Mr. C. S. Lewis's Argument that 'Naturalism' is Self-Refuting," in G. E. M. Anscombe, *The Collected Papers of G. E. M. Anscombe Volume II: Metaphyics and the Philosophy of Mind* (Oxford: Basil Blackwell, 1981), 224–32.

102. For two quite different views on the philosophical significance of Anscombe's criticisms, see Beversluis, *Rational Search*, 58–83; and Victor Reppert, *C. S. Lewis's Dangerous Idea: In Defense of the Argument from Reason* (Downers Grove, IL: InterVarsity Press, 2003), 45–71.

103. Anscombe, *Collected Papers*, ix.

104. The revised chapter is either ignored or overlooked by S. T. Joshi in his crude discussion of Lewis's argument from reason in "Surprised by Folly: C. S. Lewis," in S. T. Joshi, *God's Defenders: What They Believe and Why They Are Wrong* (Amherst, NY: Prometheus Books, 2003), 105–27.

105. Another relevant and useful discussion may be found in William Hasker's *The Emergent Self* (Ithaca, NY: Cornell University Press, 1999), 64–75.

106. Lewis, *Miracles*, 22.

107. Ibid.

108. In his response to Anscombe's criticism, Lewis noted that "*valid* was a bad word for what I meant; *veridical* . . . would have been better" (Anscombe, "A Reply," 231).

109. Lewis, *Miracles*, 23. As Beversluis points out (see *Rational Search*, 75), this claim is, strictly speaking, false. However, I do not think that this particular mistake is fatal to Lewis's argument. The essential point is that there must be some suitable perceived evidential or logical relationship between the propositions involved in the various thoughts if a given series of thoughts is to constitute reasoning that leads to knowledge – and this seems correct.

110. Ibid., 24, my addition.

111. Ibid., 25. Reppert suggests that from this point Lewis's argument runs as follows: "But if naturalism is true, then this type of causation, according to Lewis, is impossible. Events in nature are determined by the previous position of material particles, the laws of nature, and (perhaps) a chance factor. In that situation, according to Lewis, the object that is known determines the positive character of the act of knowing. But in rational inference what we know is a logical connection, and a logical connection is not in any particular spatio-temporal location." (Reppert, *Dangerous Idea*, 64) An interesting argument – but I see nothing in what Lewis says to indicate that he actually makes such an argument in *Miracles*.

112. Anscombe, "A Reply," 231.

113. Lewis, *Miracles*, 26.

114. Ibid., 27–8.

115. Beversluis appears to have missed both points. He suggests that Lewis's revised argument relies on the false claim that reasons must have causes and that this fact destroys the validity of reasoning (see Beversluis, *Rational Search*, 73–4). It should be clear from my reconstruction of Lewis's argument that in my view, Lewis's argument does not rely on any such claim.

116. Lewis, *Miracles*, 27.

117. Ibid., 43–4.

118. Ibid., 28.

119. Ibid.

120. Ibid., 25.

121. Ibid., 28.

122. Ibid.

123. Ibid., 37–8. For Reppert's discussion of intentionality, see *Dangerous Idea*, 74–6.

124. In his discussion of Lewis's argument from reason, Joshi describes Lewis as "cataclysmically ignorant" of the relevant scientific knowledge and characterizes his knowledge of science as "feeble to nonexistent" (Joshi, *God's Defenders*, 111). These are strong words, but I think that Joshi fails to grasp the complexity and subtlety of Lewis's argument.

125. C. S. Lewis, *Surprised by Joy: The Shape of My Early Life* (New York: Harcourt, 1955), 208.

126. For Plantinga's most recent presentation of the argument, together with a slew of critical responses to it and Plantinga's replies to those criticisms, see J. K. Beilby (ed.), *Naturalism Defeated? Essays on Plantinga's Evolutionary Argument Against Naturalism* (Ithaca, NY: Cornell University Press, 2002). For my own attempt to refute Plantinga's argument, see Erik Wielenberg, "How to Be an Alethically Rational Naturalist," *Synthese* 131:1 (April 2002), 81–98.

127. For one accessible and interesting attempt, see Daniel Dennett, *Kinds of Minds* (New York: Basic Books, 1996).

128. This is a crude rendering of a line of reasoning found in William Rowe, "The Problem of Evil and Some Varieties of Atheism," *American Philosophical Quarterly* 16 (1979), 335–41. This kind of argument is a version of the evidential problem of evil.

129. Daniel Howard-Snyder uses this phrase in his introduction to *The Evidential Argument from Evil* (Bloomington and Indianapolis: Indiana University Press, 1996), xvii.

130. Colin McGinn, *The Mysterious Flame: Conscious Minds in a Material World* (New York: Basic Books, 1999), 45–6.

131. Steven Pinker also develops this theme in *The Blank Slate: The Modern Denial of Human Nature* (New York: Viking, 2002), 239–40.

132. Reppert, *Dangerous Idea*, 13.

133. Lewis, *Surprised by Joy*, 17.

134. Ibid., 17–8. Joy also makes an appearance in *Till We Have Faces* when Psyche describes a kind of longing that she felt when she was at her happiest; see C. S. Lewis, *Till We Have Faces* (New York: Harcourt, 1984), 74.

135. Lewis, *Surprised by Joy*, 222.

136. Ibid., 238.

137. Ibid., 230.

138. Samuel Alexander, *Space, Time, and Deity*, Vol. II (New York: Macmillan, 1950), 374.

139. Ibid., 374–8.

140. As far as I can tell, Beversluis gave the argument this name; see his critical discussion of it in Beversluis, *Rational Search*, 8–31.

141. Peter Kreeft, "C. S. Lewis's Argument from Desire," in M. H. MacDonald and A. A. Tadie (eds.), *G. K. Chesterton and C. S. Lewis: The Riddle of Joy* (Grand Rapids, MI: Eerdmans, 1989), 249.

142. Lewis, *Mere Christianity*, 136–7.

143. Ibid., 135.

144. Lovell, *Philosophical Themes*, Chapter 6, 132.

145. Bertrand Russell, "From 'My Mental Development' and 'Reply to Criticisms'," in Greenspan and Andersson (eds.), *Russell on Religion*, 29.

146. C. S. Lewis, "The Weight of Glory," in *The Weight of Glory and Other Addresses* (New York: HarperCollins, 2001), 32–3.

147. From this point on I drop the cumbersome expression "natural and innate desires" and speak simply of "natural desires"; the shorter phrase is to be understood as shorthand for the longer, more cumbersome one.

148. Robert Holyer defends this line of reasoning in "The Argument from Desire," *Faith and Philosophy* 5:1 (January 1988), 61–70, particularly 68.

149. Lovell, *Philosophical Themes*, Chapter 6, 134; also see Kreeft, "Argument from Desire," 255.

150. See Kreeft, "Argument from Desire," 269.

151. See Wielenberg, *Value and Virtue*, 93, 122.

152. This way of formulating the inductive case is based on the discussion of inductive reasoning found in Howard Kahane, *Logic and Philosophy: A Modern Introduction*, sixth edition (Belmont, CA: Wadsworth, 1990), 336–42.
153. Holyer, "Argument from Desire," 69–70.
154. Of course, if there are characteristics that are conceptually linked to swanhood, we will be able to infer that the swan has those – for example, we can be sure that the swan is a physical object. But this point will not save the argument from desire, as there is little plausibility in the claim that it is a conceptual truth that natural desires can be satisfied.
155. Lovell, *Philosophical Themes*, Chapter 6, 140.
156. Ronald W. Dworkin, *Artificial Happiness: The Dark Side of the New Happy Class* (New York: Carroll & Graf Publishers, 2006), 8.
157. Wright, *Moral Animal*, 369. Interestingly, Lewis describes much the same phenomenon as one of the possible ways of dealing with the experience of Joy in *Mere Christianity* under the title of "The Fool's Way"; see Lewis, *Mere Christianity*, 135.
158. Lewis, *Surprised by Joy*, 170.
159. Ibid.
160. This is not to say that *theism itself* lacks empirical evidence; rather, my claim here is that there is no empirical evidence (beyond Joy itself) to support the specific hypothesis that God instilled Joy in human nature.
161. Kreeft, "Argument from Desire," 258.
162. Lovell, *Philosophical Themes*, Chapter 6, 141.
163. For useful discussions of some of the causes of our false beliefs, see Wright, *Moral Animal*; and Pinker, *Blank Slate*, particularly Chapters 12 and 13. For discussions of family conflict and phobias, see Buss, *Evolutionary Psychology*, Chapters 7 and 8 (families), and pages 90–5 (fear).
164. See Arthur Koestler, *The Ghost in the Machine* (New York: Macmillan, 1967), particularly Part 3, "Disorder," 225–339. I discuss some similar ideas (in much less detail) in Wielenberg, *Value and Virtue*, 127–42.
165. See Buss, *Evolutionary Psychology*, 28–9.
166. See, for instance, Pinker, *Blank Slate*.

3. Miracles

1. Graham Greene, "The Second Death," in Graham Greene, *Collected Short Stories* (New York: Penguin Books, 1986), 156.
2. Ibid., 157.
3. Ibid., 158.
4. Ibid. At the conclusion of the story, the narrator remembers being cured of his blindness, indicating that the miracles were real – and the dying man's fears well founded.

5. Similar issues are raised by Quentin Tarantino's 1994 film *Pulp Fiction*, in which hired killers Vincent and Jules take different views about whether their unlikely escape from a hail of bullets constitutes a miracle.

6. This very question is raised in Lewis's *The Lion, the Witch, and the Wardrobe*, the first book in the *Chronicles of Narnia* series. For a useful discussion, see Thomas D. Senor, "Trusting Lucy: Believing the Incredible," in Greg Bassham and Jerry Walls (eds.), *The Chronicles of Narnia and Philosophy* (Chicago: Open Court, 2005), 27–40.

7. Samuel Clarke, "A Discourse Concerning the Unalterable Obligations of Natural Religion, and the Truth and Certainty of the Christian Revelations," in John Earman (ed.), *Hume's Abject Failure: The Argument against Miracles* (Oxford: Oxford University Press, 2000), 120.

8. Thomas Sherlock, *The Tryal of the Witnesses of the Resurrection of Jesus*, eleventh edition (1729), in Earman (ed.), *Abject Failure*, 131.

9. Ibid., 132.

10. Earman, *Abject Failure*, 16.

11. Ibid., 18.

12. David Hume, *Dialogues Concerning Natural Religion*, second edition (Indianapolis: Hackett, 1998), 154.

13. Ibid. It is interesting to compare these remarks to Philo's remarks concerning the connection between general laws and suffering in the *Dialogues*; see Hume, *Dialogues*, 70–1.

14. C. S. Lewis, *Miracles: A Preliminary Study* (New York: HarperCollins, 2001), 156.

15. Ibid.

16. Ibid.

17. Ibid.

18. Ibid., 156–7.

19. Earman, *Abject Failure*, vii.

20. Ibid., 73.

21. Robert Fogelin, *A Defense of Hume on Miracles* (Princeton, NJ: Princeton University Press, 2003), 3.

22. David Hume, "Of Miracles," in Hume, *Dialogues*, 122.

23. Ibid., 108.

24. Ibid.

25. Contra Earman; see Earman, *Abject Failure*, 23.

26. More precisely, P(the sun will not rise tomorrow/observed constant conjunction of night followed by sunrise) = n, where n is extremely small but greater than zero. For a defense of this interpretation, see Fogelin, *Defense*, 47–53.

27. Hume, "Of Miracles," 108.

28. Ibid., 111. In a footnote (112, n. 4), he offers a more restrictive definition, declaring a miracle to be "a transgression of a law of nature by a particular volition of the Deity, or by the interposition of some invisible

agent." However, Hume seems to use the looser definition of "miracle" throughout the essay.

29. See Earman, *Abject Failure*, 12; and Fogelin, *Defense*, 27.
30. Hume, "Of Miracles," 111. Note that what is given here is a necessary condition on a law of nature, not a complete definition.
31. Ibid.
32. Ibid., 112, emphasis added.
33. Ibid., 109.
34. For a useful discussion of this point, see Fogelin, *Defense*, 24–9.
35. Hume's claim here is quite plausible; for an account of many such debunked miracles, see Karen Armstrong, *A History of God* (New York: Ballantine Books, 1993).
36. Hume, "Of Miracles," 114–15.
37. Ibid., 114.
38. Ibid., 113.
39. Ibid., 114.
40. Ibid., 113.
41. Foeglin, *Defense*, 29.
42. Hume, "Of Miracles," 112.
43. Ibid., 108.
44. Ibid., 122.
45. Here is another similar example: Despite the general unreliability of reports found in tabloids, they sometimes report events that actually occurred. And one can often pick out which reports are accurate based on the nature of the events reported.
46. Fogelin, *Defense*, 31.
47. Hume, "Of Miracles," 122, emphasis added.
48. Lewis, *Miracles*, 2. This passage explains why the subtitle of *Miracles* is *A Preliminary Study*. It is a *philosophical* study that is preliminary to any *historical* inquiry into the Christian miracles.
49. Ibid, 5. Unlike Hume, Lewis does not think that a miracle necessarily violates some law of nature, and the analyses of miracle offered by the two thinkers seem to differ. However, we can safely ignore this disagreement, since the two thinkers agree that the Resurrection of Christ is a miracle.
50. Ibid., Chapter 8.
51. Ibid., Chapter 11.
52. Ibid., 159.
53. Ibid.
54. Ibid., 162.
55. Ibid., emphasis added.
56. Fogelin discusses this objection of Lewis's in Fogelin, *Defense*, 19.
57. Ibid., 162–4.
58. Hume, "Of Miracles," 108.
59. Lewis, *Miracles*, 162.

60. See Steve Lovell, "Philosophical Themes from C. S. Lewis" (Ph.D. dissertation, University of Sheffield, 2003), Chapter 4, 75.
61. Hume, "Of Miracles," 109.
62. Lovell, *Philosophical Themes*, Chapter 4, 76.
63. Lewis, *Miracles*, 166.
64. Ibid., 168.
65. C. S. Lewis, *Mere Christianity* (New York: HarperCollins, 2001), 25.
66. Lewis, *Miracles*, 170.
67. Ibid., 171.
68. More precisely: Hume thinks the relevant claim of conditional probability is P(miracle M occurred/past experience), whereas Lewis thinks the relevant claim is P(miracle M occurred/M's level of fitness).
69. Ibid., 170.
70. Ibid., 173.
71. Ibid., 175–6.
72. Ibid., 178.
73. Ibid.
74. Ibid., 179.
75. Ibid., 180.
76. Ibid., 181.
77. Ibid., 180.
78. Ibid., 190.
79. Ibid., 188.
80. Ibid., 191.
81. Ibid.
82. Ibid.
83. C. S. Lewis, *The Problem of Pain* (New York: HarperCollins, 2001), 77–8.
84. Lewis, *Miracles*, 213.
85. Ibid., 159.
86. Interestingly, it appears that Lewis actually accepts Hume's official conclusion. Hume and Lewis agree that religious testimony *alone* is never enough to make it reasonable to believe that a miracle occurred, but Lewis thinks that fitness and testimony together can do the trick. However, Hume's argument actually supports a stronger conclusion than the one he officially draws. If Hume's argument succeeds, it shows that it is reasonable to believe that all religious testimony in support of miracles is false. This does conflict with Lewis's position, which explains why Lewis is so concerned to criticize Hume's reasoning.
87. Ibid., 170.
88. Charles Taliaferro arrives at a similar conclusion in his discussion of Hume's argument against miracles; see Charles Taliaferro, *Evidence and Faith: Philosophy and Religion since the Seventeenth Century* (Cambridge: Cambridge University Press, 2005), 197.
89. Terence Penelhum, "Hume's Criticisms of Natural Theology," in James F. Sennett and Douglas Groothius (eds.), *In Defense of Natural Theology: A*

Post-Humean Assessment (Downers Grove, IL: InterVarsity Press, 2005), 25.

90. Hume, "Miracles," 123–4.
91. Hume's writings do, of course, include criticisms of natural theology. His *Dialogues Concerning Natural Religion* contains criticisms of the main theistic arguments that were popular at the time, most notably the argument from design (for more on this, see Chapter 4, section 4.3). Penelhum argues that section XI of Hume's *Enquiry Concerning Human Understanding* (which immediately follows "Of Miracles") is also intended to undermine the argument from design; see Terence Penelhum, "Religion in the *Enquiry* and After," in *Themes in Hume: The Self, the Will, Religion* (Oxford: Oxford University Press, 2000), 222–43.
92. Lewis, *Mere Chrstianity*, 52–3.
93. See R. B. Bernstein, *Thomas Jefferson* (Oxford: Oxford University Press, 2003), 139–40 and 179.
94. See Daniel Howard-Snyder, "Was Jesus Mad, Bad, or God? . . . or Merely Mistaken," *Faith and Philosophy* 21:4 (October 2004), 456–79.
95. Richard Chessick, "Who Does He Think He Is: Remarks on the Psychology of Jesus," *American Journal of Psychoanalysis* 55:1 (March 1995), 36.
96. Lewis, *Miracles*, 174.
97. Lewis, *Problem of Pain*, 13.

4. Faith, Design, and True Religion

1. Charles Freeman suggests that the roots within the Christian tradition of such a view of faith can be found in the writings of Paul the Apostle; see Charles Freeman, *The Closing of the Western Mind: The Rise of Faith and the Fall of Reason* (New York: Vintage Books Freeman, 2005), 119–20.
2. A. C. Grayling, "Faith," in *Meditations for the Humanist: Ethics for a Secular Age* (Oxford: Oxford University Press, 2002), 117.
3. Quoted in Freeman, *Western Mind*, 272.
4. Bertrand Russell, "The Existence and Nature of God," in L. Greenspan and S. Andersson (eds.), *Russell on Religion* (New York: Routledge, 1999), 94.
5. Bertrand Russell, "Can Religion Cure Our Troubles?," in *Why I Am Not a Christian and Other Essays on Religion and Related Subjects* (New York: Simon & Schuster, 1957), 194.
6. Ibid., 197. For a useful discussion of the connection between the view Russell criticizes here and the horrors of Stalinism, see Jonathan Glover, *Humanity: A Moral History of the Twentieth Century* (New Haven, CT and London: Yale University Press, 2000), 274–82.
7. Bertrand Russell, "What I Believe," in *Not a Christian*, 56

8. Bertrand Russell, "The Value of Free Thought," in A. Seckel (ed.), *Bertrand Russell on God and Religion* (Amherst, NY: Prometheus Books, 1986), 239.

9. Ibid., 240.

10. Ibid., 253–4.

11. C. S. Lewis, *Mere Christianity* (New York: HarperCollins, 2001), 138.

12. C. S. Lewis, *The Screwtape Letters* (New York: Touchstone, 1996), 59. Victor Reppert argues that this view of faith is also evident in *The Chronicles of Narnia*; see Victor Reppert, "The Green Witch and the Great Debate: Freeing Narnia from the Spell of the Lewis-Anscombe Legend," in Greg Bassham and Jerry Walls (eds.), *The Chronicles of Narnia and Philosophy* (Chicago: Open Court Press, 2005), 260–72.

13. C. S. Lewis, "Man or Rabbit," in *God in the Dock: Essays on Theology and Ethics* (Grand Rapids, MI: Eerdmans, 1970), 108–9.

14. Lewis, *Mere Christianity*, 139. For a similar definition, see C. S. Lewis, "Religion: Reality or Substitute?," in *Christian Reflections* (Grand Rapids, MI: Eerdmans, 1995), 42.

15. Lewis, *Mere Christianity*, 140.

16. Ibid., 139.

17. Ibid.

18. Lewis, "Reality or Substitute," 43.

19. Lewis, *Mere Christianity*, 141.

20. Lewis, *Screwtape Letters*, 19.

21. Ibid., 21.

22. Bertrand Russell, "Why I Am Not a Christian," in Greenspan and Andersson (eds.), *Russell on Religion*, 90.

23. Lewis, *Mere Christianity*, 141.

24. Bertrand Russell, "The Sense of Sin," in Greenspan and Andersson (eds.), *Russell on Religion*, 189–90.

25. John Beversluis, *C. S. Lewis and the Search for Rational Religion* (Grand Rapids, MI: Eerdmans, 1985), 93.

26. C. S. Lewis, "On Obstinacy in Belief," in *The World's Last Night and Other Essays* (New York: Harcourt, 1955), 17.

27. Ibid., 21.

28. Lewis, *Mere Christianity*, 138.

29. Lewis, "Obstinacy," 22.

30. Ibid., 27.

31. Ibid., 25.

32. Ibid., 23.

33. Ibid., 24–5.

34. Daniel Howard-Snyder, "God, Evil, and Suffering," in Michael J. Murray (ed.), *Reason for the Hope Within* (Grand Rapids, MI: Eerdmans, 1999), 113.

35. The interpretation of Lewis's view I am arguing for here is very similar to the view put forth by Stephen Wykstra in "The Humean Obstacle

to Evidential Arguments from Suffering: On Avoiding the Evils of 'Appearance'," *International Journal for Philosophy of Religion* 16 (1984), 73–93.

36. Lewis, "Obstinacy," 21 (emphasis added).
37. In fact, there is a tremendous amount of literature concerning arguments along these lines; a healthy chunk of this literature is conveniently gathered together in Daniel Howard-Snyder (ed.), *The Evidential Argument from Evil* (Bloomington: Indiana University Press, 1996).
38. Lewis, "Obstinacy," 19–20. I said that these remarks are *almost* absolutely correct because Lewis makes the false assumption that Christianity and atheism are the only options. So there are far more than the four predicaments Lewis identifies.
39. See, for instance, David Hume, *Enquiries Concerning Human Understanding and Concerning the Principles of Morals*, third edition, ed. L. A. Selby-Bigger (Oxford: Oxford University Press, 1975), 165.
40. Ibid., 96.
41. Ibid., 41.
42. Ibid., 110.
43. David O'Connor, *Hume on Religion* (New York: Routledge, 2001), 9.
44. Hume, *Enquiries*, 279.
45. Ibid., 14.
46. Ibid., 12.
47. Ibid.
48. H. O. Mounce, *Hume's Naturalism* (New York: Routledge, 1999), 15.
49. Hume, *Enquiries*, 34.
50. Ibid.
51. Ibid., 37. This point should sound familiar; recall that Lewis argued that we can know that the future will resemble the past only if we know that naturalism is false.
52. Ibid.
53. Ibid., 41.
54. Ibid., 43–4.
55. Ibid., 45.
56. In his earlier work *A Treatise of Human Nature*, Hume reserves the term "knowledge" for "relations . . . which [depend] solely upon ideas"; David Hume, *A Treatise of Human Nature*, second edition, ed. L. A. Selby-Bigge (Oxford: Oxford University Press, 1978), 70. Beliefs formed on the basis of inductive reasoning are not in this category, and so, strictly speaking, the Hume of the *Treatise* would not count them as instances of knowledge. However, in the *Treatise* Hume seems to want to count as knowledge only beliefs that are absolutely certain, beyond any possible doubt, whereas in the *Enquiry* he seems to use "knowledge" in a looser sense – one that is closer to ordinary, nonphilosophical usage. Thus, when I attribute to Hume the view that custom can produce knowledge, I am using "knowledge" in the looser sense.

57. See Hume, *Enquiries,* 104.
58. When I speak of warrant, I mean *epistemic* warrant – warrant as the thing that turns true belief into knowledge.
59. See, for example, Alvin Plantinga, "Reason and Belief in God," in J. Sennett (ed.), *The Analytic Theist: An Alvin Plantinga Reader* (Grand Rapids, MI: Eerdmans, 1998), 102–61.
60. Thus, Hume holds the view that H. O. Mounce calls "epistemological naturalism," according to which "our knowledge depends on what is given us by nature" (Mounce, *Hume's Naturalism,* 11).
61. It is important to note that though there is no evidence that bestows warrant on such beliefs, it does not follow that *nothing* gives them warrant; they may have warrant derived from another source. For more on this, see Plantinga, "Reason and Belief."
62. This indicates how Hume would answer the question from the end of Chapter 3: What is the basis of our belief that nature is uniform? Hume's answer: It is a properly basic belief, one that we can know even though we cannot infer it from other things we know.
63. Bertrand Russell, "The Faith of a Rationalist," in Seckel (ed.), *Bertrand Russell on God and Religion,* 88. Also see Bertrand Russell, *The Problems of Philosophy* (Oxford: Oxford University Press, 1959), 111–12.
64. C. S. Lewis, *Miracles: A Preliminary Study* (New York: HarperCollins, 2001), 54. Also see C. S. Lewis, "Why I Am Not a Pacifist," in *The Weight of Glory* (New York: HarperCollins, 2001), 66.
65. David Hume, *Dialogues Concerning Natural Religion,* second edition (Indianapolis: Hackett, 1998), 15.
66. Ibid., 18.
67. Some qualifications may be required here; for instance, the principle holds only when the creations in question represent the best work of which the two designers are capable. But nothing in what follows depends on this point.
68. Ibid., 16.
69. Ibid., 23.
70. Ibid., 25.
71. O'Connor, for instance, refers to it as "Cleanthes's second design argument"; see O'Connor, *Hume on Religion,* 77–93. Charles Taliaferro also sees the irregular argument as one that, unlike Cleanthes's earlier argument, is based on an inference to the best explanation; see Charles Taliaferro, *Evidence and Faith: Philosophy and Religion since the Seventeenth Century* (Cambridge: Cambridge University Press, 2005), 186.
72. This seems to be Gaskin's position; see J. C. A. Gaskin, *Hume's Philosophy of Religion,* second edition (Atlantic Highlands, NJ: Humanities Press International, 1988), 51, 129.
73. See Hume, *Treatise,* 103–4.
74. Hume, *Enquiries,* 43–4.
75. Hume, *Dialogues,* 25.

76. Ibid., 26. Hume makes very similar remarks (in his own voice) in *The Natural History of Religion*. See David Hume, *Dialogues and Natural History of Religion*, ed. J. C. A. Gaskin (Oxford: Oxford University Press, 1993), 137.

77. Gaskin and O'Connor both argue that in Hume's view, belief in God is not what Gaskin calls a "natural belief." Both argue that belief in God fails to meet one of the conditions required for it to be a natural belief: that it be universally accepted (see Gaskin, *Hume's Philosophy of Religion*, 122–3; and O'Connor, *Hume on Religion*, 92). The passage I just quoted suggests Hume's *explanation* of why belief in God does not satisfy this universality requirement.

78. Hume, *Dialogues*, 26.

79. Ibid.

80. William Lad Sessions, *Reading Hume's Dialogues: A Veneration for True Religion* (Bloomington: Indiana University Press, 2002), 83.

81. Hume, *Dialogues*, 23.

82. See Parts VI, VII, and VIII, respectively.

83. Ibid., 53.

84. Ibid., 77.

85. Ibid., 79.

86. Gaskin in Hume, *Natural History*, xxiii.

87. O'Connor, *Hume on Religion*, 195.

88. Sessions, *Reading Hume's Dialogues*, 185.

89. "Hollowing out" is O'Connor's expression; see O'Connor, *Hume on Religion*, 197.

90. Hume, *Dialogues*, 80–1. I will ignore the question of whether the disagreement Philo describes is properly characterized as a purely verbal one.

91. Ibid., 80.

92. Ibid., 81. We see Philo here explicitly alluding to two of his earlier proposed alternatives to the design hypothesis.

93. Ibid.

94. Ibid. This is in direct contrast with Lewis's insistence that God's goodness cannot be entirely unlike human goodness.

95. Ibid., 66.

96. Ibid., 88.

97. Ibid.

98. Jerry Walls has made the interesting suggestion that if we also include the moral nature of human beings as described by Hume in the data under consideration, the proper conclusion to draw is that the cause of the universe is actually evil (because it constructed us such that we care deeply about human happiness, while the cause itself cares nothing for human happiness). For this argument, see Jerry Walls, "Hume on Divine Amorality," *Religious Studies* 26 (June 1990), 257–66. Walls's ultimate conclusion is that "the only kind of God we can plausibly believe in is a

perfectly good God" (ibid., 265), but this conclusion relies on a kind of moral argument that, as far as I can tell, renders the Humean argument entirely superfluous. Because our concern here is with Hume's actual position, I will not consider Walls's argument in any detail.

99. Hume, *Dialogues*, 88.

100. Hume, *Natural History*, 134.

101. Ibid., 136, 138, 142, 150, 153, 154, 155, 159, 183.

102. Ibid., 153.

103. Susan Neiman, *Evil in Modern Thought: An Alternative History of Philosophy* (Princeton, NJ: Princeton University Press, 2002), 167.

104. Hume, *Natural History*, 25.

105. O'Connor reaches a somewhat similar conclusion, although he focuses on just two of the three ideas I have identified (skepticism and design) and suggests that perhaps Hume never arrived at a settled position, but instead was "genuinely of two minds, at once inclining two contrary ways" (O'Connor, *Hume on Religion*, 218). For a somewhat different interpretation, see Terence Penelhum, "Natural Belief and Religious Belief in Hume's Philosophy" and "Religion in the *Enquiry* and After," both in *Themes in Hume: The Self, the Will, Religion* (Oxford: Oxford University Press, 2000), 204–43. At the end of the latter essay, Penelhum concludes that Hume was probably a "closet atheist" (242).

106. Hume, *Dialogues*, 69.

107. Lewis, *Mere Christianity*, 29.

108. Russell, "Existence and Nature," 98.

109. Russell, "Not a Christian," 82. Russell made similar remarks twelve years later; see Russell, "Existence and Nature," 94.

110. Ibid., 96.

111. Russell, "Free Thought," 257.

112. Russell, "Not a Christian," 81.

113. See, for example, Peter van Inwagen, *Metaphysics* (Boulder, CO: Westview Press, 1993), 132–48.

114. Russell, "Free Thought," 258.

115. John Stuart Mill, "Theism," in *Three Essays on Religion* (Amherst, NY: Prometheus Books, 1998), 176–7.

116. Lewis, *Problem of Pain*, 18.

117. Lewis, *Screwtape Letters*, letter VIII, 41.

118. Russell, "Free Thought," 261.

119. Bertrand Russell, "A Free Man's Worship," in *Not a Christian*, 105–6.

120. Hume, *Dialogues*, 37–8.

121. Kurt Vonnegut, *The Sirens of Titan* (New York: Dell Publishing, 1998).

122. Douglas Adams, "So Long, and Thanks for All the Fish," in *The Ultimate Hitchhiker's Guide to the Galaxy* (New York: Ballantine Books, 2002), 610.

123. Hume, *Dialogues*, 88.

124. Romans 1:20.

125. This may explain why many contemporary Christian apologists advance cumulative-case arguments of which design arguments constitute just one part; see, for example, James Sennett, "Hume's Stopper and the Natural Theology Project," and R. Douglas Geivett, "David Hume and a Cumulative Case Argument," both in James F. Sennett and Douglas Groothius (eds.), *In Defense of Natural Theology: A Post-Humean Assessment* (Downers Grove, IL: InterVarsity Press, 2005), 82–104 and 297–329.

126. Sessions, *Hume's Dialogues*, 196.

127. Hume, *Dialogues*, 88.

128. Ibid., 88–9.

129. Hume, *Enquiry Concerning Human Understanding*, 132–48.

130. Ibid., 146.

131. Hume, *Dialogues*, 89.

132. Ibid., 4.

133. Ibid., 12, emphasis added.

134. Globalization only makes the need for reason more obvious; even if there were only one alleged sacred text, reason would still be required to evaluate its authenticity.

135. Hume, "Of Miracles," in *Dialogues*, 122.

136. Hume, *Dialogues*, 58.

137. Ibid., 89.

138. Gaskin suggests a similar interpretation; see Gaskin, *Hume's Philosophy of Religion*, 227.

139. I owe this suggestion to Jordan Harp.

140. Hume, *Dialogues*, 85.

141. Ibid., 82.

142. Ibid., 85. The meaning of the remark about "fasces and axes" is that both political authority and military power should be kept out of the hands of religious leaders.

143. Hume, *Natural Religion*, 184.

144. David Hume, "Of Superstition and Enthusiasm," in *Selected Essays* (Oxford: Oxford University Press, 1998), 38.

145. Ibid.

146. Hume, *Natural Religion*, 167.

147. Ibid., 157.

148. Ibid., 212–13.

149. Ibid., 166.

150. In his 1794 work *The Age of Reason*, Thomas Paine criticizes this aspect of Christianity, referring derisively to "the Christian system of arithmetic" (Thomas Paine, *The Age of Reason* [New York: Citadel Press, 1948], 79).

151. Hume, *Natural Religion*, 184. Gaskin draws the same conclusion; see Gaskin, *Hume's Philosophy of Religion*, 191.

152. C. S. Lewis, *Surprised by Joy: The Shape of My Early Life* (New York: Harcourt, 1955), 63.

153. Bertrand Russell, "Has Religion Made Useful Contributions to Civilization?," in *Not a Christian*, 24.
154. Ibid.
155. Ibid., 47.
156. Bertrand Russell, "The Essence of Religion," in Greenspan and Andersson (eds.), *Russell on Religion*, 57.
157. Ibid.
158. Ibid., 59.
159. Ibid., 58.
160. Ibid., 60.
161. Ibid.
162. Ibid., 61.
163. Ibid.
164. Ibid., 64.
165. Ibid., 65.
166. Matthew 22:37–9.
167. Russell, "Essence of Religion," 67.
168. Ibid., 66.
169. Ibid., p. 67.
170. Ibid., 67–8. Perhaps we could call this a "Russellian Holy Trinity"?
171. Ibid., 68.
172. C. S. Lewis, "Religion without Dogma?," in *God in the Dock*, 131.
173. Russell, "Essence of Religion," 68.
174. Genesis 3:5.
175. Lewis, *Problem of Pain*, 75.
176. Russell, "Essence of Religion," 59.
177. Lewis, *Problem of Pain*, 76.
178. Ibid., 79.
179. Ibid., 88.
180. Russell, "Essence of Religion," 60.
181. Lewis, *Problem of Pain*, 89.
182. Ibid.
183. Lewis, *Screwtape Letters*, letter XIV, 59.
184. See, for example, Karen Armstrong, *A History of God* (New York: Ballantine Books, 1994), 396–9; Andrew Newberg, Eugene D'Aquili, and Vince Rause, *Why God Won't Go Away: Brain Science and the Biology of Belief* (New York: Ballantine Books, 2001); and Samuel Harris, *The End of Faith: Religion, Terror, and the Future of Reason* (New York: Norton, 2004).
185. Walter Hooper (ed.), *Letters of C. S. Lewis*, revised edition (Orlando, FL: Harcourt, 1993), 501.
186. Lewis, *The Four Loves* (New York: Harcourt Brace, 1960), 30.
187. Lewis, *Mere Christianity*, xv.
188. Ibid., xvi.

189. C. S. Lewis, "Answers to Questions on Christianity," in *God in the Dock*, 60.

190. Hooper (ed.), *Letters*, 428. In the same letter, Lewis goes on to reject pacifism and endorse capital punishment and killing in war, so his advice here does not stem from a general prohibition against all types of violence; see also Lewis, "Not a Pacifist," 64–90.

191. Lewis, *Mere Christianity*, 82–7.

192. Ibid., 83.

193. Ibid.

194. Ibid., 104–14.

195. Ibid., 112.

196. Ibid.

197. C. S. Lewis, "On the Transmission of Christianity," in *God in the Dock*, 118.

198. Ibid., 119. It should also be pointed out that Lewis's conception of Christian education is quite different from that of, say, Demea. It consists of telling the young "what the Christians say" and providing them with *arguments* in favor of Christianity (ibid., 115).

199. Hooper (ed.), *Letters*, 473.

200. Lewis, "Answers," 61.

201. Exodus 20:7.

202. C. S. Lewis, "Meditation on the Third Commandment," in *God in the Dock*, 198.

203. Ibid.

204. Ibid., 198–9.

205. Ibid., 199.

206. More precisely, all three accepted qualified evidentialism, as described earlier in section 4.2.3.

207. Lewis, "Transmission of Christianity," 117.

REFERENCES

Adams, Douglas. 2002. *The Ultimate Hitchhiker's Guide to the Galaxy*. New York: Ballantine Books.

Adams, Marilyn McCord. 1990. "Horrendous Evils and the Goodness of God," in *The Problem of Evil*, ed. Marilyn McCord Adams and Robert Merrihew Adams. Oxford: Oxford University Press.

Adams, Robert. 1999. *Finite and Infinite Goods*. Oxford: Oxford University Press.

Alexander, Samuel. 1950. *Space, Time, and Deity*, Vol. II. New York: Macmillan.

Alston, William. 2002. "What Euthyphro Should Have Said," in *Philosophy of Religion: A Reader and Guide*, ed. William Lane Craig. New Brunswick, NJ: Rutgers University Press.

Anscombe, G. E. M. 1981. "A Reply to Mr. C. S. Lewis's Argument That 'Naturalism' Is Self-Refuting," in *The Collected Papers of G. E. M. Anscombe Volume II: Metaphyics and the Philosophy of Mind*. Oxford: Basil Blackwell.

Aquinas, Thomas. 1947. *Summa Theologica*. New York: Benziger Brothers Inc.

Armstrong, Karen. 1993. *A History of God*. New York: Ballantine Books.

Augustine. 1993. *Confessions*, revised edition, trans. F. J Sheed. Indianapolis: Hackett.

————. 1993. *On Free Choice of the Will*, trans. T. Williams. Indianapolis: Hackett.

Ayer, A. J. 2000. *Hume: A Very Short Introduction*. Oxford: Oxford University Press.

Beilby, J. K., ed. 2002. *Naturalism Defeated? Essays on Plantinga's Evolutionary Argument Against Naturalism*. Ithaca, NY: Cornell University Press.

Bernstein, R. B. *Thomas Jefferson*. 2003. Oxford: Oxford University Press.

Beversluis, John. 1985. *C. S. Lewis and the Search for Rational Religion*. Grand Rapids, MI: Eerdmans.

References

Buss, David M. 2004. *Evolutionary Psychology: The New Science of the Mind*, second edition. Boston: Pearson Education, Inc.

Chessick, Richard. 1995. Who does he think he is: Remarks on the psychology of Jesus. *American Journal of Psychoanalysis* 55:1: 29–39.

Clarke, Samuel. 2000. "A Discourse Concerning the Unalterable Obligations of Natural Religion, and the Truth and Certainty of the Christian Revelations," in John Earman (ed.), *Hume's Abject Failure: The Argument against Miracles*. Oxford: Oxford University Press.

Craig, William Lane, and Sinnott-Armstrong, Walter. 2004. *God? A Debate between a Christian and an Atheist*. Oxford: Oxford University Press.

Cudworth, Ralph. 1996. *A Treatise Concerning Eternal and Immutable Morality*, ed. S. Hutton. Cambridge: Cambridge University Press.

Dawkins, Richard. 2006. *The God Delusion*. New York: Houghton Mifflin.

Dennett, Daniel. 1996. *Kinds of Minds*. New York: Basic Books.

Dostoevsky, Fyodor. 1981. *The Brothers Karamazov*, trans. A. H. MacAndrew. New York: Bantam Books.

Draper, Paul. 1989. Pain and pleasure: An evidential problem for theists. *NOUS* 23: 331–50.

Dworkin, Ronald W. 2006. *Artificial Happiness: The Dark Side of the New Happy Class*. New York: Carroll & Graf Publishers.

Earman, John, ed. 2000. *Hume's Abject Failure: The Argument against Miracles*. Oxford: Oxford University Press.

Feldman, Richard. 2003. *Epistemology*. Upper Saddle River, NJ: Prentice Hall.

Fine, Cordelia. 2006. *A Mind of Its Own: How Your Brain Distorts and Deceives*. New York: Norton.

Fogelin, Robert. 2003. *A Defense of Hume on Miracles*. Princeton, NJ: Princeton University Press.

Freeman, Charles. 2005. *The Closing of the Western Mind: The Rise of Faith and the Fall of Reason*. New York: Vintage Books.

Gaskin, J. C. A. 1988. *Hume's Philosophy of Religion*, second edition. Atlantic Highlands, NJ: Humanities Press International.

Glover, Jonathan. 2000. *Humanity: A Moral History of the Twentieth Century*. New Haven, CT and London: Yale University Press.

Goldie, Peter. 2004. *On Personality*. New York: Routledge.

Grayling, A. C. 2002. *Meditations for the Humanist: Ethics for a Secular Age*. Oxford: Oxford University Press.

Greene, Graham. 1986. "The Second Death," in *Collected Short Stories*. New York: Penguin Books.

Hare, Robert D. 1999. *Without Conscience: The Disturbing World of the Psychopaths among Us*. New York: The Guilford Press.

Harris, Samuel. 2004. *The End of Faith: Religion, Terror, and the Future of Reason*. New York: Norton.

Hasker, William. 1999. *The Emergent Self.* Ithaca, NY: Cornell University Press.

Hauser, Marc. 2006. *Moral Minds: How Nature Designed Our Universal Sense of Right and Wrong.* New York: HarperCollins.

Heumer, Michael. 2005. *Ethical Intuitionism.* New York: Palgrave Macmillan.

Holyer, Robert. 1988. The argument from desire. *Faith and Philosophy* 5:1: 61–70.

———. 1988 C. S. Lewis – the rationalist? *Christian Scholar's Review* 18:2: 148–67.

Hooper, Walter, ed. 1993. *Letters of C. S. Lewis,* revised edition. Orlando, FL: Harcourt.

———, ed. 2004. *The Collected Letters of C. S. Lewis, Volume II: Books, Broadcasts, and the War 1931–1949.* New York: HarperCollins.

Howard-Snyder, Daniel. 1996. *The Evidential Argument from Evil.* Bloomington and Indianapolis: Indiana University Press.

———. 1999. "God, Evil, and Suffering," in *Reason for the Hope Within*, ed. Michael J. Murray. Grand Rapids, MI: Eerdmans.

———. 2004. Was Jesus mad, bad, or God? . . . or merely mistaken. *Faith and Philosophy* 21:4: 456–79.

Hume, David. 1943. "My Own Life," in *The Forgotten Hume,* ed. E. C. Mossner. New York: Columbia University Press.

———. 1978. *A Treatise of Human Nature*, second edition. Oxford: Oxford University Press.

———. 1990. *Enquiries Concerning Human Understanding and Concerning the Principles of Morals,* third edition. Oxford: Oxford University Press.

———. 1993. *Dialogues and Natural History of Religion.* Oxford: Oxford University Press.

———. 1998. "Of Superstition and Enthusiasm," in *Selected Essays.* Oxford: Oxford University Press.

———. 1998. *Dialogues Concerning Natural Religion,* second edition. Indianapolis: Hackett.

Hurka, Thomas. 2001. *Virtue, Vice, and Value.* Oxford: Oxford University Press.

Joshi, S. T. 2003. "Surprised by Folly: C. S. Lewis," in *God's Defenders: What They Believe and Why They Are Wrong.* Amherst, NY: Prometheus Books.

Kahane, Howard. 1990. *Logic and Philosophy: A Modern Introduction,* sixth edition. Belmont, CA: Wadsworth.

Kant, Immanuel. 1930. *Lectures on Ethics,* trans. L. Infield. Indianapolis: Hackett.

———. 1996. *The Metaphysics of Morals,* trans. M. Gregor. Cambridge: Cambridge University Press.

Koestler, Arthur. 1967. *The Ghost in the Machine.* New York: Macmillan.

Kreeft, Peter. 1989. "C. S. Lewis's Argument from Desire," in *G. K. Chesterton and C. S. Lewis: The Riddle of Joy*, ed. M. H. MacDonald and A. A. Tadie. Grand Rapids, MI: Eerdmans.

Leibniz, G. W. 1985. *Theodicy*, trans. E. M. Huggard. LaSalle, IL: Open Court.

Lewis, C. S. 1955. "On Obstinacy in Belief," in *The World's Last Night and Other Essays*. New York: Harcourt.

———. 1955. *Surprised by Joy: The Shape of My Early Life*. New York: Harcourt.

———. 1960. *The Four Loves*. New York: Harcourt Brace.

———. 1970. "Man or Rabbit," in *God in the Dock: Essays on Theology and Ethics*. Grand Rapids, MI: Eerdmans.

———. 1970. "Meditation on the Third Commandment," in *God in the Dock*.

———. 1970. "On the Transmission of Christianity," in *God in the Dock*.

———. 1970. "Religion without Dogma?" in *God in the Dock*.

———. 1984. *Till We Have Faces*. New York: Harcourt.

———. 1995a. "The Poison of Subjectivism," in *Christian Reflections*. Grand Rapids, MI: Eerdmans.

———. 1995b. "Religion: Reality or Substitute?" in *Christian Reflections*.

———. 1996. *The Screwtape Letters*. New York: Touchstone.

———. 2001. *The Abolition of Man*. New York: HarperCollins.

———. 2001. *A Grief Observed*. New York: HarperCollins.

———. 2001. *Mere Christianity*. New York: HarperCollins.

———. 2001. *Miracles: A Preliminary Study*. New York: HarperCollins.

———. 2001. *The Problem of Pain*. New York: HarperCollins.

———. 2001. "The Weight of Glory," in *The Weight of Glory and Other Addresses*. New York: HarperCollins.

———. 2001. "Why I Am Not a Pacifist," in *The Weight of Glory*.

———. 2002. *All My Road before Me: The Diary of C. S. Lewis, 1922–1927*. New York: Harvest Books.

Lovell, Steve. 2003. "Philosophical Themes from C. S. Lewis." Ph.D. dissertation, University of Sheffield.

McGinn, Colin. 1997. *Ethics, Evil, and Fiction*. Oxford: Oxford University Press.

———. 1999. *The Mysterious Flame: Conscious Minds in a Material World*. New York: Basic Books.

Mill, John Stuart. 1998. *Three Essays on Religion*. Amherst, NY: Prometheus Books.

Miller, Caleb. 1999. "Faith and Reason," in *Reason for the Hope Within*, ed. Michael J. Murray. Grand Rapids, MI: Eerdmans.

Montaigne, de, Michel. 1966. "That to Philosophize Is to Learn to Die," in *Essays*. Chicago: The Great Books Foundation.

Mounce, H. O. 1999. *Hume's Naturalism*. New York: Routledge.

References

Neiman, Susan. 2002. *Evil in Modern Thought: An Alternative History of Philosophy*. Princeton, NJ: Princeton University Press.

Newberg, Andrew, D'Aquili, Eugene, and Rause, Vince. 2001. *Why God Won't Go Away: Brain Science and the Biology of Belief*. New York: Ballantine Books.

Nisbett, R. E., and Wilson, T. D. 1977. Telling more than we can know: Verbal reports on mental processes. *Psychological Review* 84: 231–59.

——, and Ross, L. 1980. *Human Inference: Strategies and Shortcomings of Social Judgment*. Englewood Cliffs, NJ: Prentice-Hall.

O'Connor, David. 2001. *Hume on Religion*. New York: Routledge.

Paine, Thomas. 1948. *The Age of Reason*. New York: Citadel Press.

Penelhum, Terence. 2000. "Natural Belief and Religious Belief in Hume's Philosophy," in *Themes in Hume: The Self, the Will, Religion*. Oxford: Oxford University Press.

——. 2000. "Religion in the *Enquiry* and After," in *Themes in Hume*.

Peterson, Michael L., ed. 1992. *The Problem of Evil: Selected Readings*. Notre Dame, IN: University of Notre Dame Press.

Petrik, James. 1994. In defense of C. S. Lewis's analysis of God's goodness. *International Journal for Philosophy of Religion* 36: 45–56.

Pinker, Steven. 2002. *The Blank Slate: The Modern Denial of Human Nature*. New York: Viking.

——. 2006. "Evolution and Ethics," in *Intelligent Thought*, ed. J. Brockman. New York: Vintage Books.

Plantinga, Alvin. 1998. "The Free Will Defense," in *The Analytic Theist: An Alvin Plantinga Reader*, ed. J. F. Sennett. Grand Rapids, MI: Eerdmans.

——. 1998. "Reason and Belief in God," in *The Analytic Theist*.

Plato. 1977. *Phaedo*, trans. G. M. A. Grube. Indianapolis: Hackett.

——. 2002. *Five Dialogues*, second edition, trans. G. M. A. Grube. Indianapolis: Hackett.

Reppert, Victor. 2003. *C. S. Lewis's Dangerous Idea: In Defense of the Argument from Reason*. Downers Grove, IL: InterVarsity Press.

——. 2005. "The Green Witch and the Great Debate: Freeing Narnia from the Spell of the Lewis-Anscombe Legend," in *The Chronicles of Narnia and Philosophy*, ed. Greg Bassham and Jerry Walls. Chicago: Open Court.

Rochefoucauld, François duc de La. 1959. *Maxims*, trans. L. Kronenberger. New York: Random House.

Rowe, William. 1979. The problem of evil and some varieties of atheism. *American Philosophical Quarterly* 16: 335–41.

Russell, Bertrand. 1957. "A Free Man's Worship," in *Why I Am Not a Christian and Other Essays on Religion and Related Subjects*. New York: Simon & Schuster.

——. 1957. "Can Religion Cure Our Troubles?" in *Not a Christian*.

References

———. 1957. "What I Believe," in *Not a Christian*.

———. 1959. *The Problems of Philosophy*. Oxford: Oxford University Press.

———. 1965. "How to Grow Old," in *Portraits from Memory*. New York: Simon & Schuster.

———. 1986. "The Faith of a Rationalist," in *Bertrand Russell on God and Religion*, ed. A. Seckel. Amherst, NY: Prometheus.

———. 1986. "Has Religion Made Useful Contributions to Civilization?", in *Russell on God and Religion*.

———. 1986. "The Value of Free Thought," in *Russell on God and Religion*.

———, and Copleston, F. C. 1999. "A Debate on the Existence of God," in *Russell on Religion*, ed. L. Greenspan and S. Andersson. New York: Routledge.

———. 1999. "The Essence of Religion," in *Russell on Religion*.

———. 1999. "The Existence and Nature of God," in *Russell on Religion*.

———. 1999. "From 'My Mental Development' and 'Reply to Criticisms'," in *Russell on Religion*.

———. 1999. "Science and Religion," in *Russell on Religion*.

———. 1999. "The Sense of Sin," in *Russell on Religion*.

———. 1999. "Why I Am Not a Christian," in *Russell on Religion*.

———. 2000. *Autobiography*. London: Routledge.

Sennett, James F., and Groothius, Douglas, eds. 2005. *In Defense of Natural Theology: A Post-Humean Assessment*. Downers Grove, IL: InterVarsity Press.

Senor, Thomas D. 2005. "Trusting Lucy: Believing the Incredible," in *The Chronicles of Narnia and Philosophy*, ed. Greg Bassham and Jerry Walls. Chicago: Open Court.

Sessions, William Lad. 2002. *Reading Hume's Dialogues: A Veneration for True Religion*. Bloomington: Indiana University Press.

Shafer-Landau, Russ. 2005. *Moral Realism: A Defence*. Oxford: Oxford University Press.

Sherlock, Thomas. 2000. *The Tryal of the Witnesses of the Resurrection of Jesus*, eleventh edition (1729), in John Earman (ed), *Hume's Abject Failure: The Argument against Miracles*. Oxford: Oxford University Press.

Shermer, Michael. 2004. *The Science of Good and Evil*. New York: Henry Holt & Co.

Singer, Peter. 1995. *How Are We to Live? Ethics in an Age of Self-Interest*. Amherst, NY: Prometheus Books.

Smith, Quentin. 1998. *Ethical and Religious Thought in Analytic Philosophy of Language*. New Haven, CT: Yale University Press.

Stout, Martha. 2005. *The Sociopath Next Door*. New York: Broadway Books.

Sumption, Jonathan. 1978. *The Albigensian Crusade*. London: Faber and Faber.

Talbott, Thomas. 1987. C. S. Lewis and the problem of evil. *Christian Scholar's Review* 17: 36–51.

Taliaferro, Charles. 2005. *Evidence and Faith: Philosophy and Religion since the Seventeenth Century*. Cambridge: Cambridge University Press.

Tolstoy, Leo. 1981. *The Death of Ivan Ilyich*, trans. L. Solotaroff. New York: Bantam Books.

van Inwagen, Peter. 1993. *Metaphysics*. Boulder, CO: Westview Press.

———. 1994. "Quam Dilecta," in *God and the Philosophers: The Reconciliation of Faith and Reason*, ed. Thomas V. Morris. Oxford: Oxford University Press.

———. 1995. "The Magnitude, Duration, and Distribution of Evil: A Theodicy," in *God, Knowledge, and Mystery: Essays in Philosophical Theology*. Ithaca, NY: Cornell University Press.

Voltaire. 1959. *Candide*, trans. L. Bair. New York: Bantam Books.

Vonnegut, Kurt. 1998. *The Sirens of Titan*. New York: Dell.

Wainwright, William. 2005. *Religion and Morality*. Burlington, VT: Ashgate.

Walls, Jerry. 1990. Hume on divine amorality. *Religious Studies* 26: 257–66.

Wielenberg, Erik. 2000. Omnipotence again. *Faith and Philosophy* 17:1: 26–47.

———. 2002. How to be an alethically rational naturalist. *Synthese* 131:1: 81–98.

———. 2005. "Aslan the Terrible: Painful Encounters with Absolute Goodness," in *The Chronicles of Narnia and Philosophy*, ed. Greg Bassham and Jerry Walls. Chicago: Open Court.

———. 2005. *Value and Virtue in a Godless Universe*. Cambridge: Cambridge University Press.

———. 2006. Response to Maria Antonaccio. *Conversations in Religion and Theology* 4:2: 219–24.

Woodward, Kenneth L. 2005. "Countless Souls Cry Out to God," *Newsweek*, January 10.

Wright, Robert. 1994. *The Moral Animal: Evolutionary Psychology and Everyday Life*. New York: Random House.

Wykstra, Stephen J. 1984. The Humean obstacle to evidential arguments from suffering: On avoiding the evils of "appearance." *International Journal for Philosophy of Religion* 16: 73–93.

INDEX

Index

DATE DUE
